Calderón

Plays: One

The Surgeon of Honour, Life is a Dream, Three Judgements in One

Calderón 'excels all modern dramatists with the exception of Shakespeare, whom he resembles, however, in the depth of thought and subtlety of imagination of his writings'. Percy Bysshe Shelley

Described in his own time as 'monstruo del ingenio' (monster of intellect), Calderón's plays are distinguished by brilliant symmetries and parallels in plot and sub-plot. In *The Surgeon of Honour*, *Life is a Dream* and *Three Judgements in One* he explores the extent of an individual's freedom in an hierarchical society often bound by anachronistic codes of conduct.

The translator is Gwynne Edwards, who has also translated two volumes of Lorca plays for Methuen.

Pedro Calderón de la Barca was born in Madrid in 1600, the son of the Secretary to the Royal Treasury. He studied at the Jesuit Colegio Imperial in Madrid and then studied canon law at the University of Salamanca. He began writing in 1620 and between 1625 and 1628 he served in the army in Italy and Flanders and combined the career of soldier and writer. During his life he wrote some 120 secular plays including *The Surgeon of Honour* (1635), *Life is a Dream* (1635) and *Three Judgements in One* (1635–1640?). After a series of misfortunes in his personal life, Calderón took Holy Orders in 1651 and, although he did not write again for the public theatres, he continued to produce two religious plays (*autos sacramentales*) a year for another thirty years. Calderón died in 1681.

in the same series

CALDERÓN

PLAYS: ONE

The Surgeon of Honour
Life is a Dream
Three Judgements in One

Translated and introduced by Gwynne Edwards

Methuen Drama

METHUEN'S WORLD DRAMATISTS

These translations first published in Great Britain in 1991
by Methuen Drama, Michelin House, 81 Fulham Road, London SW3 6RB
and distributed in the United States of America
by HEB Inc, 361 Hanover Street, Portsmouth, New Hampshire 03801

The Surgeon of Honour translation copyright © Gwynne Edwards 1991
Life is a Dream translation copyright © Gwynne Edwards 1991
Three Judgements in One translation copyright © Gwynne Edwards 1991
This collection and introduction copyright © Methuen Drama 1991
The translator has asserted his moral rights.

ISBN 0-413-63460-4

A CIP catalogue record for this book is available from the British Library

*The front cover shows Pablillos de Valladolid by Velasquez, reproduced by
courtesy of Museo del Prado, Madrid. The back cover shows Calderón and is
reproduced by courtesy of the Bibliotheque Nationale, Paris.*

Photoset by Rowland Phototypesetting Ltd
Bury St Edmunds, Suffolk
Printed and bound in Great Britain by
Cox and Wyman Ltd, Reading, Berks.

Contents

Chronology

1646   Death of Philip IV's son, Baltasar Carlos, heir to the throne. Closure of the theatres.

1647   Death of Calderón's elder brother, Diego. Around this time Calderón's illegitimate son, Pedro, is born, the mother possibly dying in childbirth.

1651   Calderón takes holy orders. He ceases to write for the public theatre but continues to write Court and religious plays.

1653   Becomes chaplain of the Chapel of the Reyes Nuevos at Toledo Cathedral.

1660   Death of Velázquez.

1663   Calderón returns from Toledo to Madrid. He is elected a member of the Congregation of St Peter.

1665   Death of Philip IV. The Queen, Mariana of Austria, acts as regent.

1666   Elected head of the Congregation of St Peter.

1681   Calderón dies and is buried in the church of St Salvador in Madrid.

Introduction

Don Pedro Calderón de la Barca was born in Madrid on 17 January 1600, the third of the four children of Diego Calderón de la Barca Barreda, Secretary to the Royal Treasury, and Doña Ana María de Henao y Riaño. His sister, Dorotea, would later become a nun; his elder brother, Diego, a lawyer; and his younger brother, José, an army officer. As far as Pedro was concerned, it was his mother's intention that he would become a priest, succeeding to a family chaplaincy when he became of age. Her death in 1610 led to his father's marriage to a woman who cared little for the step-children, and when he also died five years later they were brought up by one of their mother's brothers. In his will Pedro's father included an instruction that he pursue the career planned for him and threatened him with disinheritance if he continued to court a certain young woman. This brief glimpse of an authoritarian streak in his own father may account in part for the harsh and tyrannical fathers who appear so frequently in Pedro's mature drama.

He received his early education at the Jesuit Colegio Imperial in Madrid, where he already displayed great intellectual gifts, and then proceeded to study canon law at the world-famous University of Salamanca which he left at the age of nineteen, apparently without taking his degree. While at Salamanca he had landed himself in trouble with the university authorities for non-payment of rent, which had led to his imprisonment, an incident which reveals the often turbulent nature of his early life. Indeed, it was not long after returning from Salamanca to Madrid that Pedro and his brothers were involved in a murder and obliged to seek refuge in the Austrian embassy. In order to meet the demands of the victim's relatives for compensation, they were forced to sell their father's office, which would otherwise have been inherited by the elder brother, Diego.

Calderón's first literary efforts belong to 1620 when he entered some poems in the competition in honour of St Isidro, patron saint of Madrid. Two years later, when the canonization of the same saint was celebrated, he was awarded third prize in the poetry competition and praised by no less a figure than Lope de Vega, the most famous dramatist of the day, as 'Don Pedro Calderón, who, in his tender years, merits those laurels which time is accustomed to offer only to those whose hair is grey'. The first of his 120 or so secular plays also belongs to the early twenties, although they can hardly be said to anticipate the great plays that would flow from Calderón's pen some ten to fifteen years later. But this was the golden age of Spanish theatre when Lope de Vega (1562–1635) and Tirso de Molina (1581?–1648) were at the height of their powers and the appetite for new plays was insatiable. It was not surprising that in such fertile soil Calderón's self-confessed 'attraction to the stage' should flourish.

Between 1625 and 1628 he served in the army in Italy and Flanders, combining, as did others of the time, the career of soldier and writer. Back in Madrid in the following year, he was soon involved in controversy when, after his brother Diego had been stabbed by an actor, he and the police pursued the assailant into a Trinitarian convent. A celebrated preacher of the time, Hortensio Paravicino, accused them in a sermon of manhandling the nuns, a charge to which Calderón responded by satirising Paravicino's oratory in his play of 1929, *The Constant Prince*. This in turn led to the President of the Council of Castile, Cardinal Trejo y Paniagua, to rebuke Calderón for mentioning Paravicino by name but also effectively absolved him of the suggested offence. The publicity surrounding the affair must certainly have enhanced the image of an aspiring playwright.

The 1630s witnessed his increasing fame and popularity as a writer. On the one hand he wrote for the actor-managers whose companies performed in the *corrales*, the public theatres; on the other for the Court, where the opportunities for lavish spectacle were much greater; and finally for the Feast of Corpus Christi on which religious plays were performed in the open air. To the first of these three categories belong the three plays published here: *The Surgeon of Honour* (1635), *Life is a Dream* (1635), and *Three Judgements in One* (1635–40?), as well as other fine pieces such as *The Mayor of Zalamea* and *The Painter of His Own Dishonour*, both of which may have been written in the 1640s. As far as the Court theatre was concerned, the new palace of the Buen Retiro in Madrid and the ingenuity of its Italian stage-designer, Cosme Lotti, allowed Calderón to write such spectacular mythological plays as *Love, the Greatest Spell* (1635), and *The Three Greatest Wonders* (1636). The former, which dramatizes the fascination of Ulysses with the enchantress, Circe, was intended for production on a floating stage and contains such ambitious effects as the destruction of Circe's palace by fire and the appearance out of the sea of an erupting volcano. The specifically religious plays (*autos sacramentales*) and other works associated with that tradition could also be highly spectacular. *The Marvellous Magician* (1637), which has clear affinities with the Faust story, has a beautiful woman emerge from the interior of a rock and, as she is embraced by the play's protagonist, change into a skeleton.

Calderón's increasing contribution to the theatrical life of
Madrid, and of the Court of Philip IV in particular, led to his being
made a knight of the great military Order of Santiago in 1636. As a
member of that Order he participated in the early forties in the war
in Catalonia, where he served under the command of the most
powerful and influential figure of his day, the Count Duke of
Olivares. The revolt of the Catalans would continue into the fifties,
but Calderón was back in Madrid by the autumn of 1642, invalided
out of the army. A swift return to the stage was, however, delayed by
the death of the Queen in 1644 and Philip's only legitimate son,
Baltasar Carlos, two years later, events which put an end to both
public and Court performances until the end of the decade. It was a
period of relative inactivity for a dramatist who had been so
productive in the thirties.

The late forties also witnessed a series of misfortunes in
Calderón's personal life. His young brother, José, was killed in
military action in 1645 and his elder brother, Diego, died in 1647. It
was around this time too that his illegitimate son, Pedro, was born,
and it seems quite possible that the mother died either in child-birth
or shortly afterwards. At all events it was a distressing time which,
combined with the deaths of the Queen and the Prince, the general
spectacle of national decline, and the stagnation of theatrical
activity, seems to have made Calderón ponder on the purpose and
direction of his life and, in consequence, to take holy orders in 1651.
He would not write again for the public theatres, but continued to
produce two religious plays a year for the festival of Corpus Christi,
as well as elaborate pieces for the Court, for another thirty years.

In 1653 he became one of the chaplains of the celebrated Chapel
of the Reyes Nuevos in the great Cathedral at Toledo. Ten years
later, because of ill-health and the increasing difficulty of attending
rehearsals of his plays, he moved back to Madrid where Philip IV
made him one of his honorary chaplains and continued to pay him
his former salary. In the same year he was elected a member of the
Congregation of St Peter, a body of priests who were natives of
Madrid, and in 1666 he became their head.

In Madrid Calderón lived on the first floor of a small house (in
what is now the Calle Mayor), part of the endowment of a
chaplaincy in the chapel of San José in the church of San Salvador,
founded by his maternal grandmother. He continued to write two
autos sacramentales a year for the municipality of Madrid and in the
very last year of his life produced a chivalresque play in celebration
of the marriage of the Spanish King, Charles II, to Marie-Louise of

France. He died on 25 May 1681, having outlived all the other famous dramatists of the age, and was buried in the church of San Salvador.

II

The broad characteristics of the secular drama of the seventeenth century had been established gradually by a number of experimental dramatists, including Cervantes, in the last quarter of the sixteenth, and finally enshrined by the practice of the most prolific of them all, Lope de Vega (1562–1635). In a poetic essay, *The New Art of Writing Plays in this Age*, published in 1609, Lope set out the precepts which he had already observed for twenty-five years and which, he argued, responded to public taste and demand.

Above all, the new Spanish drama, like its English counterpart, dispensed with classical rules, freely mixing serious and comic elements in a way which was felt to imitate the variety of life itself, as Lope himself observed:

> The tragic and the comic mixed,
> . . .
> For such variety offers pleasure,
> The best example of it Nature.

The principle of verisimilitude or truth to life lay, indeed, at the heart of much of the reaction of Spanish writers of this time against the doctrines of neo-classicism, and was frequently cited by Lope and others as a justification for dispensing with the unities of place and time. To argue that the stage should represent only one location and that the action occurring on it should be limited to a single day, was in their view, to deny that the dramatist could, like the painter or historian, attempt a large canvas or wide-ranging chronicle. The action of Spanish plays moves constantly, therefore, from place to place, inside to outside, village to city, country to Court, while the time-scale of that action may be days, weeks, months, or even years.

At the same time much of Lope's practice stemmed from an instinctive feeling for what his audiences wanted and would tolerate. Conscious, above all, of the impatience and restlessness of his countrymen – especially when they were seated in a theatre – he recognised the need for material which would hold their interest, which on the whole meant events and characters, historical or fictitious, which were recognizably Spanish. Crucial too, of course, was the unfolding of that material in terms of structure and in recognition of the fact that only with great difficulty could the attention of any Spaniard be held for more than two hours. The three-act play – a form which has been used by Spanish dramatists down to the twentieth century – was perfected by Lope to that end, its shape and structure neatly combining pragmatic and dramatic aims. The first act, he suggested, should set out the situation, the second complicate it, and the third resolve it, but in a way which would keep the audience guessing and attentive until the very last scene. The importance of constantly holding its attention lay too behind Lope's suggestion that the stage should never be left empty.

A general concern with truth to life explains his insistence that the characters should speak in an appropriate manner: that the speech of kings should be suitably weighty, the language of lovers passionate, and the talk of servants earthy and vigorous. In conjunction with this Lope recommended that particular stanza forms, ranging from four to ten lines in length, were particularly suited to certain situations. But perhaps the most interesting feature of his theatre in this respect is his preference for, regardless of stanza form, the line of eight syllables. Shorter than the line favoured by Elizabethan dramatists, it allowed the plays of Lope and his successors to proceed with that pace and vigour required by their audiences. At the same time, the choice of verse rather than prose as a means of expression seems to undermine the claims of Lope to be seeking a drama which is true to life. Its justification lay, however, in the fact that verse had long been considered to be more pleasing to listen to than prose, and a fundamental aim of Lope's theatre was to give pleasure.

The pleasure principle explains to a large extent the enormous popularity of Lope's plays with the audiences who went to see them, but their value as entertainment should not obscure their concern to teach. At the end of his *New Art* Lope refers to the didactic function of theatre and observes that audiences welcome the spectacle of villainy punished and virtue rewarded. This dual function of the Spanish drama of that time was best expressed in the phrase 'deleitar aprovechando': 'pleasurable instruction'.

III

The dramatic formula set out by Lope and practised in his plays was adopted by all the successful dramatists of his day: Tirso de Molina (1581?–1648), Guillén de Castro (1569–1631), Pérez de Montalbán (1602–38), Luis Vélez de Guevara (1579–1644), Ruiz de Alarcón

(1581?–1639), Antonio Mira de Amescua (1574?–1644), and Calderón himself. Within the format described earlier they proceeded to develop their own particular gifts and characteristics.

The basic difference between Lope and Calderón is neatly summed up in the two phrases with which they were described in their own time: 'monstruo de naturaleza' ('monster of Nature') and 'monstruo del ingenio' ('monster of intellect'). The first encapsulates the sheer prodigality and inventiveness, as fertile as Nature itself, of a dramatist who claimed to have written more than one thousand five hundred plays at the rate of a play a day; the second the more reflective, intellectual qualities of a writer who, nevertheless, wrote more than one hundred and twenty, as well as more than seventy religious pieces.

The more studied nature of Calderón's art is explained in part by the fact that when he began writing for the stage in the early 1620s he had behind him a theatrical tradition, created by Lope and others, of more than forty years. The drama of Calderón and his contemporaries was not, therefore, as Lope's had been, one of innovation, novelty and experiment, but one of consolidation, of building upon and improving an existing edifice. The process is clearly evident in Calderón's re-working in some of his very best plays – *Life is a Dream*, *The Surgeon of Honour*, *The Mayor of Zalamea*, *The Constant Prince* – of the material of other dramatists, a common enough practice at that time, and vindicated in this case by the fact that the new play is in every respect artistically superior. But the particular character of Calderón's work, both in these reworked pieces and in totally original plays, stems from his background and temperament.

Intellectually superior to the other dramatists of his age – though this is not to underestimate the intelligence of either Lope or Tirso de Molina – Calderón's education at the Jesuit College in Madrid and then at the University of Salamanca proved crucial. Both exposed him to serious ideas and argument, and both trained him to develop and express them. It is not surprising, therefore, to discover the extent to which Calderón's drama has at its core a cluster of profound themes: the extent to which man's will is free, the transient nature of life and happiness, the conflict of reason and passion, and the complexity of life in general. If it has sometimes been argued that it was Tirso de Molina who provided the Spanish drama of his time with genuine seriousness, that argument seems extremely flimsy in the light of the consistently weighty issues and penetrating debate of Calderón's theatre.

His particular qualities of mind can be illustrated, in effect, in relation to every aspect of his plays, including plot, characters and language. Plots are distinguished above all by their meticulous craftsmanship and structure. In the case of the comedies, of which *A House with Two Doors is Difficult to Guard* is a particularly good example, the action often has the intricacy and the precision of a well-made watch. In the 'serious' plays the element of ingenuity may be smaller, but, as the brilliant symmetries and parallels of *The Surgeon of Honour* indicate, Calderón's control and sense of shape of the whole rarely fail him. In addition, many of his plays have sub-plots which deal either with the affairs of servants or important secondary characters, but these, far from being diversions, are almost always closely connected to the main plot in both a structural and thematic sense. In *Life is a Dream*, for example, the events concerning Rosaura and her father, Clotaldo – the sub-plot – constantly weave in and out of the affairs of Segismundo and his father, Basilio – the main-plot – and are intended too to develop the same themes.

Within the series of events that constitute the plot, the characters of a Calderón play also have more often than not a close and precise inter-relationship and dependence. In *Life is a Dream* Basilio's neglect of his son is also Clotaldo's neglect of his lover, Violante; the upstart servant of Act II is also the upstart soldier of Act III; and both of them reflect the arrogance of many of the principal characters. To this extent the characters of this and other plays are part of a great jig-saw, locking into each other, and without which the whole would not be complete. Like the disparate events of the plot or plots, the characters can be seen, individually and in relation to each other, as vital elements within the overall design.

Language too is often related to theme. There is thus in most of Calderón's plays a close-knit network of images which reinforce their meaning. Positive values – life, beauty, reason, love, understanding – are expressed in terms of light, dawn, sun, flame and the like; negative values – excessive passion, ambition, jealousy, hatred, obsession and the like – in terms of darkness, night, shadows, sunset and eclipse. And from this basic pattern other, more complex associations open out: the evocation of landscapes ablaze with light, colour and flowers to suggest the positive; of gloomy labyrinths, valleys and woods to embody the negative. As well as this, the structure of Calderón's language, as opposed to its meaning, is characterized by a good deal of pattern and symmetry: the structure of one line repeating that of another, words echoing words, and frequently, at the end of a long speech, a repetition of the individual objects alluded to in the course of that speech. In this sense Calderón was undoubtedly the most formal of the major Spanish dramatists of his time, exemplifying many of those stylistic features which we term baroque.

To conclude from the above that his plays are over-intellectual, his characters undeveloped and his style decorative would, however, be completely wrong. Ideas are never expounded for their own sake but are always integrated fully into and subordinated to the particular dramatic situation. Characters, in particular the principals, are not, as some critics have suggested, one-sided, but exposed by the circumstances which surround them to the most severe emotional traumas and self-examination, as the plays translated here indicate. And language, though stylized, expresses through its very pattern an enormous emotional charge which frequently seems to be seeking to burst through its formal constraints.

IV

The public theatres in which the three plays published here were presented were known as *corrales*, which, as the name suggests, were basically courtyards. In 1565 a charitable organization, the Cofradía de la Pasión y Sangre de Jesucristo, had been established in Madrid in order to help the poor, and part of its work consisted of the running of a hospital. As a fund-raising exercise the Cofradía obtained from the municipality permission to hire courtyards for the public performance of plays. Its example was followed by another organization, the Cofradía de la Soledad de Nuestra Señora, and in 1574 both came to an agreement to share the profits from the performance of plays in the city. It was in this context, therefore, that the public theatres of the sixteenth century came into being. Two of them in particular, the Corral de la Cruz and the Corral del Príncipe, founded in 1579 and 1582 respectively, came to be the focal points of theatrical life in Madrid throughout the seventeenth century.

The *corrales* were, in effect, great rectangular yards surrounded by houses of many storeys. The stage was situated at one end of the yard, its apron projecting into the auditorium. In contrast to the apron and the mid-stage, both open and uncluttered areas, the back-stage calls for special comment. At either side of it were the dressing-rooms from which the actors made their entrance onto the stage through doors or curtains, while the middle section could be curtained off to create a 'discovery-space' in which, when the curtains were suddenly whipped back, spectacular revelations could be made. The back-stage had behind it, moreover, the high wall of the houses on that side of the courtyard, and the various windows and balconies could often be brought into use in the stage-action: the top balcony representing Heaven, in contrast to the trapdoors in the stage which led to Hell, and other balconies linked to the stage by means of ladders. Yet another level could be created by means of ramps linking the stage to an area of the pit which could be roped off and in which battles or jousts could be enacted, sometimes with real horses. As the resources of the theatres developed, more ambitious effects could, of course, be achieved: rocks opening to reveal some wonderful effect or figure; transformation-devices whereby one actor might suddenly be concealed and another revealed; or cloud-machines descending from on high and bearing angels. As far as costume was concerned, there was considerable richness and variety, especially in the wealthier companies, but it was always contemporary – doublet, breeches, cloak, etc. – regardless of the period in which the action of the play might be set.

Apart from the stage area and some rows of seats at the side and back, the *corrales* were uncovered, which meant in turn that plays were performed in the afternoon; that performances took place only in favourable weather; and that there was no lighting of the stage. Much thus depended on the awareness and imagination of the audience, not least when scenes set in darkness or semi-darkness – *Life is a Dream, The Surgeon of Honour* – were played in broad daylight. Most of the audience stood in the area facing the stage and consisted of commoners who were usually noisy, attended plays armed with rattles and whistles, and were quick to show their impatience or disapproval. To the sides and the back were tiered rows of benches, *gradas*, which were clearly more expensive, and above them the windows of the houses around the courtyard which formed boxes, *aposentos*, and which could be hired annually by the more wealthy. Only in the *aposentos* were men and women found together. Elsewhere they were strictly separated, the area for women known as the *cazuela* or 'stew-pan'. The entrances to the theatre were situated at the back of the courtyard, one for men and one for women. A general entrance fee was charged and separate payment was then made for admission to different parts of the auditorium. As may be imagined, the performance of plays was witnessed by a varied and lively audience.

Acting companies had at their head a manager, known as the *autor*, though he was not usually a writer. Plays were obtained either directly from writers or existing texts were employed for productions which generally ran for two or three days. A company would consist, typically, of four young actors, including the leading man, six actresses, including the leading lady, two men specialising in elderly parts and two in comic parts. The season began after Easter and continued until the beginning of Lent the following year. As well as performing in the public theatres, the companies – particularly the two Madrid companies – could be called upon to perform at Court, a requirement which at times seriously affected the activities and fortunes of Madrid's *corrales*.

V

The Surgeon of Honour is, as its title suggests, a play in which the subject of honour looms large. Its protagonist, Don Gutierre Alfonso Solís, is a man obsessed with the need to preserve his honour and reputation. Suspecting Doña Leonor of infidelity, he had abandoned plans to marry her and married instead Doña Mencía, unaware that she had previously been courted by the King's brother, Prince Enrique. When Enrique visits her again in secret, Gutierre's suspicions of Mencía are aroused and then, despite his desire to prove her innocence, confirmed for him by subsequent events. His failure to deter Enrique convinces him that only Mencía's death will save his honour. He therefore engages a bloodletter who is forced at knifepoint to bleed Mencía to death. Proclaiming her death an accident, Gutierre considers he has avoided the scandal he feared. The King, however, suspects Gutierre's guilt, and, conscious of his earlier abandonment of Leonor, obliges him to marry her, dismissing his protests.

Despite objections which we shall consider later, the play is certainly one of Calderón's very best. Gerald Brenan observed in *The Literature of the Spanish People* (CUP, 1953): 'The play has been compared to *Othello*. In the movement of its plot, in the economy of its material, in the adjustment of the different characters to their functions in the whole, it is decidedly superior . . .' (p. 283). Michael Billington, reviewing a production of this translation at the Drama Centre, London, described the play as 'one of the most disquieting plays in all world drama . . . , a dark masterpiece' (*The Guardian*, 20 March, 1988). In terms of plot, atmosphere, characters and overall dramatic impact, Calderón's play entirely merits such praise.

The unfolding of the action is realized with economy, pace and unerring powers of dramatic construction. Act One begins by reintroducing Prince Enrique into Mencía's life, reveals her fear for her good name, and concludes by revealing why Gutierre abandoned

Leonor. Act Two begins with Enrique's visit to Mencía, focuses in its central section on Gutierre's growing but unwarranted suspicions and ends with their apparent confirmation when he pretends to be Enrique. Act Three moves quickly to Mencía's murder and ends with Gutierre's enforced marriage to Leonor. Although this summary omits all reference to minor characters and secondary actions, it suggests the concentrated thrust and momentum of the plot and Calderón's unfailing grasp of structure. But there is more to it than that, for the plot is also designed to reveal a number of clear symmetries and parallels. In Act One, for example, Leonor listens from behind a curtain to Gutierre's explanation to the King of his abandonment of her; while in Act Three Gutierre listens in identical circumstances to Enrique's account of his involvement with Mencía. Similarly, the beginning of Act Two, presenting Enrique's secret visit to Mencía in the garden, is paralleled by its conclusion when Gutierre pretends he is Enrique paying a second visit. These and other parallels have the effect of suggesting the extent to which characters and events mirror and echo each other, as if in the world of honour actions are prescribed, people reduced to puppets, and all individuality stripped away in response to rules of behaviour already set down. To this extent the plot is more than an action; it also serves as an image of the honour code itself.

In terms of atmosphere *The Surgeon of Honour* has something of a Gothic horror story, its mood evoked by the gloom of Gutierre's house and the flickering light of the lamps which illuminate it. Act Two is brilliantly effective in this respect: the tension and fear of Enrique's visit to Mencía; Gutierre's unexpected arrival, the extinguishing of the light, the attempt to smuggle Enrique out of the house, the discovery of the knife, and Mencía's panic; and, at the end of the act, Gutierre's scaling of the garden wall and calling to Mencía from the darkness. Calderón's achievement here is to communicate to and awaken in the audience the tension and apprehension of the characters themselves, building to an unbearable climax. But this in turn is capped by the second half of Act Three: Gutierre leading the blindfolded bloodletter through winding streets; the shapes barely discerned in the darkness of the bedroom as the bloodletter opens Mencía's veins; and the shocking moment when a curtain is whipped back to reveal Mencía's bloodstained corpse. Summarized in this way, the impression is easily given that this is material worthy of Edgar Allen Poe or Alfred Hitchcock at their most sensational. It is certainly high-voltage Calderón, though, as we shall see, the play's elements of 'grand guignol' are entirely redeemed by the integrity of Calderón's superb characterization. What is quite astonishing, given the number of scenes which occur in darkness, is that in a seventeenth-century production they would have been played in daylight.

The characters of the play have both a strength and a conviction which give the lie to the notion that Calderón created only types. Gutierre is a truly fascinating study of a man who, basically good, respectful, courteous and capable of affection, is destroyed by the ideology of honour to which he subscribes. The conflict of reason and doubt by which he is increasingly racked and the icy self-possession to which he finally submits single him out as a study worthy of Freud. Mencía, young, beautiful, often spirited, is from the outset fearful of Gutierre's notions of honour and thus, as events unfold, progressively prone to panic and, finally, terror. Her total helplessness and isolation in Act Three evoke that sense of waste, of goodness pointlessly and cruelly destroyed which is part of genuine tragedy, and therefore the pity that goes hand in hand with it. Other than Gutierre and Mencía, the King, Pedro of Castile, is a truly memorable creation. Feared by his subjects for his harshness, he is the King who never laughs, who in disguise stalks the streets of Seville at night in search of wrongdoers, who unpredictably gives a diamond to a poor man, and who makes a bargain with Coquín that, if he cannot make him laugh within a month, his teeth will be pulled out. There is, of course, a connection between King Pedro and Gutierre in the sense that the King – obsessive, suspicious, harsh, inflexible – creates a mood and tone that on a lower, domestic level is echoed by the husband. And it even affects Coquín, the comic character, the play's messenger of mirth who, by its conclusion, is reduced to tears. The way in which the traditional fool is given a greater depth is itself a pointer to the effectiveness of Calderón's characterization.

The language of the play has an economy and tightness that matches the swift movement of plot and sharp delineation of character. Particularly notable, as well as ironic, are the repeated medical references – Gutierre as the surgeon of honour whose cure is eventually to be found only in his wife's death. As well as that, the theme of honour itself is repeatedly expressed in images of light and darkness, the one suggestive of its value and importance, the other of its loss. To that extent the language of the play is concentrated, the range of allusion relatively narrow, but this in turn heightens its mood of fear and obsession. Calderón's style, which in other plays is often distinguished by clusters of dazzling and brilliant images, is here as spare and austere as the plot itself.

The question and treatment of honour in Spanish plays is one which has often puzzled and enraged non-Spaniards, in particular the death of an innocent wife at the hands of a suspicious husband. While praising the art of *The Surgeon of Honour*, Gerald Brenan condemned its morality, picking out in particular the premeditation and secrecy of Gutierre's completion of the murder and Calderón's failure to punish him, which implies the dramatist's approval of Gutierre's action. We are left, Brenan concluded, 'with a feeling of this gulf that separates the moral standards of this neurotic and convention-ridden country and age from those of the rest of Christendom' (p. 284).

In assuming that the portrayal of honour in this and other Spanish plays closely corresponded to the reality of Spanish life, Brenan was, in fact, misguided. Cases like Gutierre's were the exception, not the rule, were highly sensational, and the husbands involved were far from normal. But that, of course, explains why the dramatists considered these 'cases of honour' to be good material for dramatic plots and suggests that the exaggerated honour of the plays was less to do with life than dramatic convention. Indeed, from Lope de Vega onwards the source of many honour plays was not life but literature, especially the Italian short story. Similarly, Brenan's suggestion that Calderón approved of Gutierre's murder of Mencía can be shown to be erroneous, for what he shows us is the process whereby a man who is basically good and loving is destroyed by an inflexible ideology. The world of honour is one of increasing darkness and enclosure, physical and mental, its boundaries ever more constricting. The play concludes, moreover, not with Gutierre's escape from honour's imprisonment but with his delivery by the King into the cul-de-sac of his marriage to Leonor, whom he once suspected of infidelity. Calderón's view of honour is wholly negative, to be contrasted with the Christian values of love, compassion and charity embodied in the cross above Mencía's bed.

The play's bleakness poses too the question of its tragic character. For more than thirty years perceptions of the tragic nature of Spanish drama of the seventeenth century have been coloured by the insistence of the British hispanist, A. A. Parker, that its characters enjoy free will, have the ability to choose between right and wrong, and are thus, however much external events intervene, responsible for their fate. It is an argument which would therefore attribute the fate of Gutierre and Mencía to their own moral deficiencies – imprudence, rashness, pride – which combine with the faults of others to create a chain of events which ends in catastrophe. The fact that the same could be said of *Macbeth* or *Othello* to the detriment both of the plays and the breadth of Shakespeare's vision points to the narrowness of Parker's vision and demands an alternative approach. This lies, quite simply, in emphasizing not so much the moral responsibility as the complexity and vulnerability of the characters in an unstable and uncertain world. Gutierre is in many respects a good man who loves his wife and seeks to prove her innocence, not merely for the sake of his good name but also because of his love for her. But the very process is one which exposes him both to his own uncertainties and to the capricious actions of others. The spectacle of human weakness made quite helpless invites, by the end of the play, the questions which tragic drama always invites: 'Why must this be? Why is the world like this?' And the events which provoke those questions awaken too our pity and our fear. It matters not that Calderón was a Catholic of the Counter-Reformation, not that his religious plays dramatized orthodox dogma. It would have been astonishing if a man of his intelligence had not in the course of a long writing career questioned the beliefs which others held to be certainties.

VI

Life is a Dream was written in 1635, the same year as *The Surgeon of Honour*, and is undoubtedly Calderón's most famous play. Set in Poland, it tells the story of Segismundo, imprisoned in a tower from birth by his father, King Basilio, on account of omens predicting disaster. Some twenty years later Basilio has a change of heart and resolves to give his son an opportunity to rule. Transported to the palace under the influence of a drug, Segismundo awakens to a splendour he has never witnessed and, informed of his status and power, proceeds to take revenge on those who have wronged him or now displease him: he attacks his gaoler, Clotaldo; insults a prince, Astolfo; attempts to ravish Rosaura; reviles his father, Basilio; and throws a servant to his death from a window. Convinced of the truth of the prophecy, Basilio imprisons his son again and orders Clotaldo to persuade him that his experience in the palace was a dream. When he is released for a second time by soldiers supporting his claims to the throne, Segismundo cannot decide if he is awake or asleep but in either case believes he should behave more prudently. Confronted again by people he has seen before, he resists the passions of the moment and, having defeated his father, finally forgives him. The prophecy that he would see his father kneel before him comes true but vengeance is transformed into forgiveness.

The origins of Calderón's play are to be found in part in

traditional stories and legends. The story of the awakened sleeper, for example, occurs in a collection of eastern tales known as *The Syntipas* or *The Seven Wise Masters*, as well as in the *Arabian Nights*, and was echoed in the work of a number of Spanish writers from the fourteenth century. The theme of a prophecy which someone attempts to thwart but in so doing merely confirms, occurs in a collection of stories, *Barlaam and Josaphat*, and it was also dramatized by Lope de Vega in his play of that name. The notion that life is transient and dream-like is commonplace in both oriental and Christian religions and was particularly strong in the Spain of Calderón. But the direct source for *Life is a Dream* was clearly another play, *The Errors of Nature and Successes of Fortune*, which Calderón had written in collaboration with Antonio Coello in 1634. While the details of the plot are different, the basic ideas are the same: a prince who recovers the throne to which he is entitled after imprisonment in a tower; who is thought to be unfit to rule but learns to do so; and who in the process suggests that man can shape his destiny. The earlier play is also set in Poland and contains two characters called Segismundo and Rosaura, the son and daughter of a powerful courtier. But what is more important, of course, is Calderón's transformation of the source-material.

Life is a Dream is not so much the story of a prince who recovers his throne as of a man who discovers both himself and the true nature of life, who emerges from the darkness of ignorance and animal-passion into the light of reason and understanding. In doing so, moreover, he embodies one of the play's central themes that man's will is free and that his destiny lies ultimately in his own hands, not in the hands of others or the caprices of fate. And he learns too, in the process of discovering and mastering himself, that those things in life which are the objects of men's desire – power, wealth, pleasure – are fleeting and insubstantial in comparison to the permanence of spiritual values.

The themes embodied in Segismundo are at the same time and in different ways related to the experience of all the other characters in a plot that is both intricate and beautifully structured. There is, in fact, a main plot and a sub-plot, the first dealing with the affairs of Segismundo and his father, the second with the attempt of Rosaura, seduced and abandoned by Prince Astolfo, to recover her name and honour. But both are so interwoven and dependent on each other in terms of action and characters that they are, in effect, inseparable. Rosaura's final recovery of her honour is achieved through Segismundo's recovery of his throne, and his conquest of himself through an appreciation of her as a human being dependent on him.

Basilio's initial irresponsibility towards his son is paralleled by
Clotaldo's abandonment of his lover, Violante, and both are made to
confront in later life dilemmas associated with their children,
Segismundo and Rosaura. Astolfo, having abandoned Rosaura, is
another form of Clotaldo. And Clarion, the play's comic character, is
a form of them all at their most self-interested, his death opening
their eyes to their respective mistakes. Each and every character is, in
addition, the embodiment in one way or another of the central theme
of the insubstantial nature of the objectives of human aspiration:
power, wealth, pleasure, name; and each in the course of his own
experience grasps or is made to grasp that vital truth. In short, *Life is
a Dream* reveals again Calderón's sense of overall shape and the
interlocking of incident and character within it.

Segismundo himself is, like Don Juan, one of the great
characters of seventeenth-century Spanish drama, a figure of endless
fascination and appeal. Much of it lies in the sheer emotional ferocity
and unpredictability of this man-beast dressed in animal skins, as
likely to tear Rosaura to pieces as he is to be moved to open-mouthed
astonishment by her dazzling beauty. But it stems too from his
bewilderment at the sudden and extreme changes in his fortunes and
status – prison to palace, palace to prison, prison to palace – and his
uncertainty as to which is real, which false. The scale and range of
his mental and emotional conflict and the slow advance towards a
greater understanding of himself and of the world offer limitless
possibilities to an actor. The play, indeed, is full of interesting
characters: the over-confident Basilio, racked by guilt and
conscience, awakening slowly to the error of his ways; Rosaura,
spirited and passionate in her pursuit of her seducer, yet as confused
and distraught as Segismundo by the reality of her loss of honour;
Clotaldo, her father, thrown into confusion by the sudden
appearance of his child; Astolfo, superior, ambitious, insincere; and
Clarion, seeker of the temporary advantage, the instant reward,
forced to acknowledge the error of his life by the reality of his death.
Here, in the concentrated world of the play, is all the variety and
concerns of the world outside it, the mirror in which we observe
ourselves.

The brilliance of the characters has its counterpart in the
splendidly evocative settings. The scale is much larger, more epic
than that of *The Surgeon of Honour*. The opening scene, with its
suggestion of towering crags, darkness descending, a gloomy tower,
a pale flickering light, and a chained man dressed in skins, is
marvellously imaginative. Against this the sudden transition to the
palace opens up – largely through the suggestive power of the verse,

of course – an entirely different world of silks and brocades, glittering jewels, alluring music, and lovely women, creating that *chiaroscuro* effect that in its dramatic contrast is so characteristically baroque. But the true effectiveness of the settings – and this is also true of the other plays considered here – lies in the fact that while they exist in their own right as physical backdrops to the action, they are also images and reflections of the characters' emotional and mental states: landscapes of the mind. There is thus a very close association throughout *Life is a Dream* between external and internal; the sense of a journey through a changing landscape that is simultaneously an exploration of the human personality.

The language of the play is in general more stylized than that of *The Surgeon of Honour* and might well be described as 'operatic'. In this respect there are a number of long speeches – Segismundo's soliloquy, Basilio's speech to the Court in Act I; Clotaldo's opening speech, Rosaura's soliloquy, Segismundo's closing soliloquy in Act II; Rosaura's address to Segismundo, his reply, and his speech to the Court in Act III – which are the equivalent of arias and which, because of their carefully patterned structure, have a strong sense of musicality. Segismundo's opening soliloquy reveals very clearly Calderón's fondness for repetition, balance, symmetry and recapitulation, and its formal qualities are also echoed elsewhere throughout the play. The effect of such stylization is not, however, to mute the emotional impact of the lines but, by the very act of disciplining and containing that emotion, to make it more intense, just as the formal structure of the symphony heightens the impact of Beethoven's music. In emotional terms the language of the play also has a considerable range, from the unpredictable violence of Segismundo to the lyricism of his rhapsodic praise of Rosaura's beauty. The point has often been made that Calderón's style is more mannered that that of Lope de Vega, but it is also undoubtedly true that it is more dramatic and theatrical. Its demands on actors are very great indeed.

The final point to be made in relation to *Life is a Dream* is that, as the preceding discussion suggests, it dramatizes not man's downfall but his victory and is not therefore a tragedy; or, to put it a different way, it moves in its first two acts towards tragedy but then changes course, celebrating the triumph of man's free will. To that extent it is, in contrast to *The Surgeon of Honour*, the other side of the coin, a dark struggle from which Segismundo himself emerges victorious and in which others learn from his example. It is not, of course, a religious play and does not in that sense expound doctrinal truths, but it cannot be denied that in broad terms it suggests a more orthodox Calderón. If, then, *The Surgeon of Honour* suggests a questioning of belief in man's ability to fashion his destiny, *Life is a Dream* dispells that doubt.

VII

There is no evidence to indicate precisely when *Three Judgements in One* was written – it was not published until 1661 – but its style seems to suggest the 1630s, more or less the same period as *The Surgeon of Honour* and *Life is a Dream*. At all events it is one of Calderón's finest and most powerful pieces, akin to *The Surgeon of Honour* in the accumulating darkness of its last act. Act One begins with the capture of the King's ambassador, Don Mendo, and his daughter, Violante, by a group of outlaws. Their leader, Lope, spares their lives and in response is promised by Don Mendo that he will obtain Lope's pardon. Having listened to the latter's account of his drift into crime, partly because of his father's coldness towards him, Don Mendo succeeds in obtaining for the young man both the father's forgiveness and a royal pardon. Act Two portrays the tensions between father and son. Rivalry between Lope and another young man, Don Guillén, in relation to Violante leads to a confrontation in which the father takes Guillén's part and is accidentally struck – and thus dishonoured – by his son. In consequence, Lope is obliged to flee with his father's demand for vengeance and justice on his head. Act Three commences with Lope's arrest by Don Mendo, who is now Chief Justice to the King. The King himself, mindful of the father's call for justice, interrogates his wife, Doña Blanca, in an attempt to explain the hostility between father and son. She reveals that the latter, unknown to his father, is not their child but her sister's, who many years previously had been seduced and abandoned by Mendo. Aware finally that Lope is his son, Mendo, abetted by Blanca, attempts to save him. They discover too late that punishment has been exacted when the young man's bloodstained body is revealed and they are left to ponder on their own individual contribution to his death.

The plot of *Three Judgements in One* is in every respect as well shaped and constructed as that of the other two plays. Acts One and Three, for example, have clear similarities which have the effect of drawing attention to their differences. At the beginning of Act One the action takes place in the mountains where Lope's men take Mendo prisoner. Act Three begins with the same setting, but Mendo now takes Lope prisoner. The second half of Act One sees Mendo seeking and obtaining a pardon for Lope and bringing about a reconciliation with his father. Act Three sees him attempting but failing to save his life. Both roles and outcome are thus reversed, and what in Act One offered hope by Act Three offers none, the labyrinthine mountains from which escape seemed possible for both Lope and Mendo a final cul-de-sac from which there is none. The events of Act Two, culminating in Lope's argument with Guillén, which then becomes his confrontation with his father, are distinguished above all by the theatrical ingenuity of the scenes in which Lope intercedes with Violante on Guillén's behalf but is made to appear to betray Guillén by a series of fortuitous events. The intricacy of the plot here creates a sense of the characters unable to free themselves from a situation which is not of their own making, and adds to the impression created by the play as a whole of the increasing entanglement of human beings in affairs over which they have no control. The complex plot of *Three Judgements in One* is thus an image of the play's meaning.

As far as characters are concerned, there is no single character in the play to equal Segismundo or Gutierre in either scale or complexity, but this is entirely due to the fact that no single character predominates. The roles are, in effect, much more evenly distributed, making *Three Judgements* a group or corporate drama, but within that framework the characters and relationships are still very striking. The way in which Lope, in the process of growing up, becomes a pawn in his parents' bickering, plays them off against each other and, left to his own devices, drifts into crime, commencing the spiral that leads to his banishment, has a strikingly authentic and modern ring. There is doubtless something of Calderón's experience of his own father both here and in *Life is a Dream* which gives the fictional relationships an extra edge. That being so, the portrait of Lope's father, a man who cannot bring himself to express more tender feelings even though he feels them; who therefore increasingly isolates himself from those he really cares for, and is seen by others to be merely unfeeling, is as true as it is touching. But it is, perhaps, Doña Blanca who is the play's most moving character of all. Married at fifteen, denied the affection she craves, she finds compensation in her sister's company, then in the child which her sister secretly bears, passing it off as her own when she dies in childbirth. It is, of course, her need for emotional fulfillment which, centred on the child, makes her marriage colder still, transforming it into a battlefield in which, twenty years later, the child is a fatal casualty and Doña Blanca herself is left to face the emptiness of the years ahead. For Don Mendo, the lover who abandoned Blanca's sister many years ago, it is a case of a man enjoying supreme good fortune suddenly made conscious of the consequences of the past and, for all his power, unable to surmount them.

One of the most striking aspects of the play, as far as mood and atmosphere are concerned, is its sense of claustrophobia and inescapability. In purely physical terms it is suggested by the rugged mountains within whose confines Lope and his outlaw followers are obliged to spend their lives. Occurring at the very beginning, this labyrinthine setting disappears with Mendo's intervention on Lope's behalf but reasserts itself after the argument with his father, and becomes in the second half of Act Three the chamber-prison in which he is held captive. The physical enclosures of the play are, though, merely the external manifestations of other ways in which the lives of the characters are circumscribed: by their circumstances, their natures and their upbringing. It is a point effectively made by the key soliloquys: Lope's account of his parents' warring relationship in Act One; Blanca's description of the coldness of her marriage and her appropriation of her sister's child. Both speeches evoke lives enmeshed and inextricably entangled, actions which provoke other actions, a chain which is ever longer but always tied to its starting-point. On the one hand, there is a sense of movement, of journeys, of distances covered; on the other, of characters who are going nowhere.

Like *The Surgeon of Honour*, *Three Judgements in One* is a play in which men's attempts to fashion happiness from the mistakes and disappointments of the past are totally thwarted. Don Mendo seeks on two occasions to help Lope, first by obtaining his forgiveness, then by trying to save his life. The young man's father is anxious that his son should settle down at home again, while Doña Blanca is overjoyed by his return. In a sense there is a momentum here for a change for the better that is stronger and that is shared by more people than is the case in *The Surgeon of Honour*, and that until the mid-point of Act Two shows every sign of being realized. In the event Lope cannot curb his resentment towards his father or his impetuosity any more than the latter can control his impatience with his son. As well as that, chance plays a vital role when the appearance of a servant in Act Two prevents Guillén from hearing Violante's reply to his petition, thus creating a fundamental misunderstanding and the subsequent crucial argument. The interaction of men's natures and external events is more than enough to frustrate good intentions, and from a point where the horizons of the play seemed to be open and full of promise they quickly become enclosed again. The similarities between *Three Judgements in One* and *Life is a Dream* merely point to their crucial differences. Both deal with a young man's attempted regeneration, as well as with a difficult father–son relationship. *Life is a Dream* celebrates Segismundo's triumph over the deficiencies of his own nature and the pressure of external events; *Three Judgements in One* is the despairing account of Lope's failure. Written at about the same time, the two plays suggest that Calderón was obsessed with the same fundamental questions – the extent of man's freedom, the mystery of life itself – and that, in exploring them, he found no single or simple answer.

VIII

Of all the dramatists of the Spanish Golden Age, Calderón has undoubtedly made the greatest impact outside Spain. The Baroque characteristics of his drama could hardly be expected to appeal to the neo-classical temperament of the eighteenth century, but were acclaimed in the nineteenth, especially in Germany and England. In 1808 August Wilhelm Schlegel gave his 'Lectures on Dramatic Art and Literature' in Vienna, and observed of Calderón:

> All the writers of that day wrote in a kindred spirit; they formed a true school of art. Many of them have peculiar excellences, but Calderón in boldness, fullness and profundity, soars beyond them all; in him the romantic drama of the Spaniards attained the summit of perfection.

It was a view echoed by Friedrich Schlegel, Lessing, Goethe and others, suggesting that the German temperament of that time found much in Calderón which appealed to its Romantic idealism. As far as England was concerned, Shelley noted in 1819 in a letter to Thomas Peacock:

> He excels all modern dramatists with the exception of Shakespeare, whom he resembles, however, in the depth of thought and subtlety of imagination of his writings . . .

As the translator of a number of scenes from Calderón's *The Marvellous Magician*, Shelley must also be regarded as a significant pioneer of Calderonian drama in England.

To emphasize the German and English contribution to the wider recognition of Calderón's genius is not to say that other countries neglected it, for both in Europe and beyond the importance of his theatre has increasingly been recognized. Jerzy Grotowski's production of *The Constant Prince* in 1965 is frequently considered to be the peak of Laboratory Theatre's acting style and the distillation of Grotowski's work. *Life is a Dream* in particular has been translated into many languages and presented in many countries throughout the world, with the Polish production by the Stary Theatre of Cracow at the Edinburgh Festival in 1989 being one of the most recent. For the purposes of this volume, though, it is worth considering in a little more detail the fortunes of Calderón in Great Britain over the last century or so.

As far as translations are concerned, Edward Fitzgerald's *Six Dramas of Calderón* was published in 1853, and between 1853 and 1873 Denis Florence McCarthy published five volumes of Calderón plays containing eleven secular and three religious pieces. Since then various British and American translators have produced translations of individual plays, sometimes published individually, sometimes included with works by other dramatists in miscellaneous collections. The best-known of these is probably Roy Campbell, the English poet, whose versions of *Life is a Dream* and *Love after Death* were published in 1959 by Eric Bentley in *The Classic Theatre: Volume III: Six Spanish Plays*. It remains a curious fact, though, that for more than a hundred years no British publisher has produced a volume specifically dedicated to Calderón.

Interest in stage-productions of Calderón has notably accelerated in Britain during the 1980s, commencing with the National Theatre's *The Mayor of Zalamea* in 1981. Three years later came the RSC's production of *Life is a Dream*, and in 1989 the National Theatre Studio's rather static *Schism in England*. Much more effective were the two productions of *The Surgeon of Honour*, the first in 1988 by the Drama Centre, London, of the text published here; the second in 1989 by 'Cheek by Jowl' of Roy Campbell's version (with the title of *The Doctor of Honour*). Equally encouraging is the fact that amateur groups are also showing interest in Calderón, as is suggested by the production in 1989 by the Southend Shakespeare Company of the text of *The Surgeon of Honour* staged previously at the Drama Centre.

IX

The problems involved in translating Calderón into English are, needless to say, considerable. Not only is a very good knowledge of Spanish essential, but also familiarity with both the Spanish and the theatre of the seventeenth century, as well as with the particular features of Calderón's style. An examination of existing translations reveals a variety of errors, including simple misunderstanding, ignorance of seventeenth-century custom and usage, failure to comprehend jokes and vulgarities, and, frequently, merely arbitrary and groundless changes. In this respect, of course, adaptation needs to be mentioned, for, as the word suggests, it is more an approximation to the original than a translation of it and, one suspects, serves as a justification for a multitude of sins, two of which are often the adapter's ignorance of the original language and his belief that he can somehow improve the original play.

A major problem concerns length of line, metre and rhyme. The dramatists of the Golden Age greatly favoured a line of eight syllables with no regular stress-pattern, a variety of stanza forms ranging from four to ten lines and involving complex rhyme-schemes, and, when these were not being used, a pattern of assonance in which the same vowel sounds in words at the end of alternate lines were stressed, thereby creating a kind of rhyme. Translations into English have frequently employed iambic pentameter, with its more marked stresses, and have also tended to avoid rhyme, which is more difficult to achieve in English than in Spanish. Both decisions seem to me unwise.

In the first place Spanish words are longer than their English equivalents, so that there would be more English than Spanish words in a line of eight syllables, and more again in a line of ten syllables. To opt for iambic pentameter is thus to accept the need for unnecessary padding. Spanish dramatists favoured the octosyllabic line for its crispness and pace. To use a longer line is to sacrifice that inherent quality of the Spanish drama.

The presence of rhyme and assonance also gives Spanish plays a marked musicality. One of the problems of attempting to create end-rhymes in English is that it leads to distortion of the syntax and therefore to clumsiness rather than musicality. For that reason many translators have avoided rhyme altogether, but in so doing have sacrificed one of the principal characteristics of the Spanish original. The solution seems to me to lie in a judicious mixture of end and internal rhymes, used in a way which does not distort syntax and rhythm. If the octosyllabic line is used as well, the translator can, I believe, achieve some of the liveliness and the musicality of Calderón's original.

Gwynne Edwards, 1990

The Surgeon of Honour

Characters

THE KING, DON PEDRO
THE PRINCE, DON ENRIQUE
DON GUTIERRE ALFONSO SOLÍS
DON ARIAS
DON DIEGO
COQUÍN *a servant*
DOÑA MENCÍA DE ACUÑA
DOÑA LEONOR
INÉS *a servant*
TEODORA *a servant*
JACINTA *a servant*
LUDOVICO *a bloodletter*
A SOLDIER
AN OLD MAN
PETITIONERS

Act One

The sounds of a hunt. PRINCE ENRIQUE *falls from his horse.*
DON ARIAS *and* DON DIEGO *enter, followed by* KING PEDRO.

ENRIQUE.
    Heaven help me!

    He lies unconscious.

                In God's name! Quickly!

KING.
    What's happened?

ARIAS.
                   Prince Enrique's horse
    Has fallen. He's been badly hurt.

KING.
    Is this the way the city of Seville
    Greets me, the King of Spain? Far better
    To have stayed at home and never
    Left Castile! Enrique! Enrique!

DIEGO.
    Your majesty!

KING.
              Is there no sign
    Of recovery?

ARIAS.
             He's lost all colour
    And sense. No sign of life or movement.
    This is the gravest misfortune!

KING.
    Don Arias, hurry to the house,
    There near the road. Tell them the Prince
    Must be allowed to rest until
    He is recovered. All of you
    Shall stay with him while I go on
    Alone. Someone give me a horse.
    Though pity and fear conspire
    To blunt in me the need for haste,

The need to reach Seville and waste
No further time is greater still.
I'll take the news of this misfortune
With me.

The KING *leaves.*

ARIAS.

The episode is proof
Enough of the harshness of the King's
Condition. Who else would abandon
His brother the moment he's fallen
Into the waiting arms of death?
I swear to God . . .

DIEGO.

Take care, Arias.
Remember that the walls have ears,
The trees eyes. The man is truly wise
Who neither says nor does too much.

ARIAS.

Go quickly to the house, Don Diego.
Inform them that the Prince has fallen.
On second thoughts, perhaps the two
Of us should carry him and let
Him rest there.

DIEGO.

By far the better of
The two.

ARIAS.

Let the Prince recover.
I ask Fortune no other favour.

Exit, carrying the PRINCE. *Enter* DOÑA MENCÍA *and*
JACINTA, *her servant. A room in* DON GUTIERRE's *house.*

MENCÍA.

I watched them from the tower and saw
It happen. I've no idea who
They are but am convinced some great
Misfortune has befallen them.
A young and handsome man rode on
A horse that in its speed of flight
Seemed more a bird carried upon
The wind. Believe me, this comparison

Is truly justified, for what
Were coloured plumes that waved upon
The horse's head seemed too the feathers of
A bird now darting through the air.
On seeing them, the fields and sun
Indulged in fierce competition,
Each offering its light, the one
A dazzling array of flowers,
The other a shower of bright stars.
And so much did that plumage catch
The light, it seemed the sun itself
In all its splendour, and then a moment
Later the Spring in all its beauty.
In short, a horse encompassing
The splendour of the sun, the sky,
The earth, the wind, the bird, the beast,
The star, and finally the flower.

JACINTA.
My lady! A group of people . . .

MENCÍA.
Where?

JACINTA.
I think they must be coming here.

MENCÍA.
And carrying the injured man.
They seem quite overcome by fear.

Enter DON ARIAS *and* DON DIEGO *carrying the* PRINCE.
They place him on a chair.

DIEGO.
Since royal blood has God's authority
In every noble household, we
Were bold enough to come inside.

MENCÍA (*aside*).
I can't believe what I am seeing!

DIEGO.
The Prince, Enrique, brother to
The King, has had an accident.
A heavy fall, madam, as we
Went past the entrance to your house.
As you can see, he's badly hurt.

MENCÍA.
   This is the greatest of misfortunes!

ARIAS.
   If he can be allowed to rest
   A while on one of your beds,
   His prospects of recovery
   Will correspondingly improve,
   My lady! I can't believe it!

MENCÍA.
   Don Arias. Can this be you?

ARIAS.
   Is this some dream or fantasy
   Designed to trick both eye and ear?
   Can it be possible the Prince,
   Whose love for you is greater than
   It ever was, should come back here
   And be denied the chance of seeing you
   By this unhappy circumstance?
   It is too cruel to be true!

MENCÍA.
   This is no dream, however much
   It seems to be.

ARIAS.
                    But what are you,
   Mencía, doing here? Tell me, please.

MENCÍA.
   I'll tell you soon enough, Don Arias.
   For now, far better you attend
   Your master's needs.

ARIAS.
                          Whoever could
   Have dreamed he'd find you here?

MENCÍA.
   No more, Don Arias, please. Believe me now.
   You must be silent on this matter.

ARIAS.
   Why?

MENCÍA.
            My honour rests on it.
   Inside the bedroom there, you'll find

A bed that presently is covered by
A piece of Turkish leather, quite
Unworthy of the Prince, but he
Can rest at least and meanwhile we
Shall bring our very finest sheets,
And fresh and perfumed water suited to
This noble task.

ARIAS.

                    While that is being done,
We'll leave the Prince with you so we
Can take our leave and see if we
Can find some remedy for this, ·
If for misfortune such as this
There is a remedy.

JACINTA, DIEGO *and* ARIAS *leave.*

MENCÍA.

                    Now they are gone,
I am alone. If only I,
With honour's kind consent, could give
Free reign to my true sentiment.
If only I could voice my feelings,
Shattering the icy silence of
This prison where my passion lies
In chains, its flame but ashes, while
The dying of its embers tells
Me to remember: 'Here was love!'
But what am I now saying? What
Am I now doing, knowing who I am?
The wind must now return to me
The words it's borne away, before,
Though seeming to be lost, they say
To someone else those secret things
That never must be spoken by myself.
For if by general consent,
It is agreed I have no right
To my own feelings, I must take
My sole delight in now denying them.
Is not the only honest virtue
Virtue tested? Gold is perfected in
The crucible, the magnet tested
By iron, diamond by diamond,
Base metal in the hottest fire.

So must my self-denial be
The only test of honour's worth.
I pray to heaven, take pity on
Me now. If I must live, as I
Now die in silence, let it be!
Enrique! My lord!

ENRIQUE *opens his eyes.*

ENRIQUE.

                      Who speaks?

MENCÍA.
Good fortune . . .

ENRIQUE.

                  Must, I think, deceive me!

MENCÍA.
Spares your life, my lord.

ENRIQUE.

                    Where am I?

MENCÍA.
Where someone you already know
Is overjoyed to see your health
Restored, my lord.

ENRIQUE.

                  I could believe
It if the happiness I feel
Were not, through being mine,
To vanish suddenly. But now
I am obliged to ask myself
If I am dreaming while asleep
Or wide-awake while I now dream.
For I both seem to be awake
And still asleep. But why insist,
If putting to the test the truth
Of things involves an even greater risk?
If it is true I am asleep,
Then let me never be awake;
And if it's true I am awake,
Then never let me fall asleep.

MENCÍA.
My noble lord, your health is all
That matters now, and all of us

Must take the utmost care and prudence.
May you live long and prove the Phoenix of
Your fame and reputation, thus
In imitation of the bird
That, dying in the flames, is born
Again, rising from the ashes, child
And also father to itself.
But as for where you are, I'll tell
You afterwards.

ENRIQUE.
               I do not wish
To know, for if I am alive
And have you here in front of me,
Then I am happier than any man,
And would be happy knowing I
Am dead, when so to find myself
Bedazzled in the presence of
Angelic beauty is to be
In Heaven itself. And so to know
What causes and events explain
Both your presence here and mine,
Has no significance for me
When I am happy just to be
With you. What need is there for you
To give or me to listen to
Some complicated story?

MENCÍA (*aside*).
I fancy time will put an end
To this excessive flattery.

Aloud.

Tell me, are you feeling better now
My Lord?

ENRIQUE.
            Oh yes, Mencía! You,
I think, have helped to cure me,
Except this leg that pains me still.

MENCÍA.
The fall was heavy, sir. You need
To rest a while as quietly
As possible. I've seen to it
A bed is being made in here

Where you can be more comfortable.
You must forgive me such a small
And humble bedroom; the reason is
Quite easily explained . . . You see . . .

ENRIQUE.

You speak to me as if you are
The mistress of the house. Are you
Its owner?

MENCÍA.

   I am not, my lord.
The house does not belong to me.
You could say, though, the owner of
The house owns me.

ENRIQUE.

     But who is he?

MENCÍA.

A most distinguished gentleman,
His name Gutierre Alfonso Solís,
My husband and your loyal servant.

ENRIQUE.

You mean that you are married?

MENCÍA.

       Yes,
My lord! You must not move. You see
How weak you are. You must be still.

ENRIQUE.

I must, I must. We have to speak
Of this, Mencía!

Enter DON ARIAS *and* DON DIEGO.

ARIAS.

    My good lord!
How wonderful it is to see
You once again restored to health!
Since your health becomes our own,
We are indebted to good fortune!

DIEGO.

But in the meantime you must rest
And not attempt too much too soon.
We have prepared a bedroom, seeking
In the execution of our task

To marry practicality
To boldest imagination.

ENRIQUE.
Don Arias, get me a horse. At once.
Don Diego, get the horses ready.
We must leave this house as quickly as
We can.

ARIAS.
What do you mean, my lord?

ENRIQUE.
A horse! Get me a horse! a horse!
Immediately!

DIEGO.
You can't be serious!

ARIAS.
Listen to us!

ENRIQUE.
But can't you see
That Troy now burns? That all my senses are
Ablaze? That I, like bold Aeneas, am
Compelled to save them from the flames?

Exit DIEGO.

Don Arias, I am convinced my fall
Was not an accident, but more
A clear prophecy of death.
The heavens, I think, have now been moved
To feel for me and so decreed
That I must die while in the presence of
This woman, married recently,
So she may now from us receive
Congratulations on her marriage,
And I commiserations on
My death. The truth of it is now
Quite clear, for as the horse approached
This house, Mencía, it entered
The sphere of your influence,
And was inspired to a bold
Display of arrogance and pride.
It seemed to think itself a bird
In flight, first challenging the wind,

And then the brightness of the sun.
But then, still closer to the house,
It saw ahead of it the steep
And treacherous slopes of jealousy
That lay in wait to bring about
Its downfall; for even such an animal
Is driven mad by jealousy,
And then, however great his skill,
No horseman can control its fury or
Its speed. I thought your beauty was
Mencía, the miracle that gave
Me life again, but now
I see that my recovery
Is nothing more than your vengeance,
Designed to bring about my death.
I know, Mencía, I am dying,
And no one will remember then
That you once gave me life again.

MENCÍA.

My lord, if someone overheard
Such bitter words and accusations,
He could be easily deceived
As to my honour and my reputation.
The wind could bear your words away
And others pluck them from the air
And reassemble what they say.
I, therefore, must reply to your
Complaints and quickly give the lie
To them, in such a way that if
There's doubt in any mind about
My honesty, it shall be banished now
And give true pride of place to certainty.
I do admit, my lord, you looked
Upon me favourably once,
And chose to honour me with gifts
As generous as your affections;
But it is true, as well, that I,
Convinced that honour is a gift
More precious still, in all that time
Resisted your attentions just
As stubbornly as frozen peaks
Deny those flowers and plants that try
To cling to them. If then, unmarried, I

Rejected all those lover's favours, should
I, now that I am married, change
My mind and foolishly agree
That I instead shall be your saviour?
I am, my lord, excused that role,
But cannot, as a woman, fail
To feel concern and sympathy.
I beg you do not leave the house
Like this and put at risk the safety
Of your health.

ENRIQUE.
                    I think the risk
          Is greater to me if I stay!

          Enter DON GUTIERRE *and* COQUÍN

GUTIERRE.
          My royal lord, you bring to our house
          True majesty. I enter it
          As one who comes into the presence of
          The sun in all its fullest glory.
          I am consumed with joy, but I
          Confess my joy is sadness too,
          For as my spirits are now brightened, now
          So are they also darkened, now
          The soaring eagle that swiftly flashes to
          The sun, now the humble moth that in
          The candle's flame is burned to ash.
          I feel at once the same alarm,
          Occasioned by your fall, as has
          Been felt through all Castile, and yet
          The same relief on seeing how
          You have escaped from real harm.
          Who would have said emotions such
          As these would ever reign in such
          Complete confusion? The joy I felt
          Was at the same time deepest sadness,
          But what was sadness is now joy.
          My lord, I beg you, honour this
          Abode awhile, though it be quite
          Unworthy of your majesty.
          For as the sun illuminates
          The palace of a king, so can
          Its light, transforming dullest straw

To gleaming topaz, so create
Anew the humblest of cottages.
And since you are our Spanish sun,
It is both right and proper you
Remain with us; for if the sun creates
Its own domain, so does the presence of
The King create its palace.

ENRIQUE.

Gutierre Alfonso Solís,
I much appreciate the joy
And sorrow you have felt for me.
Such sentiments shall be engraved
Eternally upon my soul,
And prove a constant source of strength.

GUTIERRE.

Your highness greatly honours me.

ENRIQUE.

But though this house has qualities
To grace the presence of a prince,
And beauty too that might convince
Him at some other time he ought
To stay, I cannot stay a moment
Longer. My fall has been the cause
Of so much pain, I now begin
To fear for my life: not merely
On account of having fallen,
But on account of knowing too
That something I intended is
Impossible. So I must go
At once and leave this house behind.
When disappointment lies ahead,
A moment seems a century,
Each minute an eternity.

GUTIERRE.

My lord, you must have cause
Indeed to leave this house with such
Great speed, and risk the life of one
Who merits only celebration.

ENRIQUE.

I need to reach Seville today.

GUTIERRE.
> To seek some other explanation seems
> Perhaps an impropriety,
> But even so my loyalty . . .

ENRIQUE.
> Demands a clearer version of
> The story.

GUTIERRE.
> But only if your lordship
> So desires. How can I insist
> When that would be discourtesy?

ENRIQUE.
> Then listen closely now. It goes
> Like this and most concerns a friend
> Of mine, a friend so close to me
> He could quite easily have been
> My other self.

GUTIERRE.
> A happy fate,
> My lord!

ENRIQUE.
> In my own absence I
> Had placed my trust entirely in him,
> My soul, my joy, my life itself,
> Dependent on a certain lady;
> And yet this friend, no sooner had
> I gone, saw fit to take advantage of
> My absence to abuse the trust
> And confidence I'd placed in him.
> His treachery allowed another man
> To gain possession of her will,
> And soon another lover won
> That heart that I loved still. Oh, how
> Can any man who ever felt
> Such love accept such savage blows
> With calm and equanimity?

GUTIERRE.
> I doubt he ever could, my lord.

ENRIQUE.
> And so the heavens torment and mock
> Me constantly, and everywhere

I go I see my jealousy
Take shape before my eyes, and all
My fears personified, as now
I see them here in front of me.
Oh, let me leave this house! My jealousy
Goes with me now and yet I feel
Somehow . . . indeed I am convinced . . .
That much of it remains behind me.

MENCÍA.
My good lord, it's often said
A woman gives the best advice.
If you have no objection, I
Could offer an opinion that
Might, at the same time, prove a kind
Of consolation. I would advise
You set aside your jealousy,
And recommend your lordship seek
Your friend and ask him for
A simple explanation. Perhaps
He has the very best of reasons.
Perhaps you take his name in vain
When in reality he's not
To blame. You let your anger sweep
Aside your common sense, and now
Forget it is impossible
To dominate the will of someone else.
As far as your friend's concerned,
I've given you my own opinion.
As for the lady, the explanation might
Be simple too: not so much
A change of heart, more the imposition of
Another will. On that account
I think you ought to see the lady
And have, as well, her version of the story.

ENRIQUE.
It isn't possible.

Enter DON DIEGO.

DIEGO.
The horse
Is ready now, my lord.

GUTIERRE.

> But this is far too risky! You must
> Not try to mount the horse that brought
> About your fall. I beg you, take
> This mare of mine, my lord: this fair,
> Well-balanced, gentle creature,
> Always answers to her master's call.
> She knows that beast, no less than man,
> Is born to his own destiny,
> And is in every sense a prodigy.
> Observe her shape's the very best:
> So gently rounded in haunch and breast;
> So finely balanced in head and neck;
> So smooth and supple in her motion!
> In short, the perfect combination
> Of every one of nature's wondrous
> Elements: her body earth, her spirit
> Fire, her foaming mouth the sea,
> Her speed the essence of the wind.

ENRIQUE.

> Oh, Don Gutierre, the picture dazzles me!
> And yet I cannot tell which is
> The one you've drawn for me, which is
> The true reality: the mare
> Or the picture, the picture or
> The mare.

> *Enter* COQUÍN.

COQUÍN.

> Do have a care, my lord.
> It's only me. I beg you offer me
> Your hand or foot, whichever of
> Them happens to be nearer.

GUTIERRE.

> Get out, you fool.

ENRIQUE.

> No, let him stay.
> His sense of humour endears him
> To me.

COQUÍN.

> Just blame the mare for it,
> My lord. The merest mention of

Her name is quite enough to bring
Me galloping. We are twin fellows,
Her and me, except that she, of course,
Is not a fellow, strictly speaking.

ENRIQUE.

Who are you, then?

COQUÍN.

Why, can't you tell,
If you just look at me, that I
Am just the dogsbody in this
Fine house? Coquín's the name, as was
My father's too before me. One thing
I do is feed the mare, who, just
To show she's grateful for it, lets
Me share her oats – and so makes sure
I get a balanced, staple diet.
But leaving that aside, we do
Congratulate your lordship.
This is your special day.

ENRIQUE.

My day? Whatever can you mean?

COQUÍN.

As plain as the nose on your face.

ENRIQUE.

Not if the day we call our day
Is one on which we should be happy.
As far as I'm concerned, my friend,
It's only brought me misery.

COQUÍN.

But don't you see, my lord, it has
To be your day because you fell
On it, and so all calendars
Can truly say henceforth: 'Today
Is Prince Enrique's Day, but not
Because it falls on this or that;
But just because he fell on it'.

GUTIERRE.

If you intend to leave, my lord
To thus delay would not be right,
When day, invited by the ocean god
To share his cold and icy bed,
Is slipping quickly into night.

ENRIQUE.

>May God protect you, Mencía.
>To prove I value your advice,
>I'll seek the lady out. She'll have
>The opportunity to tell me what
>She meant by so forgetting me.

>*Aside.*

>The pain that trying to contain
>What cannot be revealed is scarce
>Concealed! Impossible to bear!
>What can we say of what we've seen
>Today except you win, you lose,
>And he still has his favourite mare!

Exit ENRIQUE, DON ARIAS, DON DIEGO and COQUÍN.

GUTIERRE.

>Most lovely lady, as your will
>Is mine, so mine is yours, our lives
>As one in perfect harmony;
>I know, therefore, that when I ask
>Your leave to travel to Seville
>To pay our homage to his majesty
>The King, who leaves Castile and comes
>To honour us, you'll do so willingly.
>As well as that, of course, I think
>It fitting I should also wait
>Upon the Prince, in recognition of
>The honour his misfortune has
>Bestowed upon our humble household.

MENCÍA.

>I should be angry if there were
>Some other reason here, my lord.

GUTIERRE.

>What other reason could there be?

MENCÍA.

>The hope, perhaps, that you might see
>Leonor once more?

GUTIERRE.

>   Oh, come, Mencía!
>Why do you need to mention her?

MENCÍA.

> Because you men are as you are!
> Today's love forgotten tomorrow.
> Today's pleasure, tomorrow's sorrow!

GUTIERRE.

> But then, Mencía, I could not see
> The sun, and therefore thought the moon
> Was beautiful. But now I see
> The sun and can appreciate
> How truly great the difference is
> That separates the day and night.
> To illustrate the truth of this,
> Consider how the flame burns at
> Its brightest in the dark of night,
> And seems to occupy the sphere of
> The wind; but when the sun appears,
> All other light is quickly put
> To flight and dazzled by this one
> Superior majesty. And so,
> Mencía, by analogy,
> I loved a light that seemed to be
> The sun itself, and filled me with
> A sense of wonder; until I gazed
> Upon another sun and saw
> A splendour that eclipsed all other.
> The brightest star seems loveliest
> Until we see the beauty of the sun.

MENCÍA.

> Oh this is flattery indeed!
> You ought to try your hand at poetry,
> Husband!

GUTIERRE.

>   Then you aren't happy I
> Should go?

MENCÍA.

>   I am unhappy only
> Because you want to go so much.

GUTIERRE.

> But there is no dishonesty
> In this, Mencía. Wherever I
> Go, you are with me.

MENCÍA.

                Then I am happy
To have you here when you are gone.
Goodbye, Gutierre.

GUTIERRE.

                    Goodbye, Mencía.

Exit GUTIERRE.

JACINTA.

You seem extremely sad, madam.

MENCÍA.

Yes, Jacinta. And with good cause.

JACINTA.

I cannot think what can
Have happened to distract you so.

MENCÍA.

You cannot?

JACINTA.

              No. But you can trust me.

MENCÍA.

Listen then, and you shall know
Of matters that affect my life
And honour. My birthplace was Seville,
And there it was that Prince Enrique first
Set eyes on me. He courted me,
Pursued me constantly, ignoring my
Disdain . . . Oh, such a happy, happy time!
But then he went away again,
And so my father took advantage of
His power and authority,
And gave me to Gutierre as his wife.
You see Enrique has come back.
I cannot love, I must obey.
There's nothing else for me to say.

Exit MENCÍA *and* JACINTA. *Enter the* KING, *various petitioners.*

FIRST PETITIONER.

I humbly beg your majesty
Read my petition.

KING.
                              Let me see
    It.
SECOND PETITIONER.
        Would your majesty do me
    The honour of receiving this?

KING.
    Give it!
SECOND PETITIONER (*aside*).
                    He doesn't waste his words.

THIRD PETITIONER.
    I am . . .
KING.
                Just let the paper speak!
SOLDIER (*aside*).
    I'm frightened to approach the King.
KING.
    Why do you tremble?
SOLDIER.
                              At the sight
    Of your majesty.
KING.
                        Quite right
    And proper too! What do you want?
SOLDIER.
    I'm a poor soldier, sir. A small advance.
KING.
    Don't ask for so little. I give you a lance.
SOLDIER.
    I am most grateful, your majesty.
OLD MAN.
    I'm old and poor. I beg for money.
KING.
    This diamond is yours.
OLD MAN.
                    You give
    Me what's yours, your majesty?

KING.
>   Why be surprised? If the world were
>   A diamond, it might be your prize.

LEONOR.
>   Your majesty, I come before
>   Your royal presence filled with fear.
>   The matter concerns my honour.
>   No sooner do I mention it,
>   My words become my sighs, my sighs
>   My tears. I come to plead that God
>   And your majesty now offer me
>   The justice I deserve.

KING.
>   Arise,
>   Madam.

LEONOR (*getting up*).
>   My name is . . .

KING.
>   In good time.
>   Everyone here shall wait outside.
>   Now you may speak. If you wish to discuss
>   Honour, never make a public fuss.
>   It simply gives them extra food
>   To chew on afterwards. What's more,
>   It makes no sense at all to claim
>   You wish to have your name restored,
>   And at the same time spread your shame.

LEONOR.
>   Your majesty, the whole world knows
>   You as the Just King Pedro, sun
>   And supreme planet of Castile,
>   A Spanish Jupiter whose sword
>   Of tempered steel strikes sparks and in
>   The heart of every Moor instils
>   A deep and constant fear. My name
>   Is Leonor, my claim to fame
>   The beauty on account of which
>   I am well-known in Andalusia;
>   Though, if the truth be told, my fame
>   Has less to do with beauty than
>   With fortune, for a woman's beauty

Is sometimes merely her misfortune.
A certain gentleman, your majesty,
Set eyes on me. Oh, if those eyes
Had only then been basilisks
Or deadly asps, they would have put
An end to me! But no. Instead
They fanned desire, this in turn
The fire of love, and soon this gentleman
Began to haunt the street in which
I lived, as day passed into night
And night to day. Oh, how can I
Explain to you, your majesty,
That, thus besieged by love, my need
To guard my reputation was
Quite soon in conflict with my sense
Of obligation! This in turn
Became my gratitude, and this
My love, for in the school of love
All loves are thus rewarded by degrees:
A tiny flame bursts into fire,
A gentle breeze becomes a gale,
A little cloud a mighty storm,
A glimmer of light the brightest blaze,
And so, the spark of love, once struck,
Aspires to be each one of these:
Both fire and storm and gale and blaze.
This gentleman gave me his word
He'd be my husband, throwing me
The bait these cunning fishermen
Employ to trick all honourable
Women. I find it hard to tell
Myself he lied to me, and yet
It would surprise me even more
If he had told the truth. And so
He now gained entrance to my house,
Though honour was a prize he could
Not claim and never would. But soon
The whole affair was known to everyone,
And any honour I preserved
In private was in public quickly gone.
I sought the justice I deserved.
I brought a public accusation,
But I am poor and he is rich,

And now my situation is
Impossible, for he is married.
I come to you, your majesty,
To seek the justice worthy of
A great and noble sovereign. I ask
As well, to be allowed to spend
My days within a convent. The man
Responsible for this is Don
Gutierre Alfonso de Solís.

KING.

Madam, as someone bowed beneath
The great and heavy weight of justice,
I think I understand your feelings
Perfectly. If, however, as
You state, Gutierre's married, it's
Too late for him to satisfy
Your honour; though we shall seek what justice
Possible. We need, of course, to hear
His explanation. In this you have
To trust me, Leonor, remembering
There's no occasion while I'm King
For you to say that you are weak
And he is strong. I see him coming.
He only has to see you here
To know you've told me everything.
Hide there behind the screen. If he
Hasn't seen you, he'll talk more freely.

LEONOR.

I obey at once, your majesty.

She hides. Enter COQUÍN.

COQUÍN.

Am I nothing but my master's
Shadow; off he goes and I
Must follow? God save me! It's
The King. Too late. I think he's seen me!
Oh, dear, he's looking very glum.
I wish this balcony were nearer
The ground. I'd make a run for it.

KING.

Who are you?

COQUÍN.

>   Me, your majesty?

KING.

> You.

COQUÍN.

>   Ah, well, let's see. Whoever
> You want me to be. The thing is,
> Your majesty, I met this bloke
> Quite recently, oh, very wise,
> Who told me I should be exactly what
> You wished. And so I've taken that
> Advice so seriously, that what
> I was, am now, and shall be in
> The future was, is, and shall be
> Precisely what you want. I mean,
> If you don't really want me here,
> I can be off. My feet shall be
> My guide despite the fact that I
> Can't guide my feet as quickly as I'd like.

KING.

> I didn't ask you who you'd like
> To be. I asked you who you are.

COQUÍN.

> I know you did, your majesty,
> And I'd have answered honestly
> But for the risk of being thrown
> From off this balcony because
> I've no authority to be in here.
> My job is not the sort to please
> You greatly either.

KING.

> Which is?

COQUÍN.

>   You might call me a sort
> Of messenger, a bringer of news;
> You know, the sort you have to ferret
> For, use your noddle, stick your nose
> In other people's business.
> You could say that I live in other
> People's houses, though at the moment
> It's Gutierre Alfonso Solís's.

As well as that, I am the twin
Of pleasure and every kind of mirth.
Which is to say I treat each day
As if it were an extra birthday,
And wouldn't know sorrow if he
Sat next to me, which he wouldn't, would he?
In other words, your majesty,
I'm laughter's right-hand man, jollity's
Good companion, hilarity's
Most loyal fan; which tells you why
I wasn't keen to tell you my
Identity, when it's well known
Your majesty's a king who never laughs.
In other words, I was afraid
You might not be too happy with
Me wasting your precious time.

KING.
So you, my fine fellow, hold the key
To laughter.

COQUÍN.
        So I'm told,
Your majesty. It wouldn't be
True modesty for me to say it.

KING.
In that case we shall strike a bargain.

COQUÍN.
Come again.

KING.
        You can make people laugh?

COQUÍN.
I can.

KING.
        Then every time you make
Me laugh, you'll have a bag of gold.
But if, when all of us are older by
One month, you haven't made me laugh,
Your payment shall be measured by
Your grief. My surgeon shall amuse
Himself by pulling out your teeth.

COQUÍN.
Your majesty, I think this bargain could

Be very harmful to me
Professionally speaking, not
To mention painful!

KING.

What do you mean?

COQUÍN.

A proper liability.
You see, a person shows his teeth
To others when he laughs. So what
Would I do? Give a demonstration
Of my lack of teeth and have them
Curse me for a jester in reverse?
They say you are a cruel man.
You don't just show your teeth to someone.
You insist on baring them! But what
Can I have done to you to make
You want to take away my teeth?
But still, I have no choice and must
Accept the wager – at least it helps
To get me out of here.
In any case, I've got a month
To have some fun before the surgeon
Gets his fingers on my gums.
Meanwhile, I'll see if I can't get
Some practice in. I'll have you laughing yet,
I swear it. I'm not joking.
Do you get it? I'm not Joe, King!
How could I be? My name's Coquín.

Exit COQUÍN. *Enter* ENRIQUE, GUTIERRE, DIEGO, ARIAS
and attendants.

ENRIQUE.

Welcome, your majesty.

KING.

Welcome,
Enrique. May God be with you.
I trust your health is much improved.

ENRIQUE.

So much it could not prove much better.
The shock was greater than the fall.

GUTIERRE.
>I come, your majesty,
>To kiss your hand and beg that you
>Command me as you will. To come
>Into your presence is to stand
>Before the sun itself and be
>Forever dazzled by its brightness.
>We wish your majesty good health,
>So you can rule this kingdom well,
>And all of Spain may thus acclaim
>Its greatest hero, crowned with laurel.

KING.
>I am afraid, Don Gutierre . . .

GUTIERRE.
>Why do you turn away from me?

KING.
>A grave complaint has recently been made.

GUTIERRE.
>I swear that it is quite unfounded.

KING.
>Tell me. Do you know a certain Leonor,
>A most distinguished lady of
>This city?

GUTIERRE.
>I do, your majesty.
>She is most beautiful, of true
>Nobility and faultless reputation.

KING.
>What obligation do you have
>To her that you have chosen to
>Ignore so foolishly and cruelly?
>I need a full and honest explanation.

GUTIERRE.
>If you insist, your majesty,
>I shall recount the story as
>It happened, truthfully and in
>Its every detail. It all began
>When I attended Leonor.
>I had the very best intention:
>Which was, if nothing changed that situation,

> To take her as my wife. And so
> I saw her often, visited
> Her house quite openly, and can confirm
> That neither greed nor any such
> Consideration governed me.
> But then I had a change of heart,
> No longer felt that obligation,
> And married Doña Mencía de Acuña,
> Another noble lady of
> This city. We live now in
> The countryside, outside Seville.
> Unfortunately, Leonor
> Was then advised to bring a charge
> Of breach of promise – how can advice
> Be good that in the end turns out
> So badly? The very sternest judge
> Was not convinced that I'd committed
> Any impropriety,
> Though Leonor would have you think
> The judgement bought by bribery,
> As if the beauty of a woman
> Were not itself the most effective form
> Of bribery! And knowing this,
> She seeks to have your majesty
> Now give your judgement in her favour.
> I kneel at your royal feet,
> My sword a token of my faith,
> My head the witness of my trust
> That here resides the proper seat of justice.

KING.

> What was the cause of your change
> Of heart?

GUTIERRE.

>   Your majesty, it's not
> Uncommon. On the contrary,
> It is the kind of thing that happens daily.

KING.

> Quite true. But when a man's intention
> Changes, something must have happened
> To occasion it. Is that not so?

GUTIERRE.

> I beg you, do not press me any more.

The lady is not here to face
My accusation. I'd rather give
My life than harm her reputation.

KING.
Then you admit you had good cause?

GUTIERRE.
I did. But if, in order to
Explain myself and thus remove
The stain upon my honour, I am
Obliged to state that cause, I cannot
As a man of honour, do so.

KING.
I wish to know!

GUTIERRE.
           I beg of you!

KING.
You dare defy the King? In God's name,
You inflame my anger so . . .

GUTIERRE.
Your majesty, you must not take
God's name in vain on my account.
I'd rather sacrifice my honour
Than know myself to be the cause
Of your anger. I obey.

KING (aside).
This man must state his case quite clearly,
So Leonor can verify
Its accuracy. Moreover, should
She prove the guilty one, she'll know
I know it too. (To GUTIERRE.) Recount what actually
    happened.

GUTIERRE.
I have to say, your majesty,
I visited Leonor one night,
And, entering a room, caught sight
Of someone leaving by the balcony.
I hurried after him but he
Had gone. The whole thing still remains
A mystery.

ARIAS (*aside*).
>   In God's name!
>   What is happening to me?

GUTIERRE.
>   Though Leonor attempted then
>   To prove her innocence – indeed,
>   I cannot say that I believed
>   Her truly guilty – it was enough
>   To shake my confidence in her too much
>   To warrant marriage. Love and honour seem
>   To me, your majesty, to touch
>   The soul itself, and any injury
>   To love is of necessity
>   Injurious to the soul.

LEONOR *appears from behind the screen.*

LEONOR.
>   I cannot suffer any more,
>   Your majesty, these callous blows
>   That fortune rains upon my head.

KING (*aside*).
>   The strategy is justified.
>   The lady has been nicely led!

LEONOR.
>   To listen to such slurs against
>   My name and lack the courage to
>   Reply to them is certain proof
>   Of cowardice. It matters less
>   To me to sacrifice my life,
>   If that's the price I have to pay,
>   Than suffer this attack upon my honour.
>   The man you saw was Don Arias!

ARIAS.
>   My lady! Say no more. Your majesty,
>   I beg you let me speak and so
>   Defend this lady's reputation.
>   The truth is this. Upon the night
>   In question, another lady was
>   At Leonor's, a girl I planned
>   To marry had not cruel fate
>   Cut short her lovely life. I had
>   Arranged to meet her there and gone

Inside, my eagerness to see
Her once again so great it brushed
Aside Leonor's attempts to plead
With me. And so, when afterwards
Gutierre came quite unexpectedly,
Leonor was terrified and I,
No less alarmed than she, sought refuge in
A bedroom. When woman gives a man
Advice, how soon he pays the price for it!
In short, Gutierre came into
The room and I, in order to
Avoid a needless confrontation with
The man so soon to marry Leonor,
Jumped from the balcony. But now
I answer him and ask permission of
Your majesty to let me give
The lie to any slur upon
This lady's faultless reputation.
The accusation is a lie.

GUTIERRE.
It's you who lie, sir.

They reach for their swords.

KING.
                    Both of you!
You dare behave so disrespectfully
And in my company? Does not this royal
Countenance inspire fear?
Can there be pride and arrogance
To equal this? Take them away
At once and lock them in the tower.
Be thankful I do not employ
The power I have to have your heads!

Exit the King.

ARIAS (*aside*).
On my account Leonor has lost
Her honour and her name.
I swear she will recover it
Again through me.

GUTIERRE (*aside*).
The anger of the King is not
The thing that truly saddens me:

Much more the thought that I, without
Mencía, live unhappily.

They are taken away.

ENRIQUE (*aside*).
With him a prisoner, I think
It possible the lovely lady might
Be rather lonely. A little hunting's called for.
Perhaps she'd like some company.

Exit ENRIQUE.

LEONOR.
My life is ended. May God grant
Me vengeance on this cruel, false,
Deceitful, lawless, godless man.
My honour is destroyed, yet I
Am innocent. May he be punished by
The very instrument with which
He has inflicted pain on me!
I pray to God that he be made
To feel the pain I feel, and see
His own dishonour bathed in blood.
He has ensured I can never be
The wife of anyone. The end
Of honour is the end of life.

Act Two

The garden of GUTIERRE's *country-house. Enter* JACINTA *and*
ENRIQUE.

JACINTA.
>Come with me, but quietly. Try not
>To make a sound.

ENRIQUE.
>   I promise you, Jacinta,
>My feet will barely touch the ground.

JACINTA.
>This is the garden. Now that night's
>Dark cloak conceals you and Don Gutierre
>Cannot see you, everything
>Is in your favour. You can taste
>Love's sweet delight and honeyed pleasure.

ENRIQUE.
>The liberty I promised you
>Seems poor recompense for such
>A prize as this. If there is some
>More precious gift you'd have, I place
>My life and soul at your service.

JACINTA.
>My mistress comes alone at night,
>She sits a while before going in.

ENRIQUE.
>Be quiet, do not speak so loud.
>I fear the wind is listening.

JACINTA.
>I must go back before I'm missed,
>So I cannot be blamed for this.

>*Exit* JACINTA.

ENRIQUE.
>Love shall guide my steps. These leaves
>Shall be my hiding-place, though I
>Can scarcely claim to be the first

Who from their safety dared to turn
His face towards the beauty of the sun.
Let Acteon be my witness!

Enter DOÑA MENCÍA *and servants.*

MENCÍA.
Silvia, Teodora, Jacinta!
JACINTA.
What is your wish, my lady?
MENCÍA.
                              Bring
Some light and keep me company.
I wish to overcome the sadness that
Gutierre's absence causes me.
Let Nature prove itself superior to
The things that Art considers it
Can offer us. Teodora!

TEODORA.
                              Yes,
My lady?
MENCÍA.
           Can the music of
Your voice succeed in banishing
My sadness?
TEODORA.
                My only wish is that
Both word and melody combined
Shall prove a source of instant gladness.

TEODORA *sings and* MENCÍA *falls asleep.*

TEODORA.
'Oh nightingale, your lovely song
Now fills this place with happiness.
Oh nightingale, don't leave us now,
For we would feel such deep sadness.'
JACINTA.
Enough, Teodora. Sleep already gives
Sweet solace to her gentle soul.
When sorrows find their consolation,
Who would dare awaken them?

TEODORA.
>We'd best go quietly, so she
>Might have the opportunity to rest.

JACINTA (*aside*).
>And someone else, who's desperate,
>The chance to be my lady's lover.
>The downfall of such noble honour!

Exit the servants. Enter ENRIQUE.

ENRIQUE.
>She is alone. Must I believe
>That fortune favours me? But now
>I am embarked upon this course,
>I pray that both the time and place
>Assist me now. Mencía!

MENCÍA (*awakening*).
>Heavens!

ENRIQUE.
>Do not be frightened!

MENCÍA.
>What is this?

ENRIQUE.
>A sudden boldness, madam, best
>Explained by all the time I've spent
>In hopeless longing, cruel pain.

MENCÍA.
>You, my lord!

ENRIQUE.
>You must be calm!

MENCÍA.
>Here in my house?

ENRIQUE.
>Don't be alarmed!

MENCÍA.
>You dared to enter . . .

ENRIQUE.
>Madam, listen!

MENCÍA.
>Where only he would venture who
>Would dare destroy the reputation of

A lady, and thoughtlessly offend
The precious honour of a man
Who is amongst his majesty's
Most noble and most loyal subjects.

ENRIQUE.

I was persuaded by your own
Advice: that I should go and ask
The lady who abandoned me
For some more satisfactory
Account of her offence against
My love. Is that not so?

MENCÍA.

I am to blame. But since I must
Absolve myself of blame, I ask
You have regard for my good name
And reputation.

ENRIQUE.

How can you think
That I have no regard, when I
Know well how jealously you guard
The precious jewel of your reputation?
That's why I thought it best to come
Alone and not to tell the rest
About my little hunting expedition.
I do not wish to kill my prey;
I wish to see my lovely heron speed
Away through skies of blue and soar
Towards the golden palace of the sun.

MENCÍA.

The heron does, my lord, have this
Ability. They say that instinct drives
It to aspire to the heavens,
Like some bright comet lacking its
Bright tail of fire, winged lightning
Without its flame, or feathered cloud
Possessing instinct, or fiery flash
Endowed with spirit. But soon
It's seen by birds of prey who block
Its path, and even though it tries
To fly away from them, it's said
That it already knows the hawk
On whose account it soon must die.

And so the heron will not stay
To fight, but, seized by fear, trembles in
Its flight, and losing heart and strength,
Feels death is slowly drawing near.
So I, on seeing you so close,
Am overcome by sudden fear,
Believing my own death is near.
And as the heron knows the hawk,
So now my fears are telling me
That for my death, my lord, you soon
Shall bear responsibility.

ENRIQUE.
I came to speak to you. I shall
Not lose this opportunity.

MENCÍA.
How can the heavens refuse to help
Me now? I'll call for help.

ENRIQUE.
                              Do that,
Mencía, you destroy yourself.

MENCÍA.
Let savage beasts now rescue me!

ENRIQUE.
My fury would be such, no beast,
However wild, would dare to touch me.

GUTIERRE's *voice is heard off-stage.*

GUTIERRE.
Coquín! Come! Hold the horse! Go knock
The door!

MENCÍA.
                Great heavens! Gutierre!
My life is at an end.

ENRIQUE.
                              I am
Convinced that misery is all
My fate intends.

MENCÍA.
                        What will become
Of me if he now finds you here?

ENRIQUE.
> Then tell me what I am to do.

MENCÍA.
> You have to hide at once.

ENRIQUE.
>   A man
> Of my nobility must hide?

MENCÍA.
> The honour of a lady begs
> You to. For you to try to leave
> Would be the proof that I attempted to
> Deceive my husband. The servants let
> You in but did not know what they
> Were doing. It isn't safe to leave.

ENRIQUE.
> Then tell me what to do.

MENCÍA.
>   Go to
> My room and hide behind the screen.

ENRIQUE.
> Until this moment I'd not known
> What fear means. I do believe
> A husband's bravery goes far
> Beyond the call of common duty!

> *He conceals himself.*

MENCÍA.
> I am innocent and yet
> Am made to suffer so unfairly,
> What must the poor woman feel
> Who fears because she's truly guilty?

> *Enter* GUTIERRE *and* COQUÍN.

GUTIERRE.
> Mencía, I embrace you joyfully
> A thousand times.

MENCÍA.
>   My lord, you seek
> To imitate the vines that here
> Surround us and persistently
> Embrace each other.

GUTIERRE.
                    But I do not
    Pretend, Mencía. I come to see you.

MENCÍA.
    You flatter me, husband, as much
    As any eager, constant lover.

GUTIERRE.
    I do not cease to be a lover
    Simply because I have become a husband.
    The truth is beauty merits flattery,
    Moreover, constantly invites it,
    Often ignores the risk to it,
    And thus creates the opportunity
    Where it may flourish.

MENCÍA.
                              I am
    Indebted to you, husband.

GUTIERRE.
                           And I
    To one who is both gaoler and
    Good friend. But if he's freed my body from
    Their chains, he's made my eager soul
    A prisoner by giving me
    This chance to see you once again
    And feel such happiness as this.

MENCÍA.
    Whoever felt such joy?

GUTIERRE.
                           As I
    Do now. I think this gaoler has,
    In offering me freedom, offered me
    The greatest favour any man can give.
    I had no soul when I was prisoner,
    For you possessed my soul entirely.
    And so, to grant me freedom was
    To give the opportunity
    Whereby both soul and body might
    In your presence once again
    Achieve their proper harmony.
    Mencía, my very being has
    Endured such great injury,

My body incarcerated there,
My soul entrusted to your care.

MENCÍA.
They say two instruments in tune
Are able to communicate
Quite perfectly through every sound
They make; for when the one is played,
The sound is carried on the wind
And wounds the other, which then will play
In sympathy. My own experience now
Bears witness to the truth of this,
For as you, husband, suffered there,
So correspondingly I suffered here.

COQUÍN.
Oh, yes. And I have suffered too,
My lady. Not a soul to share
My misery! I'm on my own
I am, tormented by the thoughts
That fill my head, and wondering
Who cares if poor, unfortunate Coquín's
Alive or dead?

MENCÍA.
                    What is the matter, Coquín?

COQUÍN.
Not what's the matter. More what's not
The matter! The pity is, you see,
The King loves me like his own brother,
But if this caper carries on
Much longer, I'm inclined to think
My master here will be a goner,
And I'll be gone a good deal sooner!

MENCÍA (to GUTIERRE).
I am afraid you took me by surprise,
Gutierre. Not expecting company,
I have no food prepared for you.

GUTIERRE.
Then let the servants see to it.

MENCÍA.
No. I insist, for I must always be
Your loyal servant. But let Jacinta come
With me. (*Aside.*) While I have strength, I have

To seek some remedy for my
Affliction. Honour, please protect
Me now. The course of action I
Must take affects my reputation.

Exit MENCÍA *and* JACINTA.

GUTIERRE.

Coquín, stay here with me, and be
Quite sure that you behave as I
Expect you to. I gave my word
That we'd be back in prison by
The time it's light. I shall enjoy
What little of the night is left to me.

COQUÍN.

D'you know what, master? I've just had
The best idea ever in
The history of intellectual
Endeavour. Your life depends on it.
You'll never rest until you've heard the ins
And outs of it.

GUTIERRE.

Oh, very well, just tell
Me what it is.

COQUÍN.

A simple strategy,
Whereby a man survives a prison-life
Without the slightest injury
To either hide or hair.

GUTIERRE.

Which is?

COQUÍN.

Quite simple really. Don't go back there.
Look at yourself. You're in good shape.
Tip-top condition. To keep your health,
Not going back's the best solution.

GUTIERRE.

You are in serious danger, fool,
Of losing yours. You dare suggest
That I betray the gaoler when
I've given him my word? To do
So would but compromise my honour.

COQUÍN.
>If I'm quite honest, master, I
>Just wonder if his majesty
>The King is quite the fellow I
>Considered him to be. As well
>As that, I feel obliged to ask
>Myself what has this honour lark
>To do with me? I've got a mind
>To jack it in and not go back.

GUTIERRE.
>You'd leave me go?

COQUÍN.
>   I might well do.

GUTIERRE.
>You know what they would say of you.

COQUÍN.
>So let them say it if they want to.
>Am I to suffer horribly
>So people can talk well of me?
>If I could only find something
>To recommend my suffering,
>Or maybe have a choice and say
>Which bit of it I might prefer,
>Well maybe I'd agree to it.
>But as I see it, life's a rough
>Old game. I start with what I think's
>A winning hand and place my bet;
>Before I know it I'm in debt.
>And if I lose this jolly game,
>I'll be an old-age pensioner
>Before I pay it off again.

Enter MENCÍA *alone, extremely agitated.*

MENCÍA.
>Gutierre! Quickly! Come at once!

GUTIERRE.
>In heaven's name! What has happened? Tell
>Me.

MENCÍA.
>   A man!

GUTIERRE.

What can you mean? A man?

MENCÍA.
A man was hidden in my room.
I took him by surprise. He drew
His cloak across his face as soon
As I went in.

GUTIERRE.

Shall I believe
What I am hearing now, or do your words
Astonish me so much I am
Deceived by them? A man concealed?
You say his cloak across his face?

MENCÍA.
I saw him clearly.

GUTIERRE.

My heart is turned
To ice. Come, bring the light.

COQUÍN.

What me?

GUTIERRE.
You must come with me. Quickly now.
Do not be frightened.

MENCÍA.

Are you really such
A coward? Draw your sword. Go with
Him. I shall bring the light.

She takes the lamp and, without being seen, puts out the light.

The lamp's gone out.

JACINTA enters, guiding ENRIQUE.

GUTIERRE.
The light is what is needed most.
No matter. We shall do without.

Exit GUTIERRE.

JACINTA (*to* ENRIQUE, *aside*).
This way, my lord. Just follow me.
I know each nook and cranny of
The house. You'll soon be safely out.

While GUTIERRE *has gone out through one door,* JACINTA
takes ENRIQUE *out through the other.* GUTIERRE *enters
again and seizes* COQUÍN.

COQUÍN.
I don't know where I am.

GUTIERRE (*aside*).

This is the man.

COQUÍN.
Master, listen!

GUTIERRE.

Until we get
Some light, I'll hold him tight, see who
He is and kill him afterwards.

COQUÍN.
Believe me, master. You don't know
What you are doing.

MENCÍA (*aside*).

Oh, heavens! What will
Become of me if he discovers him?

Enter JACINTA *with a lamp.*

GUTIERRE.
At last some light to tell us who
This creature is.

COQUÍN.

This creature's me,
Master. I've told you that already.

GUTIERRE.
You? Fool! How can it possibly
Be you?

COQUÍN.
Because it is. I told
You, didn't I?

GUTIERRE.

I heard, yet thought
The man who spoke was not the man
I held. Oh, how can anyone
Have patience to endure this
In such blind ignorance?

MENCÍA (*to* JACINTA).

Has he gone,
Jacinta?

JACINTA.

Yes, madam. It is done.

MENCÍA.

That this should happen while you are
Away! It's best you search the house.
Your absence may be known to thieves
And lead them to believe they have
A better chance to steal from us.

GUTIERRE.

I shall investigate. The heavens
Are witness to my anger. That knowledge of
My absence should lead anyone
To contemplate an outrage such as this!

Exit GUTIERRE *and* COQUÍN.

JACINTA.

What made you take so great a risk?
It might have lost your reputation.

MENCÍA.

I think that, on the contrary,
It offers me salvation.

JACINTA.

You think so, madam?

MENCÍA.

If I'd said nothing to Gutierre,
He could so easily have thought
Me guilty of some indiscretion,
Perhaps some dark conspiracy
With someone else. On that account
I thought it better to invent
The story of a thief and so
Deceive Gutierre with the truth.

Enter GUTIERRE, *a dagger concealed beneath his cloak.*

GUTIERRE (*to* MENCÍA).

The man you thought you saw was some
Illusion, some trick invented by
A fearful imagination.

I found no sign of anyone,
Nor evidence to indicate
Your story has a basis in
Reality. (*Aside.*) The truth is that
My dear wife deceives me. I found
This dagger there, which fills
My mind with fear and suspicion,
And seems a fateful premonition of
My death. But there is time enough
To think of this. (*To* MENCÍA.) Mencía, come.
The night begins to slip away,
Wrapped in its cold, dark cloak. The day
Advances slowly. The time has come
For me to go, though sorrow is
The greater now in consequence
Of your fear. But go I must.

MENCÍA.

Then let a wife who truly loves
You, now embrace you.

GUTIERRE.

                    Mencía . . .

As he is about to embrace her, MENCÍA *sees the dagger.*

MENCÍA.

Gutierre! Why this dagger? Why
Kill me? I swear I have done nothing in
My life that could offend you. Please!
I beg you! Please!

GUTIERRE.

                  Mencía, what
Disturbs you so? What is the cause of such
Great fear?

MENCÍA.

             I saw you with the dagger bathed
In my own blood, and I lay there
At your feet, your own wife, dead.

GUTIERRE.

I found the dagger in the house.
I brought it with me.

MENCÍA.

               Then I suppose

That I imagined it. Forgive me!

GUTIERRE.
Imagination is your own
Worst enemy.

MENCÍA.
I have done nothing to
Offend you.

GUTIERRE.
Mencía, I believe you.
There is no need for explantion.
It's frequently the case that fear is
The cause of all our darkest visions.

MENCÍA.
I think my sadness, coupled with
My loneliness, have worked upon
My mind and placed before my eyes
This dark and fearful deception.

GUTIERRE.
Then if I can, I'll come again
Tonight, Mencía. God be with you.

MENCÍA.
And God go with you too, Gutierre.

Aside.

Oh, I am so afraid! My fears begin
To overwhelm my common-sense.

GUTIERRE (*aside*).
Oh, honour, you and I must speak
About these things in confidence.

They exit in different directions. Enter DON DIEGO *and the*
KING. *The* KING *carries a circular shield. He wears a red cloak
which he now removes.*

KING.
Don Diego, take my shield. I've spent
The night examining the streets
Of this great city, and thus am properly
Informed of all that may have recently
Occurred. Seville's a place where things
Are changing all the time. I need
To know what's happening, not just

For information, but in case
Decisive action must be taken.

DIEGO.

Of course, your majesty. The King
Must always be the Argos of
His kingdom, ever watchful, as
The eyes upon your sceptre indicate.
Have you seen much so late at night?

KING.

I have seen many men who by
Their actions throw all caution to
The wind; and women too who, by
Removing veils, display much indiscretion.
There is much music, dancing, gaming,
And voices imploring the passer-by
To try his luck; and then there are
Those men who seem to spend their time
In merely boasting. This has become
The fashion here, and since I find
It tiresome, it forced me to
Confront a crowd of them, so that
It can't be said the King does not
Attempt to test the Christian blood
Of those around him.

DIEGO.

             It's far too great
A risk, your majesty.

KING.

               I think
The contrary is true, Diego.
If all of them have such fine breeding,
Why fuss about a little bleeding?

Enter COQUÍN.

COQUÍN (*aside*).

To tell the truth, I didn't want
To go back to that prison, for
The very simple reason I
Prefer it here. I thought it best
To listen first and get a few
Opinions on it. Hey, hang on
A minute. Here's a fellow of

Great wit and jest approaching – the King
Comedian! On which account I think
It best that I be going.

KING.

Coquín.

COQUÍN.
My lord.

KING.

How goes it?

COQUÍN.

I shall reply
As any poor student might.

KING.
What's that?

COQUÍN.

'De corpore bene',
But 'de pecuniis male'.

KING.
If that's the case, you may regale
Me with some witty story. Tell
The tale amusingly enough
To make me laugh, this bag of gold
Will soon be your property.

COQUÍN.
Well what about your majesty
Considering the leading part
In our hilarious comedy,
'The King Called Angel'? No, I know,
Not funny. You'd much prefer a comic story.
I'll tell you one that really has
A funny ending – and it's pithy.

KING.
Proceed then with it. I expect
It to be constantly amusing.

COQUÍN.
Right, here it is, your majesty.
I saw this eunuch getting out
Of bed, and on his upper lip
A really flash moustache-protector.
Now there's a thing that should amuse you:

A great moustache-protector with
No proper home to go to! And so
I thought the following might please you.

Aside.

Come on now. Pedro, I'm not asking for
A palace; just a flicker of
A smile across your miserable face.

Aloud.

'In my opinion, Floro, your house
Cannot have any furniture,
If I'm to judge by your front door.
I mean to say, to have a meal,
You have to have a proper menu.
To have a fruit you have to have
A shell. And if you haven't, anyone
Will tell you there's no point in it.
To reap your harvest, you must sow
Your fields. So if you want to grow
A beard, Floro, just take care
Your chin has got some hair on it
To start with.'

KING.

                Quite unfunny!

COQUÍN.

                            Don't
You think it's worth the money then?

Enter ENRIQUE.

ENRIQUE.

I come to greet your majesty.

KING.

Enrique. I trust that you are well.

ENRIQUE.

I am, and your manner tells
Me you are too. There is a matter I,
With your permission, must discuss
With you – concerning Arias.

KING.

Of course, Enrique. But the man

Is under your protection. If
You wish, you may release the two
Of them. I place their lives, as well
As their reconciliation in
Your hands.

ENRIQUE.

May God protect your majesty,
And grant you long and happy life
From this day to eternity.

Exit the KING.

Go to the tower, Don Diego,
Inform the gaoler that the prisoners
Must be brought here. (*Aside*) Heaven grant me patience
To endure misfortune; and prudence too
To bring about its resolution.

Exit DIEGO.

Coquín, what are you doing here?

COQUÍN.

Why, trying not to hear what you
Were saying, sir, and wishing I
Was far away in Flanders.

ENRIQUE.

But why would you want that?

COQUÍN.

Because
The King's the very wonder of
The animal world, that's what.

ENRIQUE.

Explain to me.

COQUÍN.

Consider Nature, my good lord.
The bull's allowed to snort, the lion roar,
The oxen moo, the donkey bray,
The dog bark, the cat mew, the bird sing,
The horse neigh, the pig grunt, the wolf howl,
And yet, of all these creatures there
Is only one that is allowed
To laugh, which Aristotle in
His wisdom dubbed the laughing animal,

And that, of course, is man.
The King, however, proves a great
Exception to this rule and will
Not laugh, not even for his fool.
I am obliged on that account
To look for stories that much sharper, thus
Extracting from those lips
The faintest sign of royal laughter.

Exit COQUÍN. *Enter* GUTIERRE, ARIAS *and* DIEGO.

DIEGO.
The prisoners are here, my lord.

GUTIERRE.
We are most grateful to you, sir.

ARIAS.
Today you make us truly happy.

ENRIQUE.
I've managed to persuade the King
To treat you somewhat less severely.
You must be friends and not forget
That both of you are in my debt.

GUTIERRE (*aside*).
We shall behave, my lord, most properly.
Heaven help me if what I am seeing now
Is true!

ENRIQUE.
            You must shake hands on this.

ARIAS.
I offer you my hand, Gutierre.

GUTIERRE.
And I my arms, Don Arias,
In token of my true affection, we
Shall now be friends, and only death
Shall bring about our separation.

ARIAS.
Then let this gesture be a confirmation of
Our true and everlasting friendship.

ENRIQUE.
Then it is settled. Both of you
Are honourable men and conscious of
Your obligation to each other.

It is important you should both
Be friends. If either of you finds
Some fault with this, I'll have you state
The nature of your main objection.

GUTIERRE.
I give my word, my lord, I shall
Respect the vow of friendship I
Have taken. All my actions shall
Be proof of everything
That you expect of true nobility.
The man would be a fool who dared
Betray your loyalty or sought
To make an enemy of you.
I am a man of principle,
And thus obliged to keep the promise I
Have made. But who, in any case,
Would be as bold or foolish as
To have a man as powerful as you
Become his own worst enemy?
The wise and prudent man would be
Regarded as insane, and never look
Upon your lordship's face again.
It follows, then, if I am guilty of
Some indiscretion which offends
You so, I'd rather see the light
Of heaven denied to me than be
Obliged to face my lord once more.

ENRIQUE (aside).
This man is guilty of too great
A protestation. He promises
Too much and gives me every cause
For great suspicion. (Aloud.) Come, Don Arias.
There are many things we must discuss.

ARIAS.
I come at once, my lord.

Exit ENRIQUE, DIEGO and ARIAS.

GUTIERRE.
Enrique's silence points to his
Acceptance of my explanation.
But this is little consolation for
The agony of heart and mind

In which I find myself. But now
I am alone, I can at last
Express my feelings. God! Who can
Contain within a single speech,
Or hope to limit to a space
As small as human reason can
Embrace the sorrows and the fears
That now crowd in on me, and like
Some bold, advancing army seek
To bring about my end! For now
My feelings seek to break their bonds;
My poor heart dissolves in tears
And rushes to appear at
The windows of my soul, which are
My eyes. Oh, eyes, you have good cause
To weep! Do not let shame or sense
Of guilt keep you from weeping now.
This is a time when neither weakness nor
Great courage should prevail, but each
Of them respect the other. It is,
Though, also true that for the sake
Of honour, I must now avail
Myself of courage, not allow
My sentiments to take possession of
My being. The man who cries aloud
For justice fails to see beyond
The futile satisfaction of
His feelings. We, instead, by carefully
Examining the implications of
The question, seek to find the truth,
And see if there is no solution to
Resolve my constant doubts and fears.
I pray there is some simple answer
To exonerate my wife's behaviour.
The first thing in her favour is
The fact that when I reached my house
Last night, the door was opened to me and
I found her lying there, not suddenly
Disturbed but quietly asleep.
Again, as for the presence of
A stranger in the house, did not
My wife, informing me of it,
Conduct herself most properly?

And then, when suddenly the light
Went out, can it be proved that it
Was not quite accidentally?
As for this dagger, it could be
Some servant's property; and even if
We now admit its similarity
To Prince Enrique's royal sword,
There is no proof that it is his.
There could, there very well might be
Another sword exactly like it.
Its workmanship is not so good
As to exclude the possibility
It could belong to someone else,
Though if I now admit the truth,
I do believe – if only I did not! –
The dagger is Enrique's, and
That he, most cunningly concealed,
Was present somewhere in my house.
But even if he were, it does
Not prove Mencía was to blame.
Is not a bag of gold the key
That opens grasping servants' hearts
And paves the way to their disloyalty
To us? Of course! This is the answer to
My question, so obvious and so clear in
Its implications for Mencía,
I am amazed I had not thought
Of it before. And so there is
No need to take the matter any further.
What sense is there in that when all
The evidence suggests her innocence,
And there is no one in this world
Who could succeed in darkening
The brightness of her purity?
But wait. Does not a black cloud pass
Sometimes across the sun, cut out
Its light and freeze its lovely warmth?
Oh what unjust decree declares
That innocence should suffer so?
But honour, you are in great danger here,
Your precious health placed constantly
At risk when there's no guarantee
That, balanced on the edge of life,

Your end will not come suddenly.
For since it is a woman gives
You vital breath, it follows your
Existence is a living death.
But honour, we shall find the cure for
This serious malady, and since
The symptoms indicate an illness whose
Considerable gravity
Is not in question, we'll prescribe
A medicine whose aim must be
Its limitation. As the doctor and
Physician of my honour, I'll
Prescribe at first a goodly dose
Of silence mixed with caution.
Then, secondly, the application to
My wife of soothing flattery
And various kinds of pleasantry,
So that the illness is denied
The opportunity to spread.
There's nothing that inflames a woman more
Than when a husband demonstrates
To her his anger and suspicion.
Tonight I shall go home again.
I'll enter secretly, to see
If I can diagnose the true
Cause of my malady. Until
I'm able to, I shall conceal
This pain, this hurt, this misery,
This ache, this anguish, agony,
This nightmare, fear, jealousy.
Did I say jealousy? Let me
Retrieve the word at once. But no!
For if it is a poison now
Conceived within but did not kill
Me when I uttered it aloud,
To swallow it again could bring
About my death. For it is said
That if the viper comes across
Its fatal poison somewhere else
And swallows it, this guarantees
Its end. So if I spoke the word,
It is enough. And when a husband knows
A symptom of his illness is

His jealousy, he knows there is
No easy cure to be found,
And that the surgeon of his honour must
Employ more drastic remedies.

Exit GUTIERRE. *Enter* DON ARIAS *and* DOÑA LEONOR.

ARIAS.

You must not think that I, because
I have not spoken to you since,
Deny my obligation to
Your name and honest reputation.
For when a creditor is owed
So much, the debtor knows full well
He cannot hope, were he to sell
His goods, to satisfy in full
An obligation of that kind.
But even though I cannot pay
The debt as I would like, you will
Observe I do not run away.
I both admit my obligation,
And offer you some satisfaction.

LEONOR.

Don Arias, it is I who am
In debt to you, and in the balancing
Of our accounts have benefited most.
For even though Gutierre can
Be counted as a loss, I think
I can see profit in it too.
For if the loss includes my name
And reputation, I by that
Same token profit by the fact
I have avoided marriage to a man
Whose life is ruled by his suspicions.
The fault was mine, and so I pay
The penalty. I can complain
Only of myself and cruel destiny.

ARIAS.

But Leonor, it isn't true.
And more than that, it would be wrong
Of you to try to say I'm not
To blame and thus deprive me of
This opportunity of stating my

Intention. My feelings are much less
Of obligation than of love.
I state them in all honesty.
I, who once destroyed your life,
Ask only that you be my wife.

LEONOR.

Don Arias, I am naturally
Grateful. You honour me with this
Proposal more than I could ever hope
To say. It's something I appreciate
And swear I cherish dearly,
But something, I'm afraid, I can't
Accept. And if you ask me why,
It's not because if I said 'yes'
It would not make me much more happy.
It is because your actions gave
Gutierre reasonable cause
To think of me as badly as
He does. And so, if I agreed
To marry now, it would confirm
What he believes, and he, absolved
Of blame in his relationship
With me, could with good cause accuse
Me of disloyalty to him.
I cannot treat so lightly what
He's done to me, and will not help
Him clear his name when he will not
Agree to clear mine. For if,
As things now stand, some people judge
Him badly, they shall not, on my account,
Begin to think of him more kindly.

ARIAS.

My dear Leonor. Your attitude
Is foolish. The disappointment of
A former love can now be banished by
The new, and no one will think ill
Of you again. It would be worse
By far if someone who imagined you
To blame in this were now to have
His doubts confirmed by your actions.

LEONOR.

But don't you see, Don Arias?

How can a lover who prescribes
A course of action that will only harm
Me ever be considered wise?
What was believed an indiscretion then
Is still an indiscretion now.
And more so if what proved to be
The food of fond imagination now
Becomes for some the certainty
And confirmation of their fears.
And it can only harm you too.

ARIAS.

For me, Leonor, you were innocent
On that occasion and, I swear,
Will always be. The truth is I
Have never known a lover quite
So foolish, so absurdly cautious,
So ridiculously jealous, who,
Once married, has not suitably
Been punished by the heavens above.
Gutierre will, I think, be proof
Of this, Leonor. The man who thinks
The worst when he sees someone leave
A lady's house might well commit
An even greater folly when
The same thing happens in his own.

LEONOR.

Don Arias, I refuse to listen to
Such unjust criticism of
Gutierre. He is a perfect gentleman,
A man who was and always will
Prove faithful to his obligations.
And he is someone too who, be
It by recourse to sword or force
Of argument, will not allow
A prince to harm his reputation.
If you believe, Don Arias, that
You soothe my anguish, better that
You think again. To tell the truth,
You lose, not gain, by this, for any man
Who calls himself a gentleman
Would not speak badly even of
An enemy. As for myself,

Although he has dishonoured me,
And I would gladly put an end
To him with my own hands, I cannot speak
So badly of his sense of honour.
You ought to know, if you do not,
That if you ever love someone,
There is no joy in his misfortune.

Exit LEONOR.

ARIAS.

What else was there that I could say
To her? I've made a terrible
Mistake in saying what I did;
For when a woman argues for
The sake of honour, who dares hope
He can persuade her differently?
I'll ask the prince if someone else
Can take responsibility
For this. The light begins to fade.
The night advances quickly now.
It's best I go and if the prince
Agrees with me, I'll try to put
The matter to Gutierre.

Exit DON ARIAS. *Enter* GUTIERRE, *as though climbing over a wall.*

GUTIERRE.

The night is still and wrapped in silence.
I feel for it the reverence of
A man who worships shadows and
Adores the grave-like darkness that
Obliterates all human life.
I come in total secrecy.
My wife is unaware that I am here,
And that the King has set me free.
It is important she should be
At ease and act quite naturally.
I am the surgeon of my honour,
And so I seek the remedy
For my dishonour. I come to see
The patient at the very hour
When, on the previous night, the first
Attack of jealousy was felt;

For if it comes again, the pain
Will help me diagnose its origin.
I have gained entry to my house
By first avoiding the front door
And scaling secretly the garden-wall
So I would not be seen. Oh, it
Would seem the greatest novelty
To any man to know the nature of
What ails him most and never feel
The pain. It cannot be! And he
Who says it can deceives himself.
Oh, how can anyone who is
Unhappy keep his tears to himself?
How can the man who claims that he
Will never speak of jealousy
Expect us to accept his word
For that? Let him now stand before
Me and confess the fact and see
If I believe him! To suffer,
And not to speak of suffering!
Whoever heard of anything
So blatantly in contradiction of
The facts? But here is where she comes
At night. How still it is! No breath
Of wind disturbs or moves the leaves.
Honour, tread softly now; for jealousy
Must have the silent step of thieves.

He discovers MENCÍA *asleep.*

Oh, sweet Mencía! Why do you
So test my love and trust so much?
I see my honour is intact.
I shall turn back. The need for such
Examination, for such stealth, begins
To fade when honour's in good health.
But why no servant with her? Might
It be that she is waiting for? . . .
Oh, unjust thought! Oh, cruel fear!
Why must you mock me constantly?
I cannot go. Suspicion haunts
Me still, ignores the evidence,
Demands that I again apply
My common-sense to all the facts.

I must put out the light. (*He does so.*) Oh, this
Is to obliterate both light
And reason, to be twice blind
When this occasion calls for even
Greater clarity of mind! I shall
Call out to her, but in a voice
That sounds like someone else. Mencía!

MENCÍA *is awakened.*

MENCÍA.
    Who calls? Is someone there?

GUTIERRE.
                    Do not
    Be frightened.

MENCÍA.
          Who is it that calls?

GUTIERRE.
    My lady, only me.

MENCÍA.
    Of course, my lord. Who else would come
    So boldly at this hour?

GUTIERRE (*aside*).
    She recognizes me.

MENCÍA.
               Who else
    Would dare come here and place my honour at
    So great a risk, I am obliged
    To sacrifice my life for it?

GUTIERRE (*aside*).
    These words are music to my ears.
    How well I did to test my wife!

    Aloud.

    Mencía, trust me. Do not fear.

MENCÍA.
    My fear is such it overwhelms me.

GUTIERRE.
    Display the utmost bravery.

MENCÍA.
    What explanation can you give . . .

GUTIERRE.
    Why, none.

MENCÍA.
                    Oh, noble prince?

GUTIERRE (*aside*).
    Oh, noble prince! Am I to think
    My ears are playing tricks on me?
    I now begin to hear the voice
    Of doubt again, the whisper of
    Suspicion softly speak to me.

MENCÍA.
    I cannot think you wish to put
    My life in danger once again.
    How can you come here every night? . . .

GUTIERRE (*aside*).
    Too much to bear!

MENCÍA.
                    Have us put out
    The light so you can hide? . . .

GUTIERRE (*aside*).
                                    Oh, heavens!

MENCÍA.
    Have me then risk my life so you
    Escape?

GUTIERRE (*aside*).
            I pray, destroy me now!

MENCÍA.
    Then lie for your benefit in order to
    Deceive Gutierre?

GUTIERRE (*aside*).
                    I cannot bear
    This misery! Why cannot death
    Come now? Why cannot my last breath
    Consume this woman, making my
    Own death the end of life for her?
    That he comes here is no surprise to her,
    Nor does she seek to hide from him.
    Oh, I am lost! For she is sorry
    Only because she is obliged
    To hide this man from me. Oh, vengeance! You

> Must correspond in every sense
> And match the magnitude of this offence!

MENCÍA.

> My lord, you must go quickly now.

GUTIERRE (*aside*).

> My anger burns me with its fire.

MENCÍA.

> No one must see you here with me.

GUTIERRE (*aloud*).

> I have to have a better reason.

MENCÍA.

> Gutierre is expected soon.

GUTIERRE (*aside*).

> Oh, who has patience to endure this?
> The man whose prudence guarantees
> That he extracts a final vengeance!

> *Aloud.*

> You can be sure he will not come.
> I left him with a friend of mine,
> And in the meantime told him he
> Should keep an eye on him for me.

> *Enter* JACINTA.

JACINTA (*aside*).

> Someone speaks to her. Who can it be?

MENCÍA.

> Someone's coming.

GUTIERRE.

> > What shall I do?

MENCÍA.

> You have to hide. Go quickly. Avoid
> My bedroom. Somewhere else. Hurry!

> GUTIERRE *hides.*

MENCÍA.

> It's only you, Jacinta.

JACINTA.

> > Yes, my lady.

MENCÍA.
>It seems that, while I was asleep,
>The wind blew out the lamp. I bid
>You go, Jacinta. Bring another.

GUTIERRE (*aside*).
>Its flame shall be my anger!
>But if I try to hide I shall
>Be seen; Mencía will be told
>Of it and realize her part
>In this affair is known to me.
>She must not know, and so cannot
>Offend me twice, the first time by
>Intention, the second thinking I
>Have somehow given her permission.
>Oh, no. I need to put a brave face on.
>Her death, in any case, will not be long.

>*Exit* GUTIERRE.
>*Aloud*.

>Is someone here? What's happening?

MENCÍA.
>Gutierre! What other shock can fate
>Now have in store for me?

GUTIERRE.
>Is there no light at this late hour?

>*Enter* JACINTA *with a lamp, and* GUTIERRE *from the opposite direction.*

JACINTA.
>Here is the lamp, my lady.

GUTIERRE.
>   Mencía!

MENCÍA.
>Husband! My joy and glory! Welcome!

GUTIERRE (*aside*).
>How cunningly the lady feigns!
>I think I have to do the same!

MENCÍA.
>How did you enter?

GUTIERRE.
>   I used the key

To the garden door. For some time now
I've thought it best to have it with me,
In case there's some emergency.
How have you spent the evening?

MENCÍA.

Oh, nothing I could call exciting.
I came into the garden to enjoy
The fountains, but the wind blew out
The lamp.

GUTIERRE.

　　　　　The wind is cold tonight,
As if there is some fierce storm
In store for us. It has a coldness and
A knife-like edge that promises
To snuff-out lights and possibly
Extinguish even life itself.

MENCÍA.

What do you mean, Gutierre? Am I
To think your words contain some truth
Now meant for me?

GUTIERRE.

　　　　　Have you not seen
A flame burn bright, be suddenly
Extinguished by a gust of wind,
And then another brighter flame
Burst quickly into life again?
See how the one begins to blaze,
The other splutters and is dead.
The wind's soft tongue has blown out your light,
And now has given me that light instead.

MENCÍA (*aside*).

What can he mean? (*Aloud.*) I think your words,
Gutierre, hide much more than they
Reveal, as if you feel the pangs
Of jealousy.

GUTIERRE (*aside*).

　　　　　It is the pain
Of wounded honour strikes me now!
No man grows wise from jealousy.

Aloud.

Mencía, do you know what jealousy
Is like? Thanks be to God I do
Not know! For if I did . . .

MENCÍA (*aside*).

Please God,
Protect me now!

GUTIERRE.

What are you, jealousy?
No more than atoms, particles
Of air, the tiny seeds that grow
In our minds once they are planted there
By some misguided servant's story of
A shadow that could be, in truth.
Imaginary. Even so,
I swear my course of action would
Be such as to defy all comprehension.
These hands of mine would rip and tear
The guilty heart, devour each
And every part of it, consume
Its blood and, were it possible,
Swallow its very soul.
Oh, Mencía! Please forgive me! Do
Not pay attention to me now!

MENCÍA.
Gutierre, I am frightened.

GUTIERRE.

My dear wife,
I swear to you, you are my life
Itself, my world, my heaven. Forgive
Me now! I beg of you a thousand times!
My mind, I think, was suddenly
The plaything of the strangest vision,
Some trick of fanciful imagination.
Let me apologize. You know
I feel respect and love for you.
Forgive me this excess. I was
Distracted, not my real self.

MENCÍA (*aside*).
I feel the icy breath of fear,
A coldness deep inside me here,
A premonition of my death.

GUTIERRE (*aside*).
>I am the surgeon of my honour,
>But if I diagnose dishonour,
>The remedy shall be to bury it.

Act Three

Enter the KING *and* GUTIERRE.

GUTIERRE.
>Your majesty, the world pays homage to
>Your glory. I come to beg of you,
>As your humble subject, only
>That you let me speak to you alone.

KING.
>Of course. All of you shall wait outside.

They leave.

>You have me.

GUTIERRE.
>You are, your majesty,
>Our true Apollo; but, more than that,
>Our Spanish Atlas, for you bear upon
>Your shoulders the great burden of
>The world, the shining sphere of
>The heavens. I place before you now
>The wreckage of my ruined life,
>Battered by constant storms, if anyone
>Can call this life. And do not be
>Surprised to see these eyes of mine
>Should speak their sorrow too, for love
>And honour can – it comes as no
>Surprise to anyone – allow
>A man to weep; and I possess
>Them both, for I have love and honour.
>As someone of most noble birth
>And origin, I am a man
>Of honour; as someone who now has
>A wife, I have discovered love.
>The one inherited, the other
>Cultivated, I have them both
>And treasure them in equal measure,
>Until a cloud, now darkening
>This heaven of mine, begins to cast

Its shadow over both, first threatening
The perfect splendour of my wife
And then the brightness of my honour.
How can I give a true impression of
My anguish? . . . I am distressed . . . the more
Because I am compelled to tell
You that the man you are obliged
To bring to justice for his part
In this is . . . your brother, Prince
Enrique . . . not because I think
My honour can oppose his power,
Your majesty; but so that he
Who has the power knows what honour means
To me. I am dependent on
You both, as much for life as honour,
Believing that prevention is
By far the surest form of cure.
For if it proved the case that this
Disease could not be cured,
That only honour's death was guaranteed,
Then I would put an end to it,
Make sure my honour was cleansed with blood
And covered by the earth! Oh, do
Not fear! I speak of my own blood, not Prince
Enrique's. I promise you, I guarantee
The Prince's safety. I only ask
You to believe this dagger that
I hold, this silvery tongue of steel,
Is his. It is the evidence
Of your brother's presence in my house.
I only ask you test the truth
Of this.

KING.
       I promise you, Gutierre, I
Shall see to it. You are a man
For whom your honour has the splendour of
The sun itself. You can, I swear,
Be quite assured that your honour . . .

GUTIERRE.
I do not doubt, your majesty.
Nor is there any need for you
To guarantee my honour's not

Affected. For if the Romans thought
That Portia and Lucretia were
The very soul and essence both
Of virtue and of chastity, I swear
That neither is as honest, true
And virtuous as my Mencía.
The reason I am here is to prevent;
I do not seek some drastic cure.

KING.

Then tell me, did you see something
That gave you cause to think there might
Be something to prevent?

GUTIERRE.

                                    No, I
Did not, your majesty; but for
A man like me to see is less
Important than to fear, suspect,
Imagine, dread, and fashion what
I fear most inside my head.
In short, I've chosen to inform
Your majesty of this in order to
Avoid an injury that has
Not yet befallen me. But if
It did, I promise I would find
The remedy myself, not then
Rely on someone else.

KING.

                              Gutierre, if,
As you now claim, you are physician of
Your honour, you must have taken steps
That help you to insure it.

GUTIERRE.

I've taken none, your majesty.
My wife has given me no cause
For jealousy, and so I've loved
Her all the more. We had, till recently,
A peaceful, pleasant country house,
And lived there happily enough;
I thought, however, she could well
Be lonely there and that a city-life
Would suit her more. She seems quite happy here,
And, having everything she needs,

Has need to envy nobody.
The husbands who deserve to suffer most
Are those who tolerate that others should
Speak openly of their affairs.
No one accuses me of that,
Your majesty.

KING.
                    The Prince is here.
If he sees you with me, he'll know
At once that he's the subject of
Our conversation. There was, you will
Recall, an earlier occasion when
Another person spoke to me of you.
I had her hide behind this screen
Where she, unseen by you, might listen to
Your explanation. Now you shall hide
As she did then, and listen to
Another person, you accusing, he
Accused. The roles are thus reversed.
But you must never show yourself.
Promise me that you'll do this.

GUTIERRE.
I swear, your majesty. I guarantee
That, come what may, I'll hold my tongue.

Enter ENRIQUE.

KING.
Welcome, Enrique. The joy I feel
On seeing you is, however, tempered by
Regret.

ENRIQUE.
            To hear it is my own
Regret, my lord. Who is to blame
For it?

KING.
            Why, you, Enrique, you.

ENRIQUE.
In that case I am sorrier still;
For if there's something I have done
Which, as you now suggest, offends
The sun, then I am banished from
Its light.

KING.

> Do you not realize
> That, more than once, avenging swords
> Have sought to right with royal blood
> Unjust offences done to them?

ENRIQUE.

> I do, your majesty. But who
> Can you be saying this about?

KING.

> You, Enrique! How could you so forget
> That honour is a sacred thing,
> The province of the soul, where I,
> The King, have no authority?
> I'll say no more.

ENRIQUE.

> > It isn't true.

KING.

> You must take greater care where love's
> Concerned and learn to act more prudently
> Where female beauty, even though
> It draws you, is impossible.
> We deal here with the soul of someone whose
> Allegiance is forever promised to
> Authority far greater than my own;
> Who, if he asks me to be fair
> And just to him, as I must be,
> Would make it difficult for me
> To spare the blood of my own family.

ENRIQUE.

> My lord, to me your word is law,
> As though your lips had written every
> Syllable upon my heart. But even so,
> You must agree to listen to
> My version of the story, for if
> You now refuse me this, how can
> It then be said you judge each case
> With total impartiality?
> The truth is that I loved the lady you
> Are speaking of, though I must doubt
> The need to justify my love
> For beauty such as hers. I loved her . . .

KING.
>There is no point. You cannot have her.

ENRIQUE.
>I know, but even so . . .

KING.
>   No more!

ENRIQUE.
>Then let me now explain it to you.

KING.
>No explanation's possible.
>There is no question that this lady . . .

ENRIQUE.
>But time and love can overcome
>All obstacles.

KING (*aside*).
>   Enough of this!
>How foolishly I hid Gutierre!

>*Aloud.*

>I ordered you to hold your tongue.

ENRIQUE.
>How can you be so angry when
>You haven't given me the chance
>To tell you everything?

KING.
>   I know
>Already! (*Aside.*) Gutierre there inside,
>And listening to this!

ENRIQUE.
>   I must
>Insist, your majesty. The girl
>I speak of was unmarried when
>I knew her first. There could be no
>Offence in that to any man
>Who later wished to marry her
>That I once loved her so.

KING.
>   I said
>Enough! I want to hear no more.
>I knew you'd tell me anything

To try to cover up your tracks.
But now, Enrique, it's the truth
I want from you, the cold, hard facts
And nothing more. You see this dagger?

ENRIQUE.
I came back home one night. I thought
It probable I'd dropped it somewhere.

KING.
Quite right, but where, Enrique, where?

ENRIQUE.
I do not know, my lord. How could I know?

KING.
Then know you dropped it where it could
So easily be stained with your blood,
Were not the man who picked it up
Both loyal to his King and good.
But even if he chose to give
The knife to me, it does not mean
That he has ceased to be the keen
And just avenger of his honour.
Observe the handle of the dagger.
It speaks of your scandalous
Behaviour, and voices loud complaints
That I, the King, am forced to hear.
Take it. Look into the mirror of
Its blade. Consider carefully
The error you have made.

ENRIQUE.
                              My lord,
I beg of you. There is no need to be
So angry. This fury . . .

KING.
                              Take the dagger!

The KING *offers the dagger to* ENRIQUE. *As* ENRIQUE *takes it, the dagger cuts the* KING's *hand.*

KING.
What treachery is this?

ENRIQUE.
                              My lord . . .

KING.

> You dare to take up arms against
> Your king? See how I bleed? I wanted you
> To see the knife. Instead you try
> To end my life.

ENRIQUE.

>   Not so. It was
> An accident, I swear.

KING.

>   Enrique! Spare
> Me, please! Or is it that in times like these
> A brother is his brother's murderer?

ENRIQUE.

> Your majesty, what makes you think
> That I intended that? It's best
> I go and find some quiet spot
> So far away you cannot think
> In your wildest dreams that I
> Can cause you harm. Imagination breeds
> In you this terrible confusion!

Exit ENRIQUE.

KING.

> What can it mean? Is this some prophecy
> That now presents me with a vision of
> My death? I seem to see my flesh
> Run red with my own blood! Oh, what
> Unhappy fantasy is this
> That floods my heart and soul with dread
> And fear strong enough to turn
> Them both to stone? I pray to God
> That such beginnings do not breed
> Such ends; that I shall never see
> My kingdom overwhelmed by rivers of
> Fresh blood!

Exit the KING. *Enter* GUTIERRE.

GUTIERRE.

>   The day is full of dark
> And terrible events. The King,
> Astonished by such portents, has
> Forgotten I was hidden there.

What can I do? Am I obliged
To hear much more of this? No, I
Shall not! Why should I ever speak of it
When it inflames my sense of injury?
Far better if I take it by
Its roots and tear it out at one
Fell swoop to stop it harming me
Forever. Mencía must die. Her blood
Shall run and bathe her breast where my
Dishonour rests; and since the prince
Has given me his knife again,
Its end shall be Mencía life.
But this must not be known to anyone.
It shall be done in secrecy,
For any loss of reputation that
So far has lacked publicity,
Must be restored as quietly
As possible. Mencía's death
Demands of me the utmost stealth.
But why am I obliged to snuff
Out breath as dear as hers? Cannot
The heavens deprive me of this life
Of mine so I may spare my wife?
Oh, why must they reserve their fury and
Their lightning for someone else
And not for me when they proclaim
That only they can show us mercy?
How cold, how empty are the heavens!
Have you no means to end my misery?

Exit GUTIERRE. *Enter* MENCÍA *and* JACINTA.

JACINTA.
    My lady, you appear strangely sad.
    What is it clouds your beauty so,
    That night and day are spent in such
    Deep sorrow?

MENCÍA.
             I really do not know.
    I only wish I could explain
    It to myself, but then I find
    The same confusion time and time
    Again. That night when I was sleeping in
    The garden . . . you may recall I thought

Enrique spoke to me (how can
I bear such misery as this?)
And you informed me he had spoken to
You too. Since then I am tormented by
The thought the man who spoke was not,
In fact, Enrique but — I am
Convinced the more I think of it — Gutierre.

JACINTA.

How could it be? Would that not be
Impossible?

MENCÍA.

So it would seem,
Jacinta, but the night was dark,
The voice that called called quietly,
My fear that he would come was such,
I am convinced he could have played
A trick on me. Not only that,
He talks to me quite happily,
But weeps when he's alone, as if
His anguish would remind his eyes
That tears cannot be disowned.

Enter COQUÍN.

COQUÍN.

Good lady.

MENCÍA.

What news is it you have
For me?

COQUÍN.

Such news as I can barely bring
Myself to speak. It has to do
With Prince Enrique.

MENCÍA.

Enough, Coquín.
I'll hear no more. The mention of
His name inflames my fears, yet fills
Me with such dread I almost freeze.

COQUÍN.

Then what you need's a cool head, madam.
My news is not to do with love,
Well, not exactly.

MENCÍA.

> You'd better tell me.

COQUÍN.

> It seems the Prince, my lady, had
> A bit of bother with the King,
> His brother. It isn't clear, though,
> If it was anything to do
> With you. It could have been another matter.
> To tell the honest truth, it's all
> A mystery. Besides, what right
> Have we comedians got to take
> The piss concerning people of
> Such obvious dignity? It went like this.
> Enrique calls to me and says,
> All in the utmost secrecy,
> Of course: 'Do me a favour. Get
> This message to Doña Mencía.
> It's on account of her I'm in
> This bother with the King, my brother.
> You have to find out where she is
> And tell her that he's banished me
> Forever to a distant place
> Where I shall not set eyes on her
> Again, and where, it shall be said,
> Enrique, on account of love, is dead.'

MENCÍA.

> Do you mean the Prince has lost the favour of
> The King on my account; that he's
> About to leave the Court? If he
> Does that, it cannot help command
> Attention and, as its consequence,
> Destroy my reputation. What
> Am I to do?

JACINTA.

> You have to try
> To stop him now.

COQUÍN.

> And how, I pray,
> Can she do that?

JACINTA.

> By asking him to stay.
> For if it's known he's gone away

On your account, how long before
The whispering tongues, as they are wont,
Begin to speak your name? As soon
As they become aware of it,
They'll know where best to fix the blame.

COQUÍN.

How can he know of this request
If he is almost ready? The last
I saw of him, he'd packed his stuff;
Was almost on his way already.

JACINTA.

Then write. Send him a note to say
He must not leave; that if he goes
Away, it risks my lady's reputation.
Don't you see? It's probably
The only chance we have to save
The situation. And as for you,
Coquín, you'll have to be the postman.

MENCÍA.

Matters of honour are fraught with danger.
But even so I am compelled
To write this letter, knowing as
I do it is the lesser of
Two ills, if either of them can
Be thought to be lesser.
Wait here. I'll go and write the letter.

Exit MENCÍA.

JACINTA.

What is the matter with you nowadays,
Coquín? What makes you so unhappy?
It's not so long ago you were
Extremely chirpy. What's come over you?

COQUÍN.

It's probably because I gave
In to my curiosity,
A very foolish thing to do,
Considering what it has done
To me.

JACINTA.

        What has it done to you?

COQUÍN.
>It's made me melancholy through
>And through. Until two years ago
>There's hardly anyone had heard
>Of it, but recently it's all
>The rage and fashion. Why, there was
>A lady, seeing how her boyfriend looked
>At her so sadly, one day said
>To him: 'The thing I fancy, darling, is
>A bit of your drooping melancholy!'
>Hey, quick. I see my master coming.

JACINTA.
>I have to go and warn my lady!

>*Enter* GUTIERRE.

GUTIERRE.
>Jacinta, wait. Where are you going?
>What makes you run away from me?

JACINTA.
>To tell my lady that I saw
>You coming, sir.

GUTIERRE (*aside*).
>   And to prove she is
>The enemy within. Why, look
>At both of them, so deathly pale
>And trembling with fear. (*Aloud*.) Come here.
>Why are you running?

JACINTA.
>   I've told you, sir.
>To tell my lady you were coming.

GUTIERRE (*aside*).
>This woman will admit to nothing.
>She seems to think I'm ignorant
>Of everything. (*Aloud*.) Come now, my good Coquín.
>I've always had great faith in you
>To tell me anything you've seen.

COQUÍN.
>You know me, sir, and all your faith
>In me has been well justified. I'd tell
>You every detail, like a shot.
>But there's no point in asking me

For anything I haven't got.

GUTIERRE.

All right, Coquín. No need to shout.
You act as if you are afraid
I've caught you out.

COQUÍN.

             It's just that I
Am naturally timid, sir.
I thought you were a ghost, and so
I wanted to get out of here.

GUTIERRE (*aside*).

The two of them make secret signs
To one another. They think that they
Can hide the truth that I shall soon
Uncover. (*Aloud.*) Both of you may leave.

Exit both.

                           Honour,

We find ourselves alone and must
Consider now how happiness
Has gone and only misery
Is left to us. But here's Mencía.
I must discover what it is
She writes so secretly.

MENCÍA.

              Heaven help me!

GUTIERRE.

Breathing still but cold as ice!

Reads.

'Your Highness.' Why, highness such as this
Is what has brought my honour low!
'For my sake, please, you must not leave
The city now . . .' Must I read more?
She begs, implores him not to leave.
Must I be made to suffer so?
I think that all my previous ills
Are nothing in comparison
To this. What if I kill her now?
But no. I must have time to think.
I shall dismiss my servants so

My sole companion shall be sorrow.
Not only that, but since I've loved
Mencía more than any woman in
My life, I'll take my leave of her
By showing that I feel true pity for
Her soul. There is still time enough
For honour's remedy to be
Applied. Her life is at an end.
Pray God her soul may still survive.

He writes and exits. MENCÍA *begins to recover.*

MENCÍA.
My lord, why do you kill me when
I'm innocent? Why do you think
Me guilty of some terrible offence?
Why do you hold this blood-stained sword
Against my breast? I give my word
To you that I am innocent.
But what is this? What am I saying? Was
Gutierre here or was I dreaming that
I saw myself now drowning in
A crimson sea of my own blood?
I think I must have fainted. Or
Was this a premonition of
My death? I am not sure, and yet
I feel that what I dreamt may well
Be true. I must destroy the letter quickly.
But this, I think, is written by
Gutierre. Its words are few. They say
That I, his wife, am soon to die.

Reads.

'My love is such it worships you,
While honour holds you in contempt.
My love demands that you shall live,
My honour that your life is spent.
Two hours of life are left to you,
Make necessary preparation,
That, though the body's doomed to die,
The soul is guaranteed salvation.'
God help me now! Where are you, Jacinta?
But no one comes. I must be here
Alone, and not a soul to listen.

The door is locked, and iron bars
Protect the window. I see my fears
Begin to form, surround me from
All sides. The room is high above
The garden. No one standing there
Below can hear my cries. What can
I do? There's no one here and yet
I see approaching death's dark shadow.

Exit MENCÍA. *Enter the* KING *and* DON DIEGO.

KING.
Are you quite sure Enrique's left
The city?

DIEGO.
                    I am, your majesty.
He left Seville this afternoon.

KING.
No doubt he thought it best to leave
As soon as possible. He thinks
He can escape from me. And did
They tell you where?

DIEGO.
                                    I think it was
Consuegra.

KING.
                    He has a country-house there.
I have no doubt my brothers will
Be hatching some conspiracy.

DIEGO.
The duty of your brothers is
To love you as a brother and
Obey you as their rightful King:
Both natural allegiances.

KING.
Who went with him?

DIEGO.
                              Don Arias.

KING.
He is Enrique's man.

DIEGO.
Let's listen to the music in the street.

KING.

> We'll hear them sing awhile. Perhaps
> Their songs will help relieve my sadness.

DIEGO.

> Perhaps, your majesty. It's said
> That music is a source of gladness.

> *Singing off.*

> 'The Prince Enrique's gone away
> King Pedro could not make him stay.
> What will his absence come to mean?
> Does it foretell dangers unseen?'

KING.

> Don Arias, there is such sadness in
> The voice. Go quickly. Bring to me
> The man to blame for madness such as this.

> *Exit both. Enter* GUTIERRE *and* LUDOVICO, *a bloodletter,
> his face covered.*

GUTIERRE.

> Come. Do not be afraid. I shall
> Uncover your face and cover mine.

> GUTIERRE *conceals his face.*

LUDOVICO.

> May heaven protect me!

GUTIERRE.

> > > > > > Nothing that
> You see must frighten you.

LUDOVICO.

> > > > > > > But, sir,
> You called on me for help, and when
> We were outside produced this knife
> And threatened me with death. You then
> Blindfolded me and having spun
> Me three times round, informed me that
> My life depends upon my eyes being bound.
> Since then we've passed through streets
> I could not see, and now that I
> Can see once more, I am the more
> Amazed to find myself in what
> Would seem to be a house quite empty but

For you. I cannot think what this
Might mean, nor why you will not let
Your face be seen. What would you have
Of me?

GUTIERRE.

Wait here a moment, patiently.

Exit GUTIERRE.

LUDOVICO.

Who can explain what mystery
Lies here? May God protect and save
Me now!

Enter GUTIERRE.

GUTIERRE.

The time has come. You have
To come with me. But first you have
To listen carefully, for if
You do not do the things I say,
This knife shall be the instrument
That lets your life-blood ebb away.
Tell me. What is it you now see?

LUDOVICO.

I see a figure, still as death,
A dark shape lying on a bed,
Candles lit on either side,
A crucifix above the head.
But who the person is I cannot say
Or guess. The face is hidden by
A veil of lace.

GUTIERRE.

You are obliged
To kill this person. It is the reason you
Are here.

LUDOVICO.

But I am meant to cure, sir.

GUTIERRE.

Proceed, by bleeding it to death.
A small incision in a vein
And all its strength shall slowly drain
Away. Be sure that the body is

Completely bled, and do not leave
Until you know for certain it
Is dead. There is no point in asking me
For mercy. If you still want to live,
There is one way: you must obey.

LUDOVICO.
I cannot do it, sir. My fears
Are such they overwhelm me.

GUTIERRE.
If I am driven to commit
More terrible atrocities,
To kill you now would be simplicity itself.

LUDOVICO.
I do not wish to die, my lord.

GUTIERRE.
Well said, my friend: then you shall be
The man who guarantees that he
Survives by making sure that
Another dies. Now go inside.
Begin. I shall be watching everything.

Exit LUDOVICO.

It is the easiest way to keep
Dishonour from becoming known.
Poison is quite easily detected,
Illness much more readily accepted as
A cause of death. If afterwards
The circumstances of Mencía's death
Are thus investigated, I
Shall say she had to lose some blood,
And that the bandages which bound
Her wounds proved not to be as good
As we had thought. To find and bring
This doctor here blindfolded was
Quite easily the best precaution.
To let him see and know what lay
In store for him would surely have been
A lack of caution on my part.
For if he ever wants to tell
What happened here, he cannot see
The victim's face nor know where this
Event took place. Moreover, when

She's dead, I'll lead him to a quiet spot
Away from here, and kill him too.
I am the surgeon of my honour, called
Upon to bleed my wife to death
If honour's life's to be restored.
For honour asks of us this price:
That precious blood be sacrificed.

Exit GUTIERRE. *Enter the* KING *and* DON DIEGO. *Singing off.*

MUSICIANS.
'The Prince is headed for Consuegra.
There you'll hear sad prophecies,
How Montiel's mysterious mountains
Soon shall see dark tragedies.'

KING.
Don Diego!

DIEGO.
                    Your majesty . . .

KING.
                              I need
To know who sings the song. He sings
Of me.

DIEGO.
          You should ignore such songs.
They know full well that singing them
Is guaranteed to make you angry.

KING.
Two men approach.

DIEGO.
                    Then we shall find
Out who they are, your majesty.

Enter GUTIERRE *with* LUDOVICO, *blindfolded.*

GUTIERRE.
Heaven guides my every step. This doctor's death
Will seal my secret even more
Securely. But who are these two men?
I must not let them see me. I'll have
To leave him.

DIEGO.
                There were two of them, my lord,
        But only one approaches now.
        The other's gone.

KING.
                                There's nothing but
        Confusion here. The moon reveals
        A form that has no face, the outline of
        A blurred and bulky shape.
        What, Diego, can we make of this?

DIEGO.
        Step back, your majesty, Let me
        Approach him.

KING.
                        Don Diego, leave me.
        You there. Speak. Or have you lost your tongue?
        Who are you?

LUDOVICO.
                        An ordinary man
        Who is amazed by what he sees,
        And cannot for that reason speak.
        Who would believe that anyone
        Like me, while walking in the street,
        Could ever meet your majesty?
        I recognize your voice quite easily —
        But now I have to speak, for I
        Must tell you of events that once
        Revealed, will be engraved upon
        The memory of everyone.

KING.
        What things are these?

LUDOVICO.
                                You shall hear everything,
        Your majesty. I think it best
        That you should hear me privately.

KING.
        Don Diego, let him speak to me.

DIEGO (*aside*).
        The night is full of mystery.
        God grant us all His tender mercy.

LUDOVICO.

    I could not see her face, but heard
    Her cry: 'Why must I die so cruelly?
    I have committed no offence.
    I pray that heaven does not demand
    From you my death.' Those were her words,
    And then her life was quickly spent.
    The man who took me there put out
    The light and, as we left, caught sight
    Of you. It was as if it caused
    In him some sudden fear, for off
    He went, and left me standing here.
    The only other thing I need
    To say, your majesty, is that
    My hands were covered with blood, and, as
    I groped my way outside, I placed
    My hands upon the door to make
    A sign that, if you needed to,
    Would help you find the house once more.

KING.

    You acted properly. This diamond
    Will grant you entry to my chamber.
    Use it if you need to speak to me.

    Exit LUDOVICO.

KING.

    Let's go, Don Diego.

DIEGO.

                What did he
    Say to you?

KING.

           The strangest thing the world
    Has ever heard

DIEGO.

           You seem unhappy.

KING.

    I am, Diego. Of necessity.

DIEGO.

    You need to rest. See how the light
    Of day now quickly turns the sky
    To gold. We have to go.

KING.

>   There is
> A certain house that I must find.
> I shall not rest until I do.

DIEGO.

> The sun appears. Everyone
> Is bound to see you.

> *Enter* COQUÍN.

COQUÍN.

>   Your majesty,
> I know that if I speak to you
> I risk some dreadful injury,
> But now I simply have to.

KING.

> What now, Coquín? Another of
> Your quite horrendous stories?

COQUÍN.

>   I swear,
> Your majesty, that this time it
> Is most unfunny. I know you think
> That I'm a clown, but want to tell
> You that, deep down, there's really quite
> A serious side to me, and what
> I have to tell you now is, not
> To put too fine a point on it,
> Well . . . pretty bloody. No, I haven't come
> To make you laugh; more to see if what
> I've got to say will break your heart.
> My master is, as you well know,
> A man suspicious of his honour, and of
> His wife, Mencía, in particular.
> Well just today, by some unlucky chance,
> He came across her just as she
> Had started putting pen to paper, which,
> It seems, consisted of a letter to
> Your brother, Prince Enrique. She begged
> Him not to leave the city, knowing well
> That people, when they heard the news,
> Would straight away believe that she's
> The one who ought to be accused
> Of it. Approaching her, Gutierre saw

How she was overcome by fear, took
The letter, thought suspicion justified,
Had all the servants leave, the doors
All locked, and him the only one
Still left inside with her. I feel
Such pity for the poor girl.
She seems so cruelly abused
By harsh, unfeeling fate, I had
To come and tell your majesty,
So you could maybe bring your strong
And mighty arm to bear on it.

KING.

How can I pay you for this show
Of sympathy?

COQUÍN.

                 I thought you might
Agree to let me keep my teeth.

KING.

It's no time to be funny, sir.

COQUÍN.

It never was, your majesty.

KING.

Come, Diego. It will soon be light.
We have to hurry. If I could find
A house where I could change my clothes,
It would assist me both to know
What secrets lie behind closed doors
As well as punish those who think
They can escape.

DIEGO.

                 The mere sight
Of you would make them tremble in
Their shoes.

COQUÍN.

                 Your majesty, the house
I spoke about. It's there, across the road.

KING.

Don Diego, wait.

DIEGO.

                 What can you see?

KING.
>Is that the imprint of a bloody hand
>Upon the door?

DIEGO.
>   It does seem so,
>Your majesty. I think it is.

KING (*aside*).
>Gutierre is the man referred
>To by the doctor as having forced
>Him bleed his wife to death. The course
>Of action I should take to punish him
>Is still unclear; and yet I am
>Convinced he has now cleansed his honour.

>*Enter* LEONOR *and a servant.*

LEONOR.
>I go to early Mass so no
>One in Seville can see or speak
>Of me again. But someone comes,
>Inés. It is his majesty.
>Why is he calling at that house?

INÉS.
>He must not see you. Hide your face.

KING.
>But rather pointless when I've seen
>You, Leonor.

LEONOR.
>   Forgive me, please.
>I did not wish to hide and not
>Pay proper homage at your feet.

KING.
>Sweet lady, such a duty as
>You have described now falls to me.
>As far as honour is concerned,
>You still remain my creditor,
>I promised you, quite properly,
>That I would see your honour is
>Restored. So shall it be, as soon
>As I can find an opportunity.

GUTIERRE (*off*).
>Please God! Unless you help me now

> I shall go mad. I beg of you,
> Send down a fatal bolt of lightning
> To end this miserable life.

KING.

> Whose is that voice?

DIEGO.

> 　　　　　　　Why, look.
> Gutierre, running from his house.

KING.

> What is the cause of this? Gutierre!

Enter GUTIERRE.

GUTIERRE.

> Your majesty, I come to tell
> Of the most terrible misfortune,
> A tragedy that cannot but
> Demand for those who hear of it
> Profoundest pity, greatest admiration.
> Mencía, my dearest wife, in whom
> The only rival to her beauty was
> Her chastity — I say so publicly —
> Whose precious life meant more to me
> Than life itself, became last night
> The victim of an unforseen
> And cruel accident, as if
> It were the whim of destiny,
> By doing this to her, to rob
> Her of divinity. She felt
> Unwell, and so a doctor, known
> Thoughout Seville to be a man
> Of reputation, thought that only if
> He bled her could he bring about
> A restoration of her health.
> As it turned out, we had no servants in
> The house to care for her, and thus,
> When I went out, to keep an eye
> On her. As soon as I awoke
> Today I went to look at her —
> How can I speak of how I found
> Her there? — the bed soaked through with blood,
> The sheets stained red, the wife I loved
> Already dead, and all her blood

Quite drained from her because the bandages
Were not secure. Oh, how can words
Express such hopelessness, the pain
And anguish of such deep distress?
Come. Gaze upon Mencía there.
The fair sun bathed in blood, the whiteness of
The moon dark red, the brightness of
The stars and lovely music of
The spheres dead. Oh why must I
Be thus denied her perfect beauty? Why
Must loveliness like hers be ravaged now,
While I am saved and thus obliged
To mourn her loss eternally?

MENCÍA's body is revealed, a bloodless corpse lying on a bed.

KING.
The tale is most remarkable!

Aside.

But prudence is required here.
His vengeance is quite admirable.

Aloud.

Conceal this vision; hide at once
This pitiful admission of
The way misfortune rules our lives,
And fills our hearts with fear for
Those things that lie in store for us.
Gutierre, you have our pity.
Your loss is great, and our duty is
To try to compensate that loss
As best we can. And so it seems
The best solution is to marry Leonor.
Do not forget, she is a creditor
To whom you owe a debt of honour.
And that will satisfy me too,
And help me keep a promise I
Once made to her.

GUTIERRE.
                    Your majesty,
It is not time to think of this.
The ashes of my tragedy
Are not yet cold. I beg you, do

Not make me keep this bargain. Give
Me time, the opportunity
To weep and find some peace again.

KING.

I have decided. See it's done.

GUTIERRE.

Your majesty. Mencía's death
Has freed me from the storm that raged
About my head. Must I set sail
Upon that sea again now she is dead?

KING.

It is your King's command.

GUTIERRE.

                            My lord,
I beg of you. Do not make this demand.

KING.

You think I am unreasonable?

GUTIERRE.

What if again I were to find
Myself in such a situation?
What if again your brother's presence in
My house inflamed suspicions . . . ?

KING.

                                 You
Should then dismiss them!

GUTIERRE.

                    And what if then,
Behind my bed, I were to find
Enrique's dagger?

KING.

                Tell yourself
Your servants have been bribed but you are wiser.

GUTIERRE.

What if, in spite of that, I were
To see Enrique night and day
Around my property?

KING.

                    Complain to me.

GUTIERRE.

And what if, having then complained,

Such action proved to be in vain?

KING.

                           You have

To trust that woman's beauty may
Accompany disdain.

GUTIERRE.

              And if,
When I went home, I found a note
Which begged the Prince to stay?

KING.

                       You know,
Gutierre, there's a sure way
To deal with it.

GUTIERRE.

             But how, your majesty?

KING.

I recommend the remedy.
You've used already.

GUTIERRE.

             Which remedy?

KING.

You have to let her bleed a little.

GUTIERRE.

What can you mean?

KING.

             But then be sure
To clean the bloodstain from your door.

GUTIERRE.

Your majesty, all men who are
Engaged in some profession place
A sign above their door which tells their trade.
My trade is honour, and my mark
As its practitioner a sign
Imprinted on my door in blood.
A man must sometimes cleanse his hands with blood
In order to protect his honour.

KING.

Then give your hand to Leonor.
Her reputation merits it.

GUTIERRE.
So be it, with the reservation that
It has been cleansed with guilty blood.

LEONOR.
On that condition I accept it.

GUTIERRE.
Do not forget. I have already been
The surgeon of my honour. It is
A skill, I promise you, that lasts forever.

LEONOR.
If I am ever sick, Gutierre, do
Not hesitate to cure me.

GUTIERRE.
Then here's my hand, my dear. And now
We end *The Surgeon of Honour*.

Life is a Dream

Characters

BASILIO, *King of Poland*
SEGISMUNDO, *The Prince*
ASTOLFO, *Duke of Muscovy*
CLOTALDO, *Segismundo's Tutor*
CLARION, *Servant to Rosaura*
ROSAURA, *Clotaldo's Daughter*
ESTRELLA, *A Princess*
SOLDIERS, GUARDS, MUSICIANS

Act One

ROSAURA *appears at the top of a mountain. She is dressed as a man. She begins to descend as she speaks the opening lines.*

ROSAURA.
> This headstrong horse must think itself
> An eagle or some fabulous beast
> That can outdash the wind for speed;
> Or lightning, perhaps, without
> Its flash of light, or scale-less fish,
> Or bird that needs no feathers for
> Its flight. You doltish creature! I
> Am here because you chose to bolt
> And bring me to this labyrinth
> Of rock and stone. Well you can stay
> And be a Phaeton to the beasts,
> While I, who have no other path
> Than that decreed by destiny,
> Shall blindly seek to find my way
> From this high peak that dares aspire to
> The sun. Is this, Poland, the way
> To greet a stranger – hardly come
> And harshly welcomed, and made as well
> To mark his presence with his blood?
> My fate bears out the common notion:
> The one who suffers most attracts
> The least compassion.

CLARION.
>   Say two, not one.
> Don't try to drop me from the sum
> Of your complaints. Since we got started,
> There's been two of us, never parted
> From each other. You and me through thick
> And thin, stiff upper-lip for everything.
> So when it's both that take a tumble,
> Don't I have the right to grumble?
> All I want's a bit of credit,
> Don't you think that I deserve it?

ROSAURA.
>I thought it better not to give
>You shares in my complaint, so you
>Might profit on your own account.
>To vent our feelings is a source
>Of such relief, so a philosopher
>Once said, true benefit's derived
>Far less from taxing others with
>Our sorrows as from seeking them
>Ourselves.

CLARION.
>   If that's philosophy,
>The bloke must be blind-drunk and crazy
>With it. I'd box his silly ears
>And take my pleasure in his tears.
>So what's our plan to be then, mistress,
>Now we're in this proper mess?
>On foot, alone, and God knows where.
>Even the sun is going elsewhere.

ROSAURA.
>Whoever saw such mysteries
>As these? If I am not deceived
>By fanciful illusion, I
>Perceive the strangest vision of
>A building in the fading light.

CLARION.
>I see it too, unless my fancy
>Shapes the very thing I want to see.

ROSAURA.
>A crude and rustic palace stands
>Amongst the bare and barren rocks,
>So small the sun disdains to look
>On it. It has in shape and form
>Such roughness that it seems itself a rock
>Now fallen at the feet of cliffs
>So high they dare to mock the sky
>Itself.

CLARION.
>   Let's go and take a look then.
>No point in just admiring.
>Maybe our luck has changed at last
>And someone'll give us bed and breakfast.

ROSAURA.

> The door is open wide, a black
> And gaping mouth, the womb from which
> The darkness of the night is born.

Rattling of chains.

CLARION.

> My God! Did you hear that, my lady?

ROSAURA.

> Yes, fear and excitement freeze me.

CLARION.

> A chain I reckon. What can it be?
> A galley-slave in purgatory?

SEGISMUNDO (*off*).

> Oh, this misery! Will someone help me!

ROSAURA.

> Listen! Such sadness in the voice.
> It seems to speak of other troubles,
> Of other cares ahead of us.

CLARION.

> Maybe, my lady. I'm just scared for us.

ROSAURA.

> Perhaps we ought to leave this place
> And not risk facing further danger.

CLARION.

> Oh yes, my lady. I approve.
> If only I could bloody move.

ROSAURA.

> But isn't that a tiny lamp
> That, like some pale and distant star,
> Sends out its beams of feeble light?
> Its flickering, instead of lighting up
> The room, seems now to flood and fill
> It with the darkness of a tomb.
> Ah, yes. Though it is far away
> And badly lit, it seems a kind
> Of prison, or if I'm not mistaken,
> A grave to house the living-dead.
> But more amazing still, I think
> I see a man inside dressed like
> An animal from head to foot,

And chained, his only company
The tiny light. This is indeed
A sight to wonder at. If there's
No way we can escape from here,
It's best we stay awhile and see
If he has anything to say.

SEGISMUNDO *is seen, dressed in skins, shackled with chains,
holding a light.*

SEGISMUNDO.
Oh this misery! Will someone help me!
Oh cruel heaven, I have the right
To know why I am treated so.
Have I somehow offended you
In being born? Though it is true.
Man's greatest crime is to be born.
And since the punishment must match
The crime in its severity,
It is appropriate that I
Should now be treated cruelly.
And yet, I wish to know as well,
If only to dispel my doubts,
What other wrong I can be guilty
Of, apart from that of being born.
Were not the rest born too? If that
Is so, do they have special rights
Which I am not entitled to?
The bird is born, its coloured plumage
The image of a feathered flower
Or winged bouquet, and soon it leaves
The quiet safety of its nest
And dares to fly away towards
The clear blue mansions of the sky.
It lacks a soul but has its freedom,
And I, who have a soul, have none.
The beast is born, so colourful
Its skin, it seems a star on earth,
The living proof of God's own worth.
But soon a need for food and drink
Awakens instincts so far hidden,
Making this once gentle creature
A cruel, cold and heartless monster.
It lacks a heart but has its freedom.

Must I, who have a heart, have none?
The fish is born, a child of spawn
And weed that cannot breathe the air,
That launched in water is a ship
Of scales to voyage everywhere,
Matching with its own ambition
The boundless vastness of the ocean.
It does not breathe but has its freedom.
Must I, endowed with breath, have none?
The stream is born, a silver snake
That winds its gentle way along,
That, sliding in amongst the flowers,
Sings to them its flattering song,
While further on the plains salute,
Offering their loyal tribute.
It has no life but has its freedom.
Must I, who have a life, have none?
Oh, I am driven to distraction!
I feel a passion in my breast
That, if unleashed, would make me pierce
It and tear my heart to pieces.
What law or justice can deny
A man the privilege that God
Has given to the stream, the fish,
The birds, and all the animals?

ROSAURA.
His words awaken in me fear
And pity too.

SEGISMUNDO.
                    Who's there? Has someone
Heard me? Is that you, Clotaldo?

CLARION (*aside*).
Go on, say yes, before he kills you.

ROSAURA.
Someone, my friend, who's also sad,
Who, passing through this cold valley,
Answers to your melancholy.

SEGISMUNDO.
Then more's the pity you must die.
No one lives to tell the story
Of my misery to someone else.

Apart from which, this trespassing
Invites these arms of mine to punish you
By tearing you from limb to limb.

CLARION.

Just tell him, mistress, I can't hear him.
Suddenly I'm hard of hearing.

ROSAURA.

I beg of you, if you have any
Pity in your heart, then let
My pleading soothe your cruelty.

SEGISMUNDO.

Who are you? Why does your voice
Move me so strangely; your presence
Suddenly disturb me; a kind
Of reverence still my hand? It's true.
I understand so little of
The world and have seen nothing of it
Save this prison, once my cradle,
Soon my grave; and since my birth,
If this can be considered birth,
Have spent my worthless life in this
Deserted place, this wilderness,
A skeleton that still has flesh,
A corpse that still lays claim to breath.
I have seen no one in this time,
Nor spoken to a single soul
Save one who knows my sorrows and
Has taught me all I know about
Both heaven and earth. My company,
So you may be the more amazed
And see me as the monster that
I am, has been these shadows, which,
In all their gloom have made me what I am:
A man who lives amongst the beasts,
A beast who lives amongst his fellow
Men. Despite this misery, I've studied
All there is to see around my prison,
The beasts, the birds, the stars, and each
Has helped to teach me something of
The workings of this world of ours;
Yet only you, of all these things,
Have been a source of softness to

My anger, of wonder to my eyes,
And pleasure to my ears. Each time
I look at you, my eyes are so
Entranced, they long to see you more,
And hunger for the sight of you,
As if they were a man to whom
Drink is forbidden, and yet he feels
Obliged to drink. So do my eyes
Absorb you now, and even though
They know this could be fatal to
Their own well-being, persist in gazing,
Considering the contemplation
Of your beauty worth the risk
To their mortality. But let
Me go on gazing even if
It means my death. I cannot tell
Which is the greater or lesser evil:
To die if I persist in looking,
Or not to look at you and die.
But that would be, much worse than death,
Despair, rage, anger, death itself.
Such is the harshness of this life.
Give pleasure to the man who cries,
But when he laughs, make sure he dies!

ROSAURA.
I see you with astonishment.
I listen to your history
With such complete amazement, I
Neither know what I should say to you
Or ask; unless it be that heaven,
Perhaps, has sent me here, so I
Should not feel pity for my own
Misfortune, but seek the consolation
Of another's misery and see
If what they say is true: that seeing
Someone else's grief must always
Offer one relief. They say there was
A wise man once who, being poor,
Had no food, and found his sustenance
In herbs and berries. 'You won't find
Any person worse than me', he'd say.
But when he turned and looked behind
He saw another man who, as

He went along, stayed close to him,
And bent to eat the leaves he'd thrown
Away. So I, complaining of
My own misfortune, was on the point
Of saying to myself: 'Oh, who
In this entire world can be
Less fortunate than I?', when your
Wretched fate became the answer
To my question, your misery
The measure of my joy; for you,
I know, would eagerly accept
My suffering as your pleasure.
If my misfortunes were to make
You happier, I'd gladly give
You some of them. Perhaps you'd like
To hear my story. My name . . .

CLOTALDO (off).
Guards! Quickly! You are paid to guard
This tower, not let people wander
In here. No doubt you thought you'd have
Some peace, unless, of course, it's just
Plain cowardice. Get hold of them!

ROSAURA.
What new confusion can this be?

SEGISMUNDO.
Oh, just one more misfortune we
Should add to all the others. All hail
My favourite jailer! His name's
Clotaldo.

CLOTALDO (off).
                     Hurry, but proceed
With care. Arrest them if you can,
But if you need to, don't think twice.
Just kill them!

GUARDS (off).
                     Come out at once, you traitors!

CLARION.
That's nice that is! What a choice it is!
You let us in here in the first place.
And now, give up or be a goner.
I've made my mind up. I surrender.

Enter CLOTALDO *with a gun, followed by soldiers whose faces will be concealed.*

CLOTALDO.

    Cover your faces properly.
    As long as you're inside no one
    Shall know your true identity.

CLARION.

    Hey, why didn't you tell me, lads?
    It's just a fancy-dress party.

CLOTALDO.

    You people. Don't you know this place
    Is out of bounds? The King's command,
    So anyone who's found here acts
    In strict defiance of the King.
    No one's allowed to see this creature,
    So if you know what's good for you,
    You won't cause any bother. Better you
    Surrender now and not persist
    In this. If you resist, this weapon has
    No other choice. I'll let it spit
    Its deadly poison, like some snake
    Of metal, and make the air the smoky
    Province of its flame.

SEGISMUNDO.

                 Stay away
    From them. Before your tyrant's hands
    Offend or cause them injury,
    These miserable chains shall see
    My death, jailer. I swear to God,
    I'll tear myself apart with them.
    My teeth, my hands shall be the weapons
    Of my own destruction before
    I let you cause these people harm.
    Far better to be dead myself
    Than left alone again amongst
    These rocks to mourn the death of others.

CLOTALDO.

    Oh, this is bravery indeed!
    But your misery, my friend,
    Is heaven's decree and there's no end
    To it. You know you were condemned

At birth to live your life out here.
You know the purpose of these chains
Is to contain your anger as
The reins control a horse. So why
Protest when there is nothing you
Can do to change the situation?
Guards! Best get him back inside again
And lock the prison door.

They close the door. SEGISMUNDO *is heard shouting.*

SEGISMUNDO.
                              Oh, you
Are wise, ungrateful heavens, to lock
Me up and rob me of my freedom,
Or I might turn against you like
Some Titan and, heaping stone on stone
To build a jasper mountain, seek
To scale its summit where I'd break
The shining windows of the sun.

CLOTALDO.
That's possibly the explanation
Of your fate. They've locked you up
To put an end to such ambition.

ROSAURA.
If pride and arrogance offend
You so, my lord, it would be foolish
Of me not to kneel at your feet
And beg for mercy. Let pity
For me rule your heart. It would
Be harsh indeed if neither pride
Nor lack of it did not find favour
In your eyes.

CLARION.
                              How very true, sir.
They've often walked the stage together
Those two, Humility and Pride.
If they don't melt your heart as they
Ought to, consider me, sir. I'm
Somewhere in between the two of them.
I'm neither over proud nor over
Humble. Make me an offer, sir,
I'll prove it to you. A nice steak?

You see, I'm not too proud to take it.
Oh, did you say shelter? Of course,
Sir. I humbly accept the offer.

CLOTALDO.
Guards!

SOLDIERS.
My lord . . .

CLOTALDO.
Take their weapons.
Cover their eyes. When they leave, they
Must have no idea where
They are or how they leave.

ROSAURA.
I give
My sword to you. You seem to have
Authority, and this must be
Surrendered only to a person worthy of
Accepting it.

CLARION.
Here, take mine too.
It's got no quality. Any silly
Fart can have it, including you.

ROSAURA.
If I must die, I leave this sword
With you as witness to the pity you
Have shown to me. It was greatly
Valued by someone else whose sword
It was and, so I'm told, its golden
Blade contains some strange and secret
History. Give me your word you'll keep
It safely. I come to Poland
In search of honour's satisfaction.
This sword has been my company
And offered me protection on
The journey.

CLOTALDO (*aside*).
This is a mystery
Indeed! Confusion merely added
To confusion! What does it mean?
What explanation can there be
For this? (*Aloud.*) Tell me, who owned the sword?

ROSAURA.
>   A lady, sir.

CLOTALDO.
>   Her name?

ROSAURA.
>   I gave
>   My word it should remain a secret.

CLOTALDO.
>   What leads you to believe the sword
>   Contains some hidden mystery?

ROSAURA.
>   Because the lady told me this:
>   'Proceed to Poland. Use whatever means
>   Or art you can to make quite sure
>   The sword is seen by everyone
>   At Court. I know that someone there
>   Will offer you protection.' She said
>   No more than that. Perhaps she thought
>   This nobleman might now be dead.

CLOTALDO.
>   My ears must be deceiving me.
>   I can't believe what they are telling me.
>   Are these things real or the product
>   Of some strange, unfathomable
>   Fantasy? This is the sword I gave
>   To Violante many years
>   Ago, so I would later know
>   Whoever happened to be wearing
>   It, and show towards that person
>   A father's love and sympathy.
>   But what am I to do in such
>   A situation as confronts
>   Me now? The bearer of the sword
>   Demands my help and yet he has
>   Condemned himself to certain death
>   By coming here. How fickle is
>   Our fate! How cruel! How can I find
>   A sensible solution to this
>   Muddle and confusion? This is
>   My son, I'm sure. The signs are clear
>   And find an echo in the beating

Of my heart. Just as a bird locked
In its cage flies furiously against
Its sides, or else a prisoner who hears
A noise tries eagerly to see
Outside his cell, so now my heart,
Imprisoned in my breast, knocks loudly,
And in its curiosity
To know what's happening, looks from
Its windows, which are my eyes, and weeps
At what it sees. What can I do?
Look on me kindly, heavens. Help me
To see this matter safely through
To its conclusion. To take him
To the King is surely to bring
About his death. And yet I cannot
Hide him from the King and still
Be loyal. Love on the one hand, on
The other, loyalty. Each pulls
Against the other to win me over,
And yet the way ahead is clear.
Is not obedience to the King
Above all other loyalties
A man may have, including life
And honour? If that is so, then
Those must live and he must die.
And furthermore, did not he speak,
As I recall, of seeking here
The satisfaction of his honour,
Which means he has no honour and by
That token cannot be my son
Or have my noble blood? Though it
Is true as well that we are sometimes
Victims of events, the prisoners
Of honour's accidents, and honour,
Being such a fragile thing, is
Broken, or tarnished by some tiny
Breath of scandal. In circumstances
Such as these, is this not all we
Can expect of any nobleman:
To make a journey such as this
For honour's sake? I swear he *is*
My son. He has my blood. His bravery
Bears witness to it. But since I am

Beset by all these doubts, I'll seek
The King, inform him he's my son,
And he can kill him if he so
Decides. If I don't hide the truth,
Perhaps the King will pity me
And feel obliged to set him free.
If so, I'll help him gain his honour,
But if the King is not disposed
To show his mercy, he shall die
And never know that I'm his father.
Both of you. You'll come with me.
I promise, you shan't lack company
In these misfortunes. To live or die,
All men have asked themselves the question.
The only problem: the solution.

Exit all. Enter from one side of the stage ASTOLFO,
accompanied by soldiers; from the other side ESTRELLA, *with
ladies-in-waiting. Music.*

ASTOLFO.
Your eyes, my lady, are the envy
Of the sun itself in brightness
And in beauty, and so the trumpets
And the drums, the fountains and the birds
Are here to welcome you and sing
Your praises. They match their harmony
To yours, and each of them in turn
Produces perfect sounds in homage
To your heavenly face, so that
The birds seem brightly feathered trumpets,
The trumpets birds of shining metal.
And so, as salvos greet a queen,
The birds Aurora, flowers Flora,
Trumpets Minerva, these bright sounds
Greet you, my lady, for you in
Your beauty are the dawn itself,
And in your spirit bold Minerva,
In sheer joy bright Aurora,
In quiet calm gentle Flora,
But most of all, of my soul ruler.

ESTRELLA.
If words, Astolfo, correspond

To deeds, such flattery as this
Is but a sign of bad intentions,
And these discordant military sounds
The measure of your future actions.
For just as this cacophony
Assaults my ears and deafens me
To sweeter sounds, so I detect,
I'm bound to say, a melody
Beneath the sweetness of your words
That growls incredibly harshly.
An animal, you know, attracts
Its prey by means of flattery
Before it kills; so any man
Who cunningly conceals his aim
In flattering and honeyed words
Before he kills, is just as beastly.

ASTOLFO.
Believe me, you are wrong, Estrella,
To doubt the honesty of my
Intentions. If you really knew me, you
Would know integrity's my second name.
I shall explain the situation.
Eustorgius the Third was King
Of Poland and left his kingdom
To his son, Basilio, whose two
Sisters were each respectively
Our mothers: yours Clorilene,
Whose goodness now enjoys a better
Life than this in heaven; and mine
Ruscinda, the younger of the two –
May heaven protect her through the years –
Who left her native country long
Ago to settle down in Muscovy.
But this is ancient history,
Simply the preface to the story
As it unfolds before us now.
Basilio, as you know, is old
And feels his years begin to weigh
Upon him heavily. As well as that, he's
Always spent his days devoted
Less to women than to books; he has
No child; and as his wife is also dead,

No heir who can succeed him legally.
In consequence we are both claimants
To the throne, you arguing that you
Are daughter to his elder sister,
Myself that though my mother was
The younger of the two, I am
A man and therefore have a stronger
Claim than you. And so Basilio,
Acknowledging our rivalry
In this, has set today aside
To judge our claims and try to reach
A satisfactory conclusion.
I, on that account, have travelled
Here from Muscovy, and that has been
My only purpose. Quite honestly,
It's not so much a case of my
Declaring war on you as your
Perfect beauty making war on me.
But why not let the god of love
Rule both our lives and in his wisdom
Realize through us the people's choice.
By which I mean that this dispute
Should end declaring you the queen,
But queen and sovereign too of my
Own destiny. And so the best
Solution's this: the King, for your
Greater honour, offers you his crown,
And my adoring love this victory.

ESTRELLA.

Who, Astolfo, can resist such pleasing
Flattery? I think I might just like
The kingdom for myself so I
Can offer it to you. Though seriously,
There's still a little something makes
Me doubt your absolute sincerity.
The locket around your neck contains
The portrait of a certain lady.

ASTOLFO.

Oh, that's quite easily explained,
Estrella . . . However, I fear
These instruments are stopping me
From doing it just now. The King,

You see . . .

Music. Enter KING BASILIO *with his Court.*

ESTRELLA.
                    Oh, wise Thales . . .

ASTOLFO.
                              Oh, great
And learned Euclid . . .

ESTRELLA.
                         Who rules amongst
The stars . . .

ASTOLFO.
                  Who governs all the planets . . .

ESTRELLA.
Who traces their paths . . .

ASTOLFO.
                              And measures
All their movements . . .

ESTRELLA.
                         Your majesty,
As ivy clings tenaciously
To some great oak, such is my loyalty
To you.

ASTOLFO.
           And I, your majesty,
Prostrate myself at your feet,
Such is my true humility.

BASILIO.
Let me embrace you both, my niece
And nephew. It makes my old heart
Glad to see you treat each other
So considerately on such
A day as this, and gives me hope
That both your rival claims can in
The end be settled amicably.
I must confess, however, that
The gravity of this affair
Weighs heavily upon my shoulders,
And so I ask you both for silence
And attention: though, as you'll see,
The things I have to tell are such

They guarantee your admiration.
Let me remind you first, beloved
Niece and nephew, illustrious Court,
Friends, subjects, relatives, that I
Throughout the world am known for my
Great wisdom, a fame I've merited
For scientific knowledge, and brush
And sculptor's chisel celebrate
For ages still to come the name
That suits me best: The Great Basilio.
The science I admire most
And earnestly pursue is subtle
Mathematics, from which a man
May learn, if he is truly wise,
To see what lies ahead of him
And thus defeat both time and fame.
For careful consultation of
My charts and tables leads to accurate
Prediction of the state of things
To come before they happen, and
Lets me steal a timely march on time itself.
These snow-white spheres up on high,
This shining canopy of sky,
Illuminated by bright sun,
And lit by moon when night has come;
These orbs as bright as diamond,
These globes of glass which stars adorn,
These fields where Zodiac-signs are formed;
All this has been for many years
My earnest study, the heavenly book
In which our fate is written by
The heavens in golden letters bold
And clear, on pages bright as sapphire.
Such is my skill, I read them all
With utmost speed; I track their course
And movement through the firmament
And heed each sign as it presents
Itself to me. If only heaven
Had put an end to me! If only
Heaven had made my ingenuity
The victim of its rage instead
Of letting it become the index
And the commentary to its secret

Pages! For if the truth be told,
The very qualities that make
Men great may, if the heavens decree,
Become the source of tragedy,
His own ability a knife
That always threatens his security,
His very knowledge a constant source
Of self-inflicted injury.
Let me be witness to the truth
Of this and ask of you that rapt
Attention be a fitting prelude
To your incredulity.
Queen Clorilene bore me a child,
A son announced by such a wild,
Extravagant display of heavenly
Portents as no man has ever seen,
And this before the child was born,
As if to say the womb that gave
Him life was simultaneously
A tomb that prophesied a death.
His poor mother, racked by dreadful
Fantasies and dreams, had visions
Of a monster that seemingly
Took human form and in the process
Of its birth ripped apart her womb,
Spilling her precious blood and, like
Some human viper, ensuring
Her end. And so the fateful moment
Of the birth arrived, accompanied
On every side by prophecies
That seemed to prove that only those
Which choose to tell the worst are true;
For when the child was born, the signs
Were such the sun itself was bathed
In blood and fought a fierce battle
With the moon in which the earth stood
In between, while both the heavenly
Bodies struggled for supremacy,
Locked in a furious struggle that
In human terms would be described
As hand-to-hand but in the case
Of these adversaries was beam-
To-beam. And then there came a great

Eclipse, the mightiest the world
Has ever seen since on that fearful
Day the sun wept with its blood for
Our Lord. So now, as then, the world
Was suddenly engulfed by fire,
And everyone was soon convinced
The end of life itself was near.
The heavens grew black, the buildings shook,
The skies rained stones, the rivers ran
With blood, and in the midst of this
Confusion of the sun my son
Was born, and gave a clear warning
Of his own condition by murdering
His mother at the very moment
Of his birth, as if to say to us:
'I am a man of natural
Ferocity. Who does
Me good, I swear I'll pay him back,
But always badly.' I hastened
To my books but everywhere I
Looked I was informed my son
Would be the boldest of all men,
The cruellest of princes, the wickedest
Of Kings, on whose account my kingdom
Would be hopelessly divided,
The very school of treachery,
The very best academy
For all imaginable vices.
As well as this, my son, inspired
By his fury, would, in the midst
Of all his hideous crimes, have me,
His father, prostrate at his feet,
And, treating this white hair of mine
As if it were some humble carpet,
Place his foot upon my royal head.
Oh, how it grieves my heart to say it!
But who would doubt a prophecy
As dark as this when his entire
Life is given to the study
Of the stars? And so, believing
What the stars foretold, that only
Tragedy would come to our royal
Household, I thought it best to shut

That beast away where he could do
No harm, and we would see if man
Was able to control the stars.
My people were informed the prince
Had died at birth. I gave the order
For a tower to be built amongst
The rocks and stones where even light
Is kept at bay by mighty crags
That bar the way to anyone
Who seeks to enter there. And laws
Were passed with due publicity,
So all would know that place was out
Of bounds and anyone who happened
To be found there knew the penalty
He'd be obliged to pay. Such is
The place where Segismundo lives
A prisoner, and wastes away
His life in utter misery,
Attended only by Clotaldo,
His jailor and his loyal teacher.
He has instructed him in all
He knows: the rudiments of learning,
The teachings of the Church, and to
This very day has been the only
Witness to his constant suffering.
But let me say three things on this.
The first concerns my love for you,
My people, and my wish to spare
You from a King who, as the prophecy
Declared, would be a ruthless tyrant.
What sort of King would you consider
Me if I had chosen to ignore
The risk and so expose my people
To the tyranny of someone else?
My second point is one that stems
From this, for I, denying to
My son the rights conferred on him
By laws both human and divine,
Deny him Christian charity;
And there is nothing that gives me
The right, by seeking to avert
His tyranny, to exercise
My tyranny on him, and in

An effort to suppress his crimes
Become myself the criminal.
And third and last of all I draw
Attention to our foolishness
In placing too much faith in what
The stars foretell; for even if
Man's inclination is the cause
Of many rash and unwise acts,
We cannot say that it in any
Way compels him to these actions.
The harshest fate, the cruellest
Of destinies, the fiercest
Of natures can in the end incline
And influence but never force
Man's will. And so, considering
These points and all their implications,
I have decided on a plan
That will demand your admiration.
Tomorrow I shall place upon
My throne, without him knowing he's
My son and your King, Segismundo,
Such is his name, and he shall rule
Instead of me and govern you,
As I have done, and you shall show
To him the loyalty you've always
Shown to me. But in relation
To this plan, I wish to mention
Three points more than correspond
To these I've made to you already.
The first is that my son, should he
Prove prudent and considerate
And thus disprove what fate has said
It has in store for him, shall be
Your rightful prince, and you shall have
As your King a man whose court
Has so far been a wilderness,
Whose only company has been
The savagery of beasts. My second
Point concerns the possibility
That he should prove to be both proud
And arrogant and boldly run
The course of all his cruel vices.
If this should be the case, I will

At least have given him the chance
To prove himself and shown to him
The mercy that a father should;
And if I were to take away
Again his power and authority,
I'd do so as a King who knew
Where duty lay, and his imprisonment
Would not be seen as cruelty
But as his rightful punishment.
The third and final point is this.
Although he is the prince by right,
My love of you is such that I
Would then bestow on you such kings
As would prove worthy of my throne:
That is to say, my niece and nephew.
Both are rightful claimants to
My throne and, being joined in holy
Matrimony, deserve this honour.
This I command as your King,
This I request as your father,
This I suggest as someone sage,
This recommend in my old age.
And if it's true, as Seneca
Once said, that every king's a humble
Slave unto his people, then I
Ask this of you as your slave.

ASTOLFO.
If it behoves me to reply
As one whose interest is now
At risk, I do so in the name
Of all those present here and ask
That Segismundo should appear.
He is your rightful son and heir.

ALL.
Our rightful prince, our very own.
He must sit upon the throne.

BASILIO.
My loyal subjects, this is true
Consideration. Thanks to all
Of you. Accompany my niece
And nephew to their chambers now.
Tomorrow you shall see my son.

ALL.

Long live our King, the great Basilio!

Exit all. As the KING *is about to leave,* CLOTALDO *enters with* ROSAURA *and* CLARION *and stops the* KING.

CLOTALDO.

I wish to speak with you, your majesty.

BASILIO.

Clotaldo, I bid you welcome.

CLOTALDO.

To kneel at your feet at any
Other time, your majesty,
Would be most welcome to this humble
Servant, but now sad fate
Deprives me of the privilege
And joy of such a happy custom.

BASILIO.

But why is that, my good Clotaldo?

CLOTALDO.

A great misfortune's come to pass,
My lord, which could quite easily
Have been my joy and happiness.

BASILIO.

Explain to me.

CLOTALDO.

This handsome youth,
Misled by curiosity
Or lack of caution, gained entrance
To the tower. He has set eyes
Upon the prince . . .

BASILIO.

Ah, well, Clotaldo.
I must confess that had it been
Another day, he'd certainly
Have seen my anger. But now I've chosen
To reveal the facts to all my people,
It doesn't really matter if
He knows what others know already.
Attend me afterwards. I have
To tell you certain things which you
Must carry out on my behalf.

I'll have you know as well that you
Shall soon be called on to perform
The most amazing feat the world
Has ever known. As for the prisoners,
I shall not punish your carelessness;
Merely grant them my forgiveness.

Exit the KING.

CLOTALDO (*aside*).
May he enjoy a thousand years
Of life and more! My luck has changed.
Good fortune smiles on me at last.
Now there's no need, I shan't reveal
To him that he's my son. (*Aloud.*) Good news
For both of you. You are free to go.

ROSAURA.
I humbly kiss your feet, my lord.

CLARION.
And I'll give 'em a miss, I think, my lord.
What's a single letter matter
If we are friends?

ROSAURA.
You've given me
My life, my lord. I am forever
In your debt. I swear that I
Shall always be your loyal and most constant
Servant.

CLOTALDO.
What I have given you
Is less than life. For any man
Of noble birth whose honour has
Been lost can scarcely claim that he
Is still alive; and since you come
In search of restitution of
Offended honour, how can I
Be said to offer life to one
Who by his own admission now has none?
A life dishonoured is no life.

Aside.

These words may stir him to some action.

ROSAURA.

I do confess that in that sense
I have no life, though you have saved
My life. But I shall seek revenge
And in the cleansing of my honour
Claim my life again so it may seem
Quite properly a gift from you.

CLOTALDO.

Then use that burnished steel. Avenge
Yourself on your enemy.
Spill his blood to cleanse your honour.
For steel that I once held – I mean
The moment now, just gone, I held
It in my hand – shall be your saviour.

ROSAURA.

I do so in your name and for
A second time accept this sword.
I shall take vengeance even though
My enemy should prove more powerful
Than I. You have my word on it.

CLOTALDO.

And is this enemy so powerful?

ROSAURA.

He is, my lord. So powerful
I hesitate to speak his name,
And so do not, but not because I doubt
The constant value of your prudence; more
Because I dare not have the favour
You have shown now turned against me.

CLOTALDO.

On the contrary, to give his name
Would be to guarantee my favour.
It would stop me helping him.

Aside.

Why won't he tell me who he is!

ROSAURA.

That being so, my lord, I would
Not want my reticence interpreted
As lack of confidence in you.
I'll have you know my enemy's

Astolfo, Duke of Muscovy.

CLOTALDO (*aside*).
My God, what is he telling me?
This is a blow far worse than I
Had thought, a mortal wound to mind
And spirit. But let's investigate
A little more. (*Aloud*.) Is it not true
That you were also born in Muscovy?
If that is so, it follows that
A natural lord can hardly be
Accused of causing injury
To you. I think you'd best go home.
Forget this rage that drives you on
So recklessly.

ROSAURA.
                        He has offended
Me, even though he is a prince.

CLOTALDO.
But he could not offend you if
He were to strike you in the face.

Aside.

Heaven spare me!

ROSAURA.
                          My injury was much
More serious.

CLOTALDO.
                    Then tell me what it was.
It cannot be much worse than what
My own imagination tells me.

ROSAURA.
Then you shall know the truth, though even
As I speak I cannot understand
Why I regard you with respect,
Why I should have for you
Such warm regard and veneration.
But if you want the truth, the clothes
I wear conceal a mystery
And do not tell you what I really am.
In other words, if I seem what
I'm not and Duke Astolfo's marriage

To Estrella is a further injury,
I've told you all you need to know.

Exit ROSAURA *and* CLARION.

CLOTALDO.
Stop! Come back! Listen to me!
Oh what a maze and labyrinth
This is, and no way out that reason
Can suggest! Oh what confusion!
My honour has been lost, the man
Who's blackened it is strong,
I his vassal, and she a mere woman.
Heaven must guide me in this matter now,
Though heaven itself may well be powerless,
When in this terrible abyss
The heavens predict catastrophe,
And all the world's a mystery.

Act Two

Enter KING BASILIO *and* CLOTALDO.

CLOTALDO.
>Everything's been done, your majesty,
>Exactly as you wished.

BASILIO.
>   Tell me,
>Clotaldo, precisely what you did.

CLOTALDO.
>First, my lord, I carefully prepared
>The drink according to instructions,
>Mixing with various sweet ingredients
>A variety of herbs which by
>Their nature have authority
>And total power over man.
>Indeed, they rob him of his speech,
>Gradually encourage sleep,
>And overcoming sense and reason,
>Render him so weak he soon becomes
>A living corpse – such is, your majesty,
>The power of the herbs I speak of.
>Nor should we doubt the truth of it,
>When long experience proves to us
>That medicine itself relies
>On Nature's secrets, and every
>Animal, plant and stone contains
>Ingredients, each of which provides
>Enormous benefit to man.
>What's more, if human ingenuity
>Has fashioned from the study of
>These things such poisons as can kill
>So rapidly, it cannot be
>Beyond the skill of man to find
>Some poison that will merely put
>To sleep. In any case, as I
>Have said, such facts as these are proven
>And well-known and need no further

Explanation. And so, your majesty,
Poppy and henbane were the herbs
That formed my potion when I took
It to the Prince. We talked a while
Of various things: of all he'd learned
From watching from the window of
His cell the silent world of sky
And mountain; of what he knew from
Studying the language and the rhetoric
Of animals and birds. But thinking
More especially of what you have
In mind for him, I sought to find
Some topic that might move his thoughts
To higher things and fixed upon
The swiftness of a golden eagle
There above, whose wings defied the sphere
Of the wind and, taking it towards
The highest regions of the sun,
Made it appear both a feathered ray
Of light and the bright tail of a comet.
I praised the boldness of the eagle's
Soaring flight, describing her as queen
Of all the birds, and rightly so
In view of her true majesty.
As for the prince, he needed no
Encouragement, for mere mention
Of the topic was sufficient
To unleash in him much evidence
Of pride and natural ambition.
His blood, in short, ran fast and
Passion moved his thoughts to topics
Worthy of a king. 'Observe', he said
To me. 'Even in the kingdom of
The birds there's one demands submission
From the rest. It offers me at least
Some comfort in my misery,
For if I now obey, it is
Because I am the slave of someone
Else. I'd never willingly submit.'
I saw how quickly thoughts of his
Imprisonment inflamed his passions,
And in those circumstances thought
It best to let him drink the potion.

No sooner had the liquid passed
His lips than all his strength began
To drain away from him, and sleep
Invade his being so entirely
That all his limbs and veins grew cold
As ice, and had I not then known
That what seemed death was just appearance,
I would have feared for his very life.
The others you'd entrusted with
The matter soon arrived and took
Him in a carriage to your Court,
Where all the majesty that any
Prince is worthy of shall now be his.
He lies upon your royal bed
Where soon the sleeping-draught will lose
Effect and he, awake, shall see
Himself attended just as if
He were himself your majesty.
If I am thought in any way
Deserving of reward for this
— Excuse the liberty — I only ask
What lies behind your plan to bring
Young Segismundo to the palace.

BASILIO.

Of course, Clotaldo, I understand
Your question very well. I'll do
My best to give you satisfaction.
The stars, as you well know, have threatened
Segismundo with a thousand
Tragedies, and though I do not think
The heavens can ever lie — indeed,
The boy's ferocity is proof
Enough that they are right — I wish
To know if prophecy is totally
Infallible, or if the exercise
Of courage, prudence and the like
May somehow modify its harsh
Decree, and thereby prove that man
Is master of his destiny.
To put this to the test I've had
The boy brought here, where he shall learn
He is my son and, knowing this,
Will have the opportunity

To prove himself. If he can show
Himself magnanimous, he shall
Be king, but if he's only cruel
And tyrannical, his chains shall once
Again become his prison. But why,
You are about to ask, must he
Be fast asleep before we put
The matter to the test? The answer
Is quite simple. If he discovers
He's my son today but learns tomorrow
He's been locked away again, the shock
Would be too great for him to bear,
And thoughts of majesty that was,
Compared with present misery,
Would lead him only to despair.
Because of that I thought we ought
To be prepared and have a plan
Whereby he can be told that what
Seemed real to him was a dream.
My plan has two advantages.
It first of all reveals to us,
When he's awake, what kind of man
He is, for he'll behave according
To his will and inclination.
But then it has the consolation too
That, though he's seen himself obeyed
And finds himself again imprisoned,
He's likely to accept it was
A dream: a natural conclusion
When everything that seems so real
In this world is nothing but a dream.

CLOTALDO.

I could find many arguments
To prove your majesty mistaken;
The time for that is gone. Indeed,
I think the Prince, awakened, now,
Begins to come towards us.

BASILIO.

I shall withdraw. Approach him as
His tutor. Inform him of the truth,
To ease the muddle and confusion of
His mind.

CLOTALDO.
>> Your majesty, I must
Have your permission.

BASILIO.
>> I think the truth
Is best. To know the situation in
Advance gives any man a better
Chance of finding a solution.

Exit BASILIO. *Enter* CLARION.

CLARION.
You'll never guess what I've put up with!
Four fierce blows from some red-headed
Halberdier, and that was just to get
In here! My God, you should have seen him!
Bright red beard, bright red livery.
You couldn't tell, quite honestly,
If his face was liveried or his
Chest bearded. Anyway, now I'm in,
I want to see what's happening.
What better seat to see the play
Than one for which you haven't paid?
Who wants to pay to get in there
When cheek will get you anywhere?

CLOTALDO (*aside*).
This fellow's Clarion, servant to
The lady whose coming here
Has brought with her my own dishonour.

Aloud.

Clarion! I say, what news?

CLARION.
>> I think
The latest information is,
My lord, that your reassurance has,
Together with your guarantee
Of vengeance, made Rosaura wear
The kind of gear that suits her best.

CLOTALDO.
I'm glad to hear of it. It avoids
Unseemliness.

CLARION.
                    As well as that,
    There's unconfirmed reports she's gone
    And changed her name, taken yours,
    Claiming she's your niece, and on
    The strength of that become a great
    Success at Court, lady-in-waiting
    To Estrella.

CLOTALDO.
                    I'm glad to hear that too.
    Naturally, my name must honour her.

CLARION.
    And news has just come in, sir, that
    She hopes it won't be long before
    You've gone and cleansed her precious honour.

CLOTALDO.
    I'm sure that will come, Clarion.
    Honour shall be redressed in time.

CLARION.
    Just one thing more. Stop press, you might
    Say — little item all to do
    With how her close association with
    You has done her such a great big favour.
    I mean by that, that she is treated like
    A queen, while I must starve to death
    From sheer hunger, no one looking
    After me, and not forgetting
    That my name is Clarion, meaning that
    My disposition is to trumpet
    Things, however accidentally,
    Like all that's happened recently
    To the King, Estrella and Astolfo.
    Thing is, you see, I'm two things really.
    — Clarion and servant — none of which
    Takes very kindly to the other;
    In short, an unfortunate mixture,
    Unless there's someone generous
    And kind enough to fix things for me.

CLOTALDO.
    You have a point, Clarion. I'll see
    What I can do to make your life

Less miserable. And in the meantime
Think it best you work for me.

CLARION.

A wise choice, sir. I do agree.
See there, my lord. It's Segismundo.

*Enter musicians, singing, and servants dressing SEGISMUNDO.
He is bewildered.*

SEGISMUNDO.

In heaven's name! What is this I see?
I am amazed and yet it does
Not frighten me. The sight that greets
My eyes . . . it seems so real, and yet
I think my eyes must be deceiving me.
Why do I find myself in this
Fine place, and dressed in satin
And brocade? Why am I waited on
By servants splendidly arrayed?
Why do I sleep and wake in such
A bed as this? Why do these people
Dress me now in all this finery?
To say I dream is to mistake
The truth of this. I am awake.
For am I not the Segismundo that
I always was? I beg you, heavens,
Dispel these doubts. I long to know
What happened to me while I slept
That I should be here now. But since
I am, what does the why and wherefore
Matter? If they insist on serving
And attending me, must I deny
Them such an opportunity?

SECOND SERVANT.

The prince seems strangely sad.

FIRST SERVANT.

                              Who wouldn't be
At such events as these?

CLARION.

                    Try me,
My friend. I think I'd fancy it.

SECOND SERVANT.

Why not approach and speak to him?

FIRST SERVANT.
>Your highness, would you have them sing
>Again for you?

SEGISMUNDO.
>   No. Make them stop
>Their singing.

SECOND SERVANT.
>   Music such as this
>My lord, will help to overcome
>Your melancholy.

SEGISMUNDO.
>   Music such
>As this, my friend, is far too jolly.
>It depresses me. I long for
>Harsh and stirring military sounds.

CLOTALDO.
>Your highness. Let me kiss your hand
>And be the first to pay you homage
>As a loyal and obedient subject.

SEGISMUNDO (*aside*).
>This is Clotaldo. Why should he
>Who treated me with such contempt
>In prison show towards me such
>Respect? What fall from tyranny
>Is this that now he only crawls?
>What mystery is hidden here
>That no one will explain to me?

CLOTALDO.
>I do not doubt, my lord, that such
>A change of fortune must create
>In any reasonable mind
>A sense of absolute confusion.
>My duty is to free you from
>Such doubt, and have you know by way
>Of explanation of these strange
>Events that you are in reality
>The Prince of Poland. I must inform
>You too that your long imprisonment
>Was due to fate's harsh prophecy
>That if the royal crown were ever
>Placed upon your head, this kingdom

Would be torn apart by constant
Tragedy. But now it is believed
That you, like any other man,
Can by your efforts overcome
The stars and, in the light of this,
And while you slept, you were transported
From your prison to the palace.
The King, your father and my lord,
Will soon attend and speak to you
Of anything you wish to know.

SEGISMUNDO.
Disloyal traitor! What else is there
To know that matters more than knowing
Who I am when this confers on me
Such power? You have betrayed your country;
In hiding me away denied
Me every privilege against
All right and reason.

CLOTALDO.
                           You are mistaken.

SEGISMUNDO.
And you are guilty of high treason:
Of blatant treachery towards
The law; of fawning flattery
Towards the King; of cruelty
To me. And so the three of us,
The law, the King, myself, hereby
Condemn you to this instant death
Between these hands.

SECOND SERVANT.
                          My lord . . .

SEGISMUNDO.
                                    Let no
One try to stop me. I swear to you,
Take one step more, I'll throw you from
The window.

FIRST SERVANT.
                 Run, Clotaldo! Save
Yourself!

CLOTALDO.
                I beg you, Segismundo,

Be less arrogant. For what seems
Real to you now may in the end
Prove nothing but an empty dream.

Exit CLOTALDO.

SECOND SERVANT.
I have to say, my lord . . .

SEGISMUNDO.
                              Out of
My way!

SECOND SERVANT.
                  He merely carried out
The orders of the King.

SEGISMUNDO.
                              A fine
Thing too if what the King commands
Is blatantly against the law!
In any case, I am his prince.

SECOND SERVANT.
I don't suppose he stopped to think
If what he did was right or wrong.

SEGISMUNDO.
Then you'd do well to stop and think,
My friend, before I put a stop
To this fine song and dance of yours.

CLARION.
In other words, old friend, old cock,
The Prince means put a sock in it!

FIRST SERVANT.
And who told you to interfere?

CLARION.
I told myself, my dear. Is that
Quite clear, eh?

SEGISMUNDO.
                  Who are you? Speak.

CLARION.
A nosey-parker, sir. First-class,
And cheeky with it. A master of
That good and true profession, sir.
I swear, sir, by my own admission.

SEGISMUNDO.
>   I think you are the only fellow
>   Here who manages to please me.

CLARION.
>   Quite so, sir. That's because I know
>   That flattery is always pleasing to
>   The Segismundos of this world,
>   And most of all to you, sir.

>   *Enter* ASTOLFO.

ASTOLFO.
>   Great Prince, how happy is the day
>   When you, bright sun of Poland, fill
>   With your dazzling light the far
>   Horizons of this blessed land.
>   For as the night is banished by
>   The sun's first golden streaks, so you,
>   Like dawn itself, appear to us now,
>   Emerging from those dark and savage peaks.
>   We bid you shine on us, and though
>   This crown is only now allowed
>   To grace your royal head, our hopes
>   Are that its splendour never sets.

SEGISMUNDO.
>   God be with you.

ASTOLFO.
>   I must assume,
>   My lord, that ignorance of my
>   Identity explains this lack
>   Of true respect. I am Astolfo,
>   A duke by birth. I come from Moscow.
>   Furthermore, my lord, we are first
>   Cousins, equal in nobility.

SEGISMUNDO.
>   You mean that 'God be with you' isn't
>   Good enough and seriously make all
>   This fuss about your noble birth
>   And rank? If we should meet again,
>   I know what I shall say to you:
>   'May God forever bid farewell
>   To you, my friend, so you shall rot
>   Henceforth in Hell'.

SECOND SERVANT (*to* ASTOLFO).
                              Attribute such
    Behaviour to his origins,
    My lord: born in a tower. You must
    Make some allowance. (*To* SEGISMUNDO.) If I
    May say so, your highness, Duke Astolfo . . .

SEGISMUNDO.
    Thinks far too highly of himself.
    You think it courtesy to greet
    His Prince and keep his hat stuck firmly
    On his head?

SECOND SERVANT.
                              He is of noble birth.

SEGISMUNDO.
    And I of nobler birth than he.

SECOND SERVANT.
    But still, my lord, you should behave
    Towards each other more respectfully.

SEGISMUNDO.
    I warn you, friend, to think again
    Before you offer me advice.

    Enter ESTRELLA

ESTRELLA.
    Your royal highness. I bid you welcome
    To the palace. My fervent wish
    Is that the happiness which marks
    This day be equalled only by
    The eminence and dignity
    With which you long may rule this kingdom.
    May your life be measured not
    By years but centuries.

SEGISMUNDO.
                              Who is
    This woman? Who can this human
    Goddess be who bids the sky itself
    Pay homage to her perfect beauty?
    Will no one tell me who she is?

CLARION.
    She is Estrella, sir. First cousin
    To yourself, and, as her name suggests,

A star, such is her beauty.

SEGISMUNDO.
Far better had you said the sun.
To gaze upon perfection such
As this is to congratulate
Myself on my good fortune, and at
The same time offer thanks to someone
Fortunate enough to be so beautiful.
And since I am unworthy of
Good fortune such as this, regard
Myself as doubly fortunate.
Estrella, envy of the sun
Itself, for when you rise to greet
The dawn, so dazzled is the sun
By your light, it turns its face
Away and seeks in ignominious
Flight its only refuge. I kiss
Your hand, this cup of dazzling snow
From which the breeze drinks pure sweetness.

ESTRELLA.
My lord, I beg you moderate
This flattery. Be more gentle.

ASTOLFO.
He takes her hand. How truly princely!

SECOND SERVANT.
Astolfo is so angry. I'll see
What I can do to stop him. Sir!
It doesn't do to be so bold
And in Astolfo's presence . . .

SEGISMUNDO.
Have I not told you more than once
You interfere?

SECOND SERVANT.
                    I merely do
My duty, sir.

SEGISMUNDO.
                    Your duty, sir,
Annoys me greatly. What duty
Can this be that pleases me so
Little?

SECOND SERVANT.
            I heard you say yourself,
    Sir, duty is the proper sign
    Of loyalty.

SEGISMUNDO.
                You also heard
    Me say I'd throw the person who
    Annoyed me from this balcony.

SECOND SERVANT.
    I doubt you'd do that with a person
    Such as me, sir.

SEGISMUNDO.
                You think not, sir?
    By God, I think we'll see to it.

He takes the servant in his arms, goes out, followed by the others, enters again.

ASTOLFO.
    My eyes cannot believe what they
    Are seeing.

ESTRELLA.
                Quickly. All of you. Stop him!

SEGISMUNDO.
    He fell like a stone to the sea
    Below. And yet the fellow thought
    It wasn't possible.

ASTOLFO.
                Control
    Your actions, sir. They indicate
    Your origins. A man must be
    As distant from an animal
    As is a palace from an isolated
    Mountain.

SEGISMUNDO.
            I think you need to take
    Your own advice, my friend, and speak
    To me with greater moderation.
    If not, you see, you might be left
    Without a head to put your hat on.

Exit ASTOLFO. Enter the KING.

BASILIO.
>   What's happened here?

SEGISMUNDO.
>   Nothing really.
>   A man got on my nerves. I threw
>   Him from the balcony.

CLARION.
>   Easy,
>   Segismundo. It's the King that you
>   Are talking to.

BASILIO.
>   No sooner here
>   Than you become responsible
>   For taking someone's life?

SEGISMUNDO.
>   He claimed
>   I couldn't do it, so I did.
>   A lesson in the art of what is possible.

BASILIO.
>   I cannot say how much this grieves me,
>   Segismundo. I hoped to find
>   In your prudent actions proof
>   Of your ability to overcome
>   The stars. Instead you offer only
>   Confirmation of a savagery
>   So great it leads to pointless murder.
>   How, then, in circumstances such
>   As these can any father offer
>   You his arms when yours, judged by all
>   We've seen, may only do him harm?
>   What man can gaze upon a knife
>   That recently has caused some fatal
>   Injury and not feel fear for his life?
>   Or who can stand upon a spot
>   Still red with blood from someone's murder,
>   And, thinking what has happened there,
>   Not feel his heart beat that much faster?
>   All men, the weak and strong alike,
>   Have this in common in their nature.
>   So I, although I long to place
>   A father's arms around your neck,

See your arms as both the instrument
And place of my own death and am
Obliged by fear to withdraw from them.

SEGISMUNDO.

What makes you think I need your arms
When I have so far been denied them?
A father who so cruelly
Abused a son; who ruthlessly
Denied his true position in
The scheme of things; who heartlessly
Reduced him to the level of
An animal. You think I care
That such a father now denies
His arms to me when he's deprived
Me of both life and liberty?

BASILIO.

Far better had I never given
Life to you; that I had never heard
Your voice or seen in any son
Such unforgivable audacity.

SEGISMUNDO.

If I had not been given life,
I'd not complain, but once you gave
Me life you had no right to take
My life away from me again.

BASILIO.

Is this the measure of your gratitude
When only yesterday you were
A poor wretched prisoner
And now you are a prince?

SEGISMUNDO.

                        What cause
Is there for gratitude when you
Saw fit to rule my life, and now
That you are old and close to death
Give me no more than what is mine
By right? For since you are my father
And my King, this sovereignty is mine
By natural decree, by law,
And I am not obliged to feel
This gratitude you think I ought

To feel. Indeed, the contrary
Is true, for you deprived
Me of my honour, liberty
And life, and now must thank me for
My generosity in not
Obliging you to pay this debt.

BASILIO.
How can I doubt the prophecy
Is true? Your pride and arrogance
Confirm its authenticity,
And heaven itself bears witness to
This animal barbarity.
But even though you know the truth
Of your birth and upbringing,
And everyone is now obliged
To treat you as a King, take heed
And pay attention to this warning:
Your passions are the source of your mistakes,
And though you are convinced you are awake,
The truth is you may well be dreaming.

Exit BASILIO.

SEGISMUNDO.
The truth is that I may be dreaming
Even though I seem to be awake?
I do not dream. I touch, I know
What I have been and what I am.
And though you may regret what you
Have done, it is too late to seek
Some easy remedy. I know
Now who I am, and you, though you
Regret the fact, can never take
From me the crown that I, by right
Of birth, do properly inherit.
And if you saw me once condemned
To spend my life in chains, the cause
Of it was merely ignorance
Of my identity. But now
I am informed of who I am,
I do declare I am a man
Who is a beast, a beast who is a man.

Enter ROSAURA, *dressed as a woman.*

ROSAURA.

    I am obliged to wait upon
    Estrella but come in fear of
    Astolfo seeing me. Clotaldo
    Says he must not recognize me
    Now, for it concerns my honour.
    And since Clotaldo is the guardian
    Of my honour and my life, I do
    My best to follow his advice.

CLARION.

    So what has pleased you most, my lord,
    Of all the things you've seen today?

SEGISMUNDO.

    Why, nothing comes as a surprise
    To me. I had imagined all
    Of it precisely as it is;
    Though if there's one thing in the world
    To wonder at, I think it is
    The beauty of a woman. I once
    Read in a book that God devoted all
    His energy to man's creation,
    For man is in himself a world
    In miniature. And yet I think
    God must have given woman more
    Attention still, for she is surely
    A tiny heaven, and since the heavens
    Embrace a beauty far superior
    To the earth, must correspondingly
    Be thought more beautiful by far
    Than man, especially if she
    Becomes the special object of
    My contemplation.

ROSAURA.

               The Prince!
    I must withdraw.

SEGISMUNDO.

              Listen to me,
    Woman! Stay! The sun must never
    Be allowed to set before its rising,
    To merge first light with evening.
    To have the dawn become before
    My very eyes the night, is to deny

Existence to the day. (*Aside*.) But what
Is this?

ROSAURA (*aside*).
          I see and yet I doubt
What I am seeing.

SEGISMUNDO (*aside*).
             I have gazed
Upon this beauty once before.

ROSAURA (*aside*).
    I've seen this pomp, this princely grandeur
    Reduced to utter wretchedness
    Within the confines of a tower.

SEGISMUNDO (*aside*).
    And seeing her once more, I feel
    As if my life has taken on
    New meaning. Woman – the word itself
    Is pleasurably soothing to a man –
    Who are you? Without me ever
    Seeing you, I'd be obliged to worship
    At your feet. I feel instinctively
    As if some bond now draws me close
    To you and, though it cannot be,
    Am half convinced that we have met
    Before. Who are you, lovely woman?

ROSAURA (*aside*).
    I must not tell him who I am.
    An ordinary woman, sir.
    A mere servant to Estrella.

SEGISMUNDO.
    Far better had you said the sun,
    For ir comparison with you
    She is a tiny star, her beauty but
    A pale reflection of your flame.
    I see how in the kingdom of
    The flowers it is the rose who's queen,
    And dazzling her commoners,
    By her beauty reigns supreme.
    I see how in the hierarchy
    Of gems the diamond is king,
    And brighter far than other stones,
    Obliges them to bow to him.

There, amongst the stars above,
I see the morning star shine bright,
While others in her heavenly court
Are humbled by her lovely light.
And there where perfect spheres spin,
The sun has true authority,
And, brightest of them all by far,
Demands their constant loyalty.
How then, if in the realm of flowers,
Jewels, stars and spheres, the fairest rules,
Must you obey someone less fair
Than you when you too are a rose,
A diamond, a star, a sun?

Enter CLOTALDO.

CLOTALDO (*aside*).
I've taught him many things, but now
I need to clip his wings. What's this?

ROSAURA.
You flatter me, my lord. If I
Do not reply, it is because
I think that silence is at times
A greater eloquence. And when
A person lacks sophistication,
He speaks much better when he holds his tongue.

SEGISMUNDO.
Wait. You cannot go. Is it your wish
To leave me in such total darkness?

ROSAURA.
I beg your leave to take my leave,
Your highness.

SEGISMUNDO.
                    To turn your back on me
Is not to ask my leave. It is
To take your leave.

ROSAURA.
                    If you refuse
To give your leave, then I shall take it.

SEGISMUNDO.
And you, on that account, shall make me
Sacrifice this courtesy to gross

Brutality. Resistance such
As this is poison to my patience.

ROSAURA.
But even if such poison has
The potency to overcome
Your patience, sir, I doubt it has
The necessary strength to touch
My honour.

SEGISMUNDO.
                        To prove to you
The contrary, I'll set aside
The deep respect your beauty makes
Me feel for you. The things that seem
Impossible appeal to me.
This very day a sevant said
I couldn't throw him from the balcony,
And now the foolish fellow's dead.
So if you want to challenge me
To throw your honour through the window,
I'll be glad to prove it to you.

CLOTALDO (aside).
He is resolved upon this course
Of action! Oh what am I to do
When for a second time I see
My honour seriously at risk,
And yet again because of passion?

ROSAURA.
I see now why the prophecy
Announces for this kingdom only
Tyranny and death and constant misery.
What else can be expected of
A man who is a man in name,
No more, and shows that cruelty
And pride, that inhumanity,
That fierce arrogance that is
The consequence of being born
Amongst wild animals?

SEGISMUNDO.
                        I spoke
To you so pleasantly because
I thought you'd find it more agreeable.

But since you now insult me so,
And find that even softer words
Are disagreeable, I'll give
You cause to think the rest of me
Much more objectionable. Close
The doors. Let no one enter here.

Exit CLARION.

ROSAURA (*aside*).
My death is near. Listen to me!

SEGISMUNDO.
I am a cruel tyrant, madam.
A woman's tears have no effect on me!

CLOTALDO (*aside*).
What's to be done in such a sorry
Situation? I'll try to stop him
Even if he kills me! My lord!
Listen! Do not act so hastily!

SEGISMUNDO.
This is the second time you've angered
Me, you old, half-witted fellow.
You underestimate my anger!
What are you doing here?

CLOTALDO.
                    I heard
The lady cry aloud and came
To tell you to conduct yourself
With greater moderation, if
You really wish to rule this kingdom.
Act sensibly, for though you seem
To be the lord and master of
This world, it may be just a dream.

SEGISMUNDO.
The more you try to disillusion me,
The more you drive me to distraction.
I'll tell you what. I'll put an end to you
And you can tell me if it's false or true.

As SEGISMUNDO *draws his dagger,* CLOTALDO *restrains
him and kneels at his feet.*

CLOTALDO.
You have no right to take my life.

SEGISMUNDO.
    Let go. Release the knife at once.

CLOTALDO.
    Till someone comes and puts a stop
    To your rage, I shan't let go.

ROSAURA.
    Oh, heavens!

SEGISMUNDO.
                    Let go, old man. You are
    A fool, and feeble too. No breath
    In you. You'd best let go, before
    These arms of mine crush you to death.

    They struggle.

ROSAURA.
    Come quickly. He's killing Clotaldo.

    Exit ROSAURA. ASTOLFO *enters as* CLOTALDO *falls at his
    feet. He steps between them.*

ASTOLFO.
    I can't believe, oh noble prince,
    You wish to bathe a sword as bold
    As yours in blood as cold as his.
    The best place for your sword is in
    Your scabbard.

SEGISMUNDO.
                    When it is covered
    In his infamous blood!

ASTOLFO.
                    He seeks
    His sanctuary at my feet.
    It is my guarantee that he'll
    Not meet his death at your hands.

SEGISMUNDO.
    Then it shall guarantee your death,
    And give me satisfaction for
    The way you've managed to annoy me.

ASTOLFO.
    If I am driven to defend
    Myself, it cannot cause offence
    To any King.

They draw swords. Enter KING BASILIO *and* ESTRELLA.

CLOTALDO.
                    My lord, do not
Provoke him any more!

BASILIO.
                              Why are
These swords drawn here?

ESTRELLA (*aside*).
                              Why, it's Astolfo!
What confusion!

BASILIO.
                    What is the cause
Of this? Speak up! Your explanation!

ASTOLFO.
        Your majesty, it doesn't matter
Now you've come.

They put away their swords.

SEGISMUNDO.
                    Your majesty,
It matters greatly that you've come.
You've stopped me killing the old one there.

BASILIO.
        You should respect such old grey hair.

CLOTALDO.
        Your majesty, it's only mine.
It doesn't matter.

SEGISMUNDO.
                    To think I should
Feel reverence for some old grey head!
The day may come when I shall tread
On yours and so avenge myself
On you for treating me unjustly.

Exit SEGISMUNDO.

BASILIO.
        Before that possibility
You'll find you are asleep again
And back where you were once imprisoned.
And though you'll think that everything

That happened here is so convincing, you'll
Soon realize that you were only dreaming.

Exit the KING *and* CLOTALDO. ESTRELLA *and* ASTOLFO
find themselves alone.

ASTOLFO.

How rarely is the prophecy
That forecasts only ills proved wrong,
Announcing doom with certainty,
Good fortune always grudgingly.
How lucky the astrologer
Who deals in tragedy, when life,
As we all learn in time, admits
No other possibility.
Consider as examples of the truth
Of this both Segismundo and
Myself, for in the two of us
You have its perfect testimony.
For him it forecast pride and death,
Misfortune, cruelty, and was
In everything it said proved right.
For me, in being fortunate
Enough to gaze upon these lovely
Eyes, compared to which the sun
And sky are but a pale shadow,
It promised triumph, happiness,
Success, and was proved right and wrong:
For if at first such beauty seemed
A promise that would ease my pain,
It follows that the end of it
Must be this terrible disdain.

ESTRELLA.

I do not doubt there is sincerity
In this, Astolfo, and yet I am
Convinced its object must be someone
Else: I think, perhaps, a certain lady
Whose portrait hangs around your neck,
While you indulge in flattery
That she, I'm sure, would much prefer.
I think you ought to seek from her
Your true reward; for in the courts
Of love the oaths and promises

Which suitors make in someone else's
Name means we should not consider them
The most reliable of witnesses.

ROSAURA *appears behind a curtain.*

ROSAURA (*aside*).
Thanks be to God. This is a sign
That destiny has nothing worse
In store for me, for who sees this
Must know there's nothing more to fear.

ASTOLFO.
The portrait shall be banished from
My breast at once, and in its place,
Estrella, your lovely face
Shall rule my heart. For where you are,
No shadow can command, nor star
Where there's a sun. Wait here for me.
I'll get the portrait. (*Aside.*) Forgive me this
Offence, Rosaura. It isn't true
That absence makes the heart grow fonder!

Exit ASTOLFO.

ROSAURA (*aside*).
What did he say to her? I couldn't
Let him see me and so heard nothing.

ESTRELLA.
Astrea!

ROSAURA.
          My lady.

ESTRELLA.
                    I'm glad you've come.
I wish to share with you a secret.

ROSAURA.
My lady. You honour me. My one
And only wish is your command.

ESTRELLA.
I haven't known you long, Astrea,
And yet I feel that I can trust
You with the key to all my safely-
Guarded secrets. I wish to share
With you a confidence I barely

Trust myself with.

ROSAURA.
                    I promise I
          Shall keep your secret safe, my lady.

ESTRELLA.
          Then listen. My cousin Astolfo
          (I call him cousin knowing that
          Certain things are better left unsaid)
          Is soon to marry me, and prove
          That fortune in a single stroke
          Can put an end to all my misery.
          But it upsets me since the day
          We met that still he wears around
          His neck the portrait of another
          Lady. I spoke to him, and since
          He is a perfect gentleman
          And fond of me, he's gone to get
          The portrait. But it's embarrassing
          To have to wait and have him place
          The picture of another woman
          In my hands. I'd rather have you
          Wait instead of me. When he comes,
          Demand the picture of him. You are
          Discreet as well as lovely, and know
          As much as I of love's complexity.

          Exit ESTRELLA.

ROSAURA.
          If only I did not! Oh, who
          Can ever be discreet and wise
          Enough, and know how to advise
          Himself in matters such as these?
          Can there be anyone more cruelly
          Abused by fate than me, more bruised
          By fortune's fierce blows, more battered
          By a hail of constant sorrows?
          What can I do to find a remedy
          For this confusion, some avenue
          Or path to lead me hopefully
          To some solution? For since the day
          I suffered one misfortune, others
          Quickly followed, and everything

That's happened to me since has been
A perfect imitation of
The first, and coming thick and fast
Upon each other, form an endless
Chain, a close-knit family in which
Each individual inherits
Further misery. This is the habit
Of the Phoenix, the one born from
The other, each drawing breath where breath
Has gone, the dying ashes of
The one a source of life and constant
Resurrection. It's said a wise
Man called them cowardly because
They never dare come singly. I call
Them bold because they constantly attack
And never show the slightest sign
Of turning back. And anyone
Whose company they share can take
Whatever risk confronts him, knowing
That they'll always daringly go
With him. I speak of this as one
Whose life misfortune has attended
Constantly and not been satisfied
Until it has reduced to misery
What joy I had. What can I do
In circumstances such as these?
To say I'm who I am would be
To cause annoyance to Clotaldo,
To whom I owe my life, my honour
And protection. To say I'm who
I'm not involves deliberate
Deception of Astolfo, and though
My voice, my words, my eyes may manage
For a while to hide the truth from him,
I doubt my soul can ever be
As totally convincing. Oh what
Am I to do? But what's the point
Of thinking what I'll do if I
Already know that when the moment
Comes I'll do what sorrow tells me to.
Who can do otherwise when sorrow
Rules his life entirely? If then
My soul lacks courage to decide

What I must do, let sorrow guide
My destiny and grief, so that,
Despite confusion, it may reach
Its true extremity. For now,
Until that moment comes, heaven help me!

Enter ASTOLFO *with the portrait.*

ASTOLFO.
The portrait, madam! Good heavens!

ROSAURA.
Why do you stare, my lord? What is
It so amazes you?

ASTOLFO.
                    Why, seeing you,
Rosaura. What are you doing here?

ROSAURA.
Rosaura? I think there must be some
Confusion on your part, my lord.
My name's Astrea, my station humble.
It hardly merits consternation
Such as this.

ASTOLFO.
                Come now, Rosaura.
The heart can never be deceived,
For though it sees you as Astrea,
It knows it loves you as Rosaura.

ROSAURA.
I do not understand you, sir,
And so have no reply for you,
Except to say I was commanded
By Estrella to wait until
You came, and in her name to ask
You for the portrait. I am to take
It to her, sir, though even in
Such trivial things as these I am
Obliged to think that destiny
Is bound to treat me cruelly.

ASTOLFO.
You are quite good, Rosaura, but what
You really need, to be an even
Better actress, is lots more practice.

    Tell your eyes to harmonize
    Their music to your voice, for if
    An instrument is out of tune
    Its discords grate most horribly,
    As now there's no accord between
    The emptiness of what you say
    And what I know you feel more deeply.

ROSAURA.
    I've told you all I want's the portrait.

ASTOLFO.
    Ah, yes. Of course. But let's continue
    The deception and see what happens
    When we take it to its logical
    Conclusion. I think, Astrea,
    You have to tell Estrella that
    I feel such genuine regard
    For her that sending her a painting
    On request seems somewhat untoward
    When I can send the real thing.
    Just take yourself to her. A special
    Gift from me, to let her see how
    You and I can both be quite original.

ROSAURA.
    If someone undertakes a task
    In all good faith, my lord, completion
    Of that task must be the only means
    Of true reward and satisfaction.
    To give Estrella the original
    And not the picture merely underlines
    My sense of failure. I'd rather take
    The portrait. Give me it.

ASTOLFO.
    If I don't, how can you take it?

ROSAURA.
    Like this. Let go!

ASTOLFO.
               No. No, Rosaura!

ROSAURA.
    No other woman lays her hands
    On it.

ASTOLFO.

    I always did admire
  Your spirit.

ROSAURA.

      Hypocrite!

ASTOLFO.

        That's quite
  Enough of that, my sweet!

ROSAURA.

         Me yours?
  Never! Never in a thousand years!

  Enter ESTRELLA.

ESTRELLA.

  Astrea, Astolfo! What are you up to?

ASTOLFO.

  Why, it's Estrella!

ROSAURA (*aside*).

       Love grant me
  Ingenuity to get my portrait
  Back. (*Aloud.*) If you wish to know, my lady,
  I am happy to explain.

ASTOLFO (*aside*).

        Astrea,
  Why do you cause me such great pain?

ROSAURA.

  You instructed me to wait and, when
  Astolfo came, obtain the portrait
  From him. I waited, as you'd said,
  And since I was alone began
  To think, as one so often does
  When on one's own, of different things;
  And since my mind was mostly occupied
  With your portrait, realized
  That in my sleeve was one of me,
  Quite similar in kind to yours.
  I thought I'd look at it – how foolish
  We can be when we're alone! – it fell,
  And, as I went to pick it up,
  Astolfo came and snatched it from me.
  Instead of giving me your portrait,

He now has mine and shows no sign
Of giving either back. I pleaded,
Begged, persuaded, and in the end
Decided I would only get
My portrait back by using force.
You see, my lady? He conceals
It in his hand. You only need
To look at it to see it's me.

ESTRELLA.
Give me the portrait.

She takes it from him.

ASTOLFO.
                    But madam!

ESTRELLA.
It does some justice to the truth.

ROSAURA.
Is it not me?

ESTRELLA.
                Quite clearly it is.

ROSAURA.
Now ask him for the other one.

ESTRELLA.
Take your portrait, Astrea. Leave us.

ROSAURA (*aside*).
My portrait is my own once more.
The next thing to be claimed is honour.

Exit ROSAURA.

ESTRELLA.
Now, Astolfo. The portrait I
Requested of you. For though
I shall not see you any more,
Or ever speak to you again,
You shall not keep my portrait.
How dare you make a fool of me
By forcing me to ask for it!

ASTOLFO (*aside*).
Good heavens! This is a fine to-do!
The fact is, dearest Estrella,
I'd do almost anything for you,

You know I would. As for the portrait,
A tiny problem, I'm afraid,
Which means it's rather difficult
To give it back to you . . .

ESTRELLA.

                              You are
The most despicable, the most
Completely unreliable
Of suitors! You can keep the portrait!
My having it would only make
Me think of how I had to come
To you like this and beg for it.

Exit ESTRELLA.

ASTOLFO.

Wait, Estrella! Listen to me!
By God! This is Rosaura's doing!
Why did you have to come to Poland,
Woman, and bring about my ruin?

Exit ASTOLFO.

SEGISMUNDO *is revealed, as in Act One, in skins and chains.*
    He is lying on the floor, asleep. Enter CLOTALDO,
    CLARION *and two servants.*

CLOTALDO.

Leave him. His arrogance and pride
Have earned their true reward.

FIRST SERVANT.

                              The chain
Is tied, my lord, exactly as it was.

CLARION.

If I was you, good Segismundo,
I wouldn't want to wake again
To see what fate had done to me,
And know the glory I once had
Is but a memory, a shadow of
A life that was, a flame whose fading seems
A prophecy of death.

CLOTALDO.

                              This fellow
Has an instinct for philosophy,
But, needs, I think, a place where he

Can be alone and dedicate
Himself to that most elevated
Study. Lock him in that room!

CLARION.

Me, sir?

Me, sir? Why me?

CLOTALDO.

Because a clarion
Placed securely behind locked doors
Has far less opportunity
To trumpet secrets to the world.

CLARION.
Did I, by any chance, lay hands
Upon my father, sir, or throw
A servant from a balcony?
I must be dreaming. Why are you
Doing this to me?

CLOTALDO.

Because you are Clarion.

CLARION.
Then I'll become a cornet, sir.
I promise. It's a quiet, weak
Instrument. You can't get a peep
Out of it. You can't, sir. Honest!

They take him away. Enter BASILIO, *his face concealed.*

BASILIO.
Clotaldo.

CLOTALDO.

Your majesty! Why have
You come?

BASILIO.

Foolish curiosity.
To see if Segismundo is awake,
And whether he accepts his destiny.

CLOTALDO.
He lies there. See how once again
He is the image of his former
Misery.

BASILIO.

This is a sight a father

Cannot bear to see. A prince, and from
The moment of his birth so cruelly
Condemned to this. Approach him. Wake him.
The opiate will soon begin
To lose effect.

CLOTALDO.
           See how he moves,
Your majesty, and now begins
To speak.

BASILIO.
           Perhaps he dreams. Let's listen
To his words.

SEGISMUNDO (*half-awake*).
             It is a righteous prince
Who punishes the tyrant's cruelty.
These hands shall wring Clotaldo's neck
And have my father kiss my feet.

CLOTALDO.
He threatens me with death.

BASILIO.
                 And me
With violence and ignominy.

CLOTALDO.
  To take my life.

BASILIO.
           To have me crawl
And humbly place my head beneath
His feet.

SEGISMUNDO.
          My triumph shall be seen
Upon the world's great stage, and when
I make my entrance there applause
Shall greet Prince Segismundo's just
And lawful vengeance on his father.

He awakens.

But what is this? Where am I?

BASILIO (*to* CLOTALDO).
He must not see me. You know what you
Must do. I'll listen to you here.

He hides.

SEGISMUNDO.
>Can this be me, a prisoner
>In chains, condemned by destiny
>To live and die in this dark tower
>When I have dreamed such things?

CLOTALDO (*aside*).
>   The time
>Has come for me to prick the bubble
>Of his dreams. Ah! Awake at last
>I see!

SEGISMUNDO.
>   I think the time has come
>For me to wake.

CLOTALDO.
>   And not before
>Time too, unless I am mistaken.
>You must have been asleep the whole
>Day long, from when I first made mention
>Of the eagle's slow majestic flight.

SEGISMUNDO.
>I think I must, yet even now
>I wonder if I have awakened,
>Or if, Clotaldo, I really am
>Asleep. For if I dreamt those things
>I touched and saw so clearly,
>Then what I see before me now
>Cannot be true reality.
>But then, this is the cruel trick
>Of destiny – that I should see
>So clearly while I'm asleep but only
>Dream when I'm awake.

CLOTALDO.
>   What did you dream?

SEGISMUNDO.
>If dream it was! I will not tell
>You what I dreamt, Clotaldo, but what
>I saw . . . and saw so clearly.
>I woke and found myself – how cruelly
>The vision stays with me! – upon
>A bed which in the brilliance of
>Its colours seemed a canopy

Of flowers woven by the Spring.
A thousand noblemen were gathered
At my feet, all of them eager
To sing my praises, call me prince
And shower me with gems and clothes
And finery, the like of which
I'd never seen. And you, Clotaldo,
Brought me news of my true destiny,
Raised me to the very peak of happiness,
Informing me, regardless of
This present misery, that I
Was Prince of Poland.

CLOTALDO.

                    Did you reward
Me well for that?

SEGISMUNDO.

                    I tried to kill
You twice. Your treachery inflamed
My anger.

CLOTALDO.

            You treated me so badly?

SEGISMUNDO.

I ruled them all, so all were victims
Of my vengeance . . . except a woman
Whom I loved . . . whose memory remains
With me and does not fade and makes
Me think that all I dreamt may well
Have been reality.

    Exit BASILIO

CLOTALDO (*aside*).
The King has left. He cannot bear
To listen. (*Aloud.*) The explanation of
Your dream's quite simple. Just before
You slept, we talked of eagles, rulers
Of the heavens, and so in sleep your thoughts
Were naturally turned to ruling
Kingdoms. But even in dream
You ought to show respect for one
Who's cared for you and brought you up.
Believe me, Segismundo, doing good
Can only bring its own reward,

Even in our dreams.

Exit.

SEGISMUNDO.
                He speaks the truth.
I must control this savagery,
This wild ambition, this ferocity
Of mine in case I dream again.
For surely I'll dream again
When this world seems so strange a place
That all our life is but a dream,
And what I've seen so far tells me
That any man who lives dreams what
He is until at last he wakes.
The King dreams he is king and so
Believing rules, administers,
Rejoices in the exercise of power;
He does not seem to know his fame
Is written on the wind and death
Will turn to ashes all his splendour.
Oh who would want to be a king
And have his power, when the dream
Of death must soon awaken him?
The rich man dreams in all his wealth,
Though riches cause him endless care.
The pauper dreams his suffering,
Complaining that the world's not fair.
The man who has success dreams too,
And so does he who strives for more.
He dreams whose heart is full of spite,
Who, hurting others, claims he's right.
The world, in short, is where men dream
The different parts that they are playing,
And no one stops to know their meaning.
I dream that I am here, a prisoner,
I dream that I am bound by chains,
When once I dreamt of palaces
Where I was king, where once I reigned.
What is this life? A fantasy?
A prize we seek so eagerly
That proves to be illusory?
I think that life is but a dream,
And even dreams not what they seem.

Act Three

Enter CLARION.

CLARION.
    Imprisoned in a blessed tower,
    And all because of what I know!
    So what would happen to me, eh,
    For what I don't know, judged by what
    They've done to me for what I do?
    Believe me, it's a liberty
    To let a man like me go hungry;
    To take my food away from me;
    To have me at death's door when all
    I want's a little more to eat.
    I'm starting to feel sorry for
    Myself, and others too, who know
    How heavily this silence weighs
    Upon a man like me whose sole
    Delight is words, whose very name
    Of Clarion tells the world, there to
    The east, the west, the north and south,
    That, even more than lack of food,
    What really chokes him most of all
    Is being forced to shut his mouth.
    Then there's the company. It's not
    Exactly aristocracy;
    More your spider, mouse, your creepy-crawly,
    But still quite tasty if you're hungry.
    As for the dreams I had last night,
    My head is ringing with the sound
    Of fanfares, stuffed with sights so strange
    I see them still: mysterious men
    In hoods, some bearing crosses, moving
    In procession, starting, stopping,
    Some collapsing at the sight of blood.
    It either means I'm slowly going mad,
    Or seeing things for sheer lack of food.
    Mind you, at least me being here's
    Made me a student of philosophy.

I mean, are thoughts of juicy steaks
So big they make your taste-buds ache,
The proof of its reality,
Or just a trick of memory?
The only thing for sure is
It gives you food enough for thought.
I'm told as well, on good authority,
That silence has become a holy
Thing that guarantees a place in heaven,
On which account I can indulge
Myself excessively, wallow in
An orgy of my silences
And not be thought to sin!
It's for my sins that I'm condemned
To this, and rightly so; for if
To gossip is the privilege
Of servants, I, by keeping my
Mouth shut, must of necessity
Be guilty of true sacrilege.

Sound of drums and voices off.

FIRST SOLDIER.
>   This is the tower. Break the door
>   Down. It's where they keep him prisoner.
>   Inside quickly.

CLARION.
>   Good lord! To judge
>   By what they say, they want to set
>   Me free. Hey, you! What do you want
>   Of me?

Enter soldiers.

FIRST SOLDIER.
>   Inside.

SECOND SOLDIER.
>   It's him.

CLARION.
>   It's me.

SOLDIERS.
>   Your highness!

CLARION.
>   I think they must be pissed on duty.

SECOND SOLDIER.
>You are our noble prince. We shall
>Accept as our ruler only he
>Who by his birth is our natural
>Lord. We'll not have any foreigner.
>We kneel in homage at your feet.

ALL.
>Long live our great and noble prince!

CLARION (*aside*).
>I think these lads may soon convince
>Me this is true. Or maybe it's
>The custom here to let a bloke
>Be prince just for a day or two
>Before he's locked away again.
>If that's the case, let's have some fun.
>It's best to play along with them.

SOLDIERS.
>Give us your feet, oh noble prince!

CLARION.
>My feet? I can't give you my feet.
>The greatest defect in a prince
>Is lack of feet, for then he is
>Defeated.

SECOND SOLDIER.
>   We have informed your father
>You shall be our prince. We shan't
>Accept the one from Moscow.

CLARION.
>   Ah, so!
>You mean you disobeyed my dad,
>And you expect me to be glad?

FIRST SOLDIER.
>We were loyal to your highness.

CLARION.
>In that case, witness my forgiveness.

SECOND SOLDIER.
>Let's go. Your kingdom awaits you.
>Long live Segismundo!

ALL.
>   Segismundo!

CLARION.
>They call me Segismundo too.
>That's what they must call every so-and-so
>Whose turn it is to be a prince.

>*Enter* SEGISMUNDO.

SEGISMUNDO.
>Who called Segismundo?

CLARION (*aside*).
>   It seems
>I am deposed already.

SECOND SOLDIER.
>   Who
>Is Segismundo?

SEGISMUNDO.
>   I am he.

SECOND SOLDIER.
>Then who is he? You dare to make
>A fool of me and give yourself
>The name of Segismundo?

CLARION.
>   Not me,
>My lord. You made a Segismundo
>Out of me. I never made a fool
>Of anyone who wasn't made
>A fool by his stupidity.
>I think we can agree on that.

FIRST SOLDIER.
>Prince Segismundo. Your father,
>King Basilio, believing fate
>Would soon fulfil its prophecy
>And he would be obliged to kneel
>At your feet in token of your victory,
>Denies what rightfully is yours.
>Instead, he'd have the Duke Astolfo
>As our prince and so informed
>His Court, but our people, learning this,
>Refused to have the foreigner
>And stormed the palace, naming you
>As their rightful ruler.
>As for ourselves, we shall ignore

What fate is said to have in store
For you. We've come to set you free,
So you can take up arms and use
Your liberty to claim your rightful
Kingdom from a man who used you just
To practice his own tyranny.
Come. We have a rebel army waiting,
Acclaiming you as their leader,
Demanding you as their ruler.

VOICES (*off*).
Segismundo! Long live Segismundo!

SEGISMUNDO.
Great heavens, must I be made to dream
Of greatness once again when I
Already know that time will prove
To me its emptiness?
Must I be made to realize
Once more that pomp and majesty,
Like shadows scattered by the wind
Are mere vanity?
Must I expose myself once more
To certain disillusionment,
Or foolishly, as all men do,
Risk all for mere disappointment?
It shall not be! It shall not be!
For if my fortune sets me free,
I know that life is but a dream
And so shall not be easily
Deceived by anything that seems
To have both form and substance,
And in reality conceals
Its emptiness. I want no hollow
Majesty, no pomp that in the end
Proves mere fantasy, no dreams
That can be scattered by the wind,
Or like the flowers of the almond-tree
That blooms too early in the Spring
Are withered by the icy wind,
And see their beauty fade, their petals fall.
I know these dreams too well. I know
How they exactly parallel
The man who sleeps. I shall not be

Deceived when, disillusioned once, I know
The whole of life is an illusion.

SECOND SOLDIER.

I swear that you are not deceived,
My lord. See there how on the peak
Of that steep mountain all your men
Now wait impatiently for you
To lead them on to victory.

SEGISMUNDO.

But I have seen such things before
With equal clarity. And what
Seemed just as real to me then
Was but a dream.

FIRST SOLDIER.

        Is it not true
That dreams are often premonitions?
Your dream may be, my lord, a happy
Sign that you are soon to be the rightful
Ruler of our kingdom.

SEGISMUNDO.

        I think I see
The wisdom of your words. And since
We live so briefly in this world,
Begin to be persuaded I
Should dream once more. But when I do,
I must remind myself that if
I live my life for pleasure's sake,
The day must come I'll find myself awake.
To be forewarned's to be forearmed,
To know this now's to mitigate
Whatever harm may come to me.
For if it's clear from the start
That what we have is ours only on
Account and, certain as it seems
To us, must one day be redeemed,
Then we can take what risk we please,
And know we cannot be deceived.
My friends, I thank you for your loyalty.
I promise you, you have in me
A prince whose boldness you can trust
Will free you from the slavery
Imposed by any foreigner.

Let trumpets sound the call to arms.
You'll see a demonstration of
My valour; how I shall be so bold
As to assault the very heavens
To see my father at my feet.

Aside.

But wait. This is a dream from which
I might quite suddenly awake.
I'd best not boast of what I'll do
In case I fail to see it through.

ALL.
Segismundo! Long live Segismundo!

Enter CLOTALDO.

CLOTALDO.
What's happening? What noise is this?

SEGISMUNDO.
Clotaldo.

CLOTALDO.
My lord! (*Aside.*) I am to be
The living proof of his ferocity.

CLARION (*aside*).
Did he say living proof? I guarantee
He'll chuck him to his certain death.

Exit CLARION.

CLOTALDO.
My lord! I kneel at your feet.
I know I am to die.

SEGISMUNDO.
Up on
Your feet, old man. Arise. I need
You with me at my side, my compass
And my guide in everything I do.
You brought me up, a true and loyal
Servant. Everything I am I owe to you.

CLOTALDO.
What do you mean?

SEGISMUNDO.
I mean I know

This is a dream, and I must do
What good I can when even in
His dreams such goodness is not lost
Upon a man.

CLOTALDO.

It pleases me,
My lord, that you should speak of virtue
As the end you seek; and since I seek
The same thing too, I know I'll not
Offend you if I say you must
Not take up arms against your father.
He is my King, this country's ruler.
I cannot help or give advice.
I'd rather die if that's the price
I have to pay.

SEGISMUNDO.

You dare defy
Me! Ungrateful traitor! (*Aside.*) But I
Must learn to hold myself in check,
Remind myself this is a dream.

Aloud.

Clotaldo, I esteem your loyalty.
Go at once. Serve your King. Our paths
Shall cross in battle once again.
Now let the drums and trumpets sound.

CLOTALDO.
I thank you for my life, my lord.

Exit CLOTALDO.

SEGISMUNDO.
Fortune, I go to reign once more.
If I am dreaming, do not let
Me wake; and do not let me dream
If I am now awake. But wake
Or dream, let's not forget that virtue
Matters most of all in all we do.
If I awake, it is its own reward;
If I'm asleep, let's win a friend or two
For when I wake.

Exit all. Drums and trumpets.
Enter KING BASILIO *and* ASTOLFO.

BASILIO.

> Astolfo, who can ever stop
> The fury of a bolting horse?
> Or hope to stem the river's flood,
> Or change its headlong, sea-bound course?
> Or catch the rock that from some peak
> Falls on our heads with such great force?
> Yet stopping these seems easier
> Then curbing my own people's anger.
> The mountains echo to their cries,
> And loyalty is split in two,
> For cries of 'Duke Astolfo' here
> Are echoed there by 'Segismundo'.
> All our hopes are dashed, the day
> Of coronation turned to tragedy,
> And all of us upon a stage
> Where we confront our destiny.

ASTOLFO.

> My lord, I set aside those hopes
> That, based upon your favour, promised
> Future happiness; for if your people
> Now reject me as their ruler,
> I'll seize this opportunity
> To show them I can be their saviour.
> Get me a horse. My speed shall be
> Like lightning, my voice like thunder.

> *Exit* ASTOLFO.

BASILIO.

> If there is risk in what's foreseen,
> For what's to be, there is no remedy,
> And he who turns his eyes away
> Precipitates catastrophe.
> Oh, this is harsh indeed! To flee
> The risk and cause the tragedy!
> For me to act so cautiously
> And bring about the ruin of my country!

> *Enter* ESTRELLA.

ESTRELLA.

> Your majesty, you must confront
> This violence that like a flood
> Now spills from street to street and promises

To drown this country in its blood.
If not, the whole of Poland will
Be covered by a crimson tide
From whose advance your majesty
Himself will find no place to hide.
Such is this spectacle it breaks
The heart of anyone who sees
The damage done to this fair land,
And cruelly offends the ears
Of him informed of it at second-hand.
See how the sun grows dark, the wind
Abates, how graves are formed by stones,
How flowers now seem wreaths, and houses tombs,
And soldiers walking skeletons.

Enter CLOTALDO.

CLOTALDO.
Thanks be to God I have arrived.

BASILIO.
Clotaldo, what news of Segismundo?

CLOTALDO.
The mob, your majesty – a wild,
Unruly, monstrous crowd – broke down
The prison-door and gave the prince
A second opportunity to rule.
He hesitated first, then boasted
How he'd bring the heavens down on our heads.

BASILIO.
Get me a horse at once. I shall
Confront the boy's ingratitude,
Defend my crown and teach him that
When science fails, the steel of King
Basilio's sword prevails.

Exit BASILIO.

ESTRELLA.
I shall accompany the King,
Belona to his sun, our name
Forever joined in history.
I'll ride as though endowed with wings,
And when the battle comes I'll prove
My spirit worthy of Athene.

Exit ESTRELLA. *Sound of trumpet and drums.*
Enter ROSAURA.

ROSAURA.
    I know your bravery is such,
    My lord, you answer battle's call
    Instinctively. But listen first
    To one who knows that we must fight
    The whole of life courageously.
    When I first came, you were much moved
    By my unhappy state and offered me
    Your pity and protection. You told
    Me I should not reveal my name,
    But living in the palace should
    Conceal myself, especially from Duke Astolfo.
    Now he knows I'm here, but even so
    He disregards my name and treats
    Me just as if I were to blame,
    For every night he meets Estrella
    In the garden. I have the key.
    I can arrange for you to find
    Them there and seize the opportunity
    To cleanse my honour. If it is true,
    My lord, that you are bold enough
    To take revenge on my behalf
    And end Astolfo's life, you'll prove
    That war is not the only place
    Where you display your bravery.

CLOTALDO.
    Rosaura, when we met I know,
    As your tears were my witness,
    I promised I'd do anything
    I could for you. My first advice
    Was that you changed the kind of clothes
    You travelled in, in case Astolfo,
    Seeing you attired as a man,
    Should think that what you wore for safety
    On the journey was merely one
    More sign of woman's levity.
    Since then I've thought how best
    Your honour's to be won again —
    You see how much I am obsessed
    With its recovery — although

It means Astolfo's certain death.
But now, though he is not the King
And there's no cause to fear him,
The thought of killing him is pure
Folly. The truth is Segismundo
Tried to murder me, but Duke Astolfo
Came to my defence, regardless of
The risk, confronting him with such
Audacity he saved my life.
How then can I, when I owe him
My life and am obliged to him
Eternally, have any thoughts
Of killing him? Is not the choice
Impossible? A daughter here,
The precious flesh and blood to which
I've given life; and there a man
To whom I owe my life. How can
These things be reconciled? Who can
Advise when in the end the arguments
Are contradictory, and I
Am twice obliged: by giving life
To you, receiving it from him?
Whichever course I take can never
Make the resolution easier
For me, for if to give is better,
It is said, than to receive, this is
An act of generosity
That guarantees my suffering.

ROSAURA.

I do not need to say to such
A man as you, my lord, that just
As giving is a noble action,
Taking is the lowest form
Of satisfaction. It follows, then,
That if Astolfo gave you life,
To ask for thanks is to deny
His generosity, while I,
Receiving from your hands the gift
Of life, accept it gratefully.
In short, while he has given you
What you in turn have given me,
You are obliged by my accepting,
Offended by his asking something

In return. What's more, if you can
Give me honour too by taking it
From Duke Astolfo, that is even
Further proof of how to give is so
Much better than merely to receive.

CLOTALDO.
But it is also true that if
The man who gives is noble-hearted,
He who takes must show his gratitude.
In giving life to you I've proved
My generosity, but owing life
To him must prove I gratefully
Accept his gift. It is the measure of
A man's nobility that he
Should give but also gratefully receive.

ROSAURA.
While it is true, my lord, you gave
Me life, you told me too that life
Dishonoured was no life at all,
And so have given me no life.
If, therefore, you would have me call
You generous and liberal,
I'd have you give me life that all
The world regards as meaningful.
If giving so ennobles man,
Then you must first be liberal,
So you may gratefully receive my thanks.

CLOTALDO.
Your argument convinces me,
Rosaura, that I must be above all
Generous. This is what I'll do.
I'll set aside sufficient money,
So you can find safe sanctuary
In a convent. Believe me, it's
The best thing possible in times
Like these that you should put your safety
First, and I, in helping you, should not
Add further to my country's troubles.
You see, the remedy is one
That leaves me loyal to the King,
Generous to you, and grateful to Astolfo.
What course could possibly suit you more?

What more could any father do?

ROSAURA.
If you were my true father, I'd
Accept this insult. But since you aren't,
I shan't!

CLOTALDO.
What can you hope to do?

ROSAURA.
I'll kill Astolfo.

CLOTALDO.
A girl of unknown
Origins displays such bravery?

ROSAURA.
See for yourself.

CLOTALDO.
What so inspires you?

ROSAURA.
I must avenge Astolfo's infamy.

CLOTALDO.
Astolfo is to be . . .

ROSAURA.
He has
Dishonoured me!

CLOTALDO.
. . . your King, Estrella's
Husband.

ROSAURA.
I swear he never shall be!

CLOTALDO.
But this is madness.

ROSAURA.
Yes, I know.

CLOTALDO.
You must forget it.

ROSAURA.
No. It isn't
Possible.

CLOTALDO.
If you persist, you'll lose

Your honour and your life.

ROSAURA.

Quite true.

CLOTALDO.
So what's achieved?

ROSAURA.

I shall be dead.

CLOTALDO.
It's lunacy.

ROSAURA.

I call it honour.

CLOTALDO.
Stupidity.

ROSAURA.

It's more like valour.

CLOTALDO.
More like frenzy.

ROSAURA.

You mean anger.

CLOTALDO.
I mean you must control this blind,
Unbridled fury.

ROSAURA.

No.

CLOTALDO.

Who is to help?

ROSAURA.
I'll help myself.

CLOTALDO.

Is there no other way?

ROSAURA.
I've told you, no.

CLOTALDO.

No possibility?

ROSAURA.
Only to be lost forever.

Exit ROSAURA.

CLOTALDO.

> Daughter, wait. If you are to be lost,
> Then we shall both be lost together.

Exit CLOTALDO.
Drums. Enter marching soldiers, CLARION, *and*
SEGISMUNDO *dressed in skins.*

SEGISMUNDO.

> If only Rome could see me now,
> Recapturing her former glory!
> How she would celebrate the spectacle
> Of someone who's a beast and yet
> Commander of a mighty army!
> Someone whose pride is such, the conquest
> Of the heavens seems but a puny victory.
> But I must banish thoughts like these,
> In case what seems so certain now
> Has vanished by the time I wake,
> And any sense of joy in what
> I had becomes the gnawing ache
> Of knowing that it's all been lost.
> Much better if we think its value small
> And not be sorry when we lose it all.

A trumpet sounds.

CLARION.

> What's this? A great big stallion galloping
> Towards us? I feel a great temptation
> To offer you a most poetic
> Version of it all, if only your
> Imagination's up to it.
> It's like a great big map this horse.
> Its body is the earth, its spirit fire,
> Its foaming mouth the sea, its breath
> The air, and all chaotically
> Thrown together; for body, spirit, foam
> And breath are but a great monstrosity
> Of earth, air, fire, water. And in
> Its colour it's a kind of patchwork,
> Dappled creature, not so much horse
> As bird that flies, that's driven on
> Relentlessly, and boldly ridden
> By . . . a woman!

SEGISMUNDO.

                Her beauty dazzles me.

CLARION.

  My God! Her ladyship, Rosaura!

Exit CLARION. *Enter* ROSAURA. *She is wearing riding-clothes and carries a sword and a knife.*

ROSAURA.

  Great Segismundo. Your majesty
  Emerges now into the daylight of
  Your deeds from the darkness of your night.
  Just as the sun awakens in
  The arms of dawn, and gives its light
  Once more to flower, land and sea,
  Encompassing the mountain tops
  With gold, the waves with brightly shining
  Silver, so you awaken to this world,
  The brightest sun in this entire land.
  I come to you pursued unhappily
  By my misfortunes, pleading that
  On that account and as a woman
  Too you'll offer me protection
  Worthy of a man as powerful
  And brave as you. Three times
  You have encountered me, three times
  Not known me since on each of them
  You saw me dressed so differently.
  At first you saw me as a man
  When in the confines of the tower
  The wretchedness of your life
  Made all my troubles seem but pleasure.
  You saw me next dressed as a woman
  In the palace, when all the majesty
  That you enjoyed proved nothing but
  An empty dream, a fantasy.
  Today I am a curious mixture of
  Both man and woman, a creature in
  Whom skirts are contradicted by
  The manly weapons of the soldier.
  I beg you, bear with me, my lord,
  If I, in order to deserve
  The more your pity and protection,
  Ask now you listen to the history

Of my misfortune. My mother was
Of noble birth, a lady at
The Court of Moscow, her life, it seems,
As darkened by unhappy fate
As graced by enviable beauty.
A certain man, on that account,
Set eyes on her – his name remains
Unknown to me, and yet I feel
What bravery is mine owes much
To him, and sometimes think that if
We lived in ancient times he would
Most certainly have been the kind
Of god who in the form of golden
Rain or mighty bull or swan deceived
The beauty of Europa. In short,
As she and Leda too in former times
Were cruelly deceived, so was
My mother now seduced by him,
The object of his cunning flattery,
The victim of his heartless treachery.
He promised her, as all men do,
He'd marry her – how could she possibly
Believe his empty words? – and as
Aeneas long ago deceived
The lovely Dido, soon abandoned her,
And left this sword which she in turn
Has handed down to me. To such
A bond, which neither marriage-vows
Nor constancy had formed, I owe
My birth, and ever since have proved
To be the image of my mother
In both my beauty and my fate.
I need to say no more, for as
My mother was so cruelly deprived
Of precious honour, so Astolfo . . .
The mere mention of his name
Enrages me . . . It fills my heart
With anger such as anyone
Is bound to feel if she is made
To name someone by whom she's been
So cruelly abused! Astolfo is
The man who won my heart, who robbed
Me of my honour, and now treats love

As if its memory is something he
Has long forgotten; for now he comes
To Poland, seeking Estrella's hand
In marriage, her rising star the witness
To my setting. Oh, who'd believe
That such a star can now divide
Two lovers once so closely allied by
Another star? I was so sad,
So desperate with grief, I thought
I would go mad. I felt as if
The chaos and confusion of the world
Was centred in this Babylon
Of mine, and though I did not speak
My griefs aloud, my manner was
Itself the clearest sign of all
I felt inside the prison of
My silence . . . until there came a day
I found myself with Violante,
Quite alone, and felt I had to say
To her what I had said to no one else.
It was as if the gates were opened
Wide, and all the pent-up sorrows there
Inside were suddenly set free.
I told her everything and felt
No sense of shame, for when we know
Another's fate has been the same
As ours, we find both comfort in
Their pain and proof that their loss
Can be the source of our gain.
She listened patiently and tried
To comfort me, recounting sorrows
Of her own. How easily the judge
Forgives if he knows he is also guilty
Of some wrong! And knowing too that she
Had let time pass and waited far
Too long in seeking restitution
Of her honour, made me leave to seek
Astolfo out and make him satisfy
His obligation to my honour.
She told me I'd be safer in
Men's clothes; she made me take the sword
You see me wearing now, and as
I left I vividly recall

How strange I thought her parting words:
'When you reach Poland, everyone
At Court must be allowed to see
This sword, for there is someone there
Who, seeing it, might well be moved
By your plight, and, knowing who
You are, consider it his proper
Duty to defend your rights.'
And so, as you already know,
I came to Poland where my horse
Ran wild and took me to your cave,
Where you were so astonished at
The sight of me. Clotaldo then,
Much moved, saw fit to beg the King
To spare my life, and when he was
Informed of who I was, advised
That I should dress accordingly
And serve Estrella in the palace.
There, ingeniously, I managed to
Upset Astolfo's plans to have
Estrella for his wife. And finally
You see me here and are once more
Confused by my identity,
The strangest mixture and anomaly
Of man and woman. As for Clotaldo,
He regards Astolfo's marriage
To Estrella as important to
The interests of State and bids
Me set aside my right to honour.
Brave Segismundo, you who seek
This just and rightful vengeance on
A father; you whom fate has now
Released from that dark tower where
You were as much a monster in
Your feelings as a rock in all
Your sufferings; I offer you
The loyalty of one in whom
The softest silk is allied to
The sharpest steel; whose costume now
Confuses chaste Diana's finery
With war-like garments of Athene.
It matters to us both, your majesty,
That we should now prevent the marriage

Of Estrella to Astolfo; to me
Because he is obliged to be
My husband; to you because to join
The kingdom they command would be
The greatest threat to your victory.
I beg you as a woman, help
Me in my quest for honour; I urge
You as a man, regain your power.
I ask you as a woman, feel
Pity for my plight; I swear
That as a man, I'll join you in the fight.
But if you think a woman is
Fair game for man's desire, I'll show
You as a man that honour is
A prize much higher in the scheme
Of things than life itself. And so
I am a woman fair enough
To be the object of your flattery,
And yet as bold as any man
To show the world my bravery.

SEGISMUNDO.
Great heavens! If I am dreaming now,
Suspend my memory! How can
So many things be part of any
Dream? If only I could now forget
Them all and so obliterate
Such thoughts as haunt me constantly!
Whoever had such doubts as these?
For if I only dreamt the majesty
I once enjoyed, how can she now
Recount so clearly the history
Of what they tell me was a dream?
I swear it was reality,
Not dream! But if it was reality,
It still confuses me that anyone
Could even think it was a dream.
Can it be possible that such
A similarity exists between
Our dreams and all the things we took
Such pleasure in that what we held
Was true proves false, and false proves true?
Must we believe that what we see
And touch and hear with clarity

Is in the end in constant doubt,
An object of uncertainty;
And thus conclude that what we thought
Must be the true original
Is nothing more and nothing less
Than some pale imitation of
Reality? If this is so,
And power and pomp and majesty
Prove in the end to have the empty
Insubstantiality of dreams,
It's best we take our pleasures as
They come and treat each one of them
As though it were a pleasurable
Dream, no sooner come than it is gone
Forever. I have Rosaura in
My power. I am entranced by her.
Why not enjoy this opportunity
And let my passion sweep aside
Such bonds of trust and confidence
As she has placed in me? This is
A dream. It would be wise to take
My pleasure now, enjoy today,
Forget tomorrow when we know
How quickly present joy is always
Turned to lasting sorrow. Though if
All this is so, I am persuaded
That the contrary is also true,
And that the greatest folly is
To sacrifice an everlasting
Glory for a temporary joy.
What man has ever tasted happiness
Who later on, when he discovers
It has gone, does not confess
That what seemed real to him then
Was nothing but a dream? If I
Must learn what I already know,
That pleasure is a flame soon turned
To ashes by a breath of wind,
Then I must seek that fame that burns
Eternally, the happiness,
The joy that is not measured by
The merely temporary. Rosaura
Has no honour. It is the duty of

A prince, therefore, to help her win
Her honour, not dishonour her.
I am decided. I shall be
The saviour of her honour first
And then my crown, and not allow
Myself to be so sorely tempted
By her beauty. Let the trumpet sound,
The battle now begin, before
Black clouds entomb the sun beneath
The ocean's icy dark-green waves.

ROSAURA.
My lord, how can you take your leave
Of me so soon? Does not my plight
Deserve a word, a glance? Why do
You close both ears and eyes to me,
As if the sight and sound of my
Complaints offended horribly?

SEGISMUNDO.
Rosaura, honour matters more
Than anything, and asks that I
Be cruel to be kind. If I
Am dumb it is because, I promise you,
My deeds, not words, have now become
The spokesman of my thoughts. And if
I do not look at you, it is
Because I do not wish to be
Distracted by your beauty when
The greater duty is to honour.

Exit SEGISMUNDO

ROSAURA.
Oh heavens, what mysteries are these?
My sorrows seem to have no end,
And all his words confuse me with
Their constant ambiguity.

Enter CLARION.

CLARION.
My lady, are you free to speak
To me?

ROSAURA.
        Why, Clarion. Where have you been?

CLARION.
> They locked me in a tower, madam,
> And dealt me such a hand of cards
> As no one ever won a game with.
> But what they didn't know was I
> Already had one hidden up
> My sleeve . . . a winning card . . . and it
> Was bound to win the game for me.

ROSAURA.
> What do you mean?

CLARION.
>   A simple matter
> Really, madam . . . to do with your
> Identity . . . and with Clotaldo's . . .

Drums off.

> What's that?

ROSAURA.
>   Can you see what it is?

CLARION.
> A great big army by the look
> Of it, and coming from the palace.
> It looks as if Basilio's made
> His mind up finally to put
> An end to mad-dog Segismundo.

ROSAURA.
> How can I be so cowardly
> As not to be at Segismundo's side,
> And help him put an end to tyranny
> That threatens both our lives?

VOICES (*off*).
> Long live Basilio!

VOICES (*off*).
>   Long live liberty!

CLARION.
> And I say long live both of them
> As long as they don't bother me
> And I can subsequently profit
> By them both. I'll keep well out of it
> And play the part of Nero. Nothing
> Bothered him, eh, fiddling away

While Rome was burning? You know what they
All say: look after number one,
'Cos no one else will do it for
You, son. I'll find a hiding-place
Behind these rocks and watch the fun
And games from where it's safe.
I don't think death will find me here.
Hey, death. You won't disturb me, will you?
Anyway, here's two fingers to you!

He conceals himself. Sound of battle. Enter the KING,
CLOTALDO *and* ASTOLFO, *fleeing.*

BASILIO.
    Can any King be so unfortunate?
    Has any father known such hate
    In any son?

CLOTALDO.
           Our army flees,
    In blind confusion.

ASTOLFO.
              The traitors have
    Possession of the palace.

BASILIO.
                In
    Every battle such as this,
    The victors boast of loyalty,
    The losers are accused of treachery.
    Clotaldo, we must flee from here
    And seek some far-off hiding-place
    That guarantees our safety from
    The vengeance of a tyrant-son.

A gun-shot off. CLARION *falls from his hiding-place,*
wounded.

CLARION.
    Will no one help me?

ASTOLFO.
              Who can this poor
    Soldier be who falls before us,
    His body stained with blood?

CLARION.
              A fellow,

Sir, who's so unfortunate, that all
His efforts to avoid his death
Have been the cause of it. I tried
To get away where I'd be safe.
Instead, I ran into the waiting arms
Of death and found there's no escape
From it. The man who thinks he can
Avoid the consequences of
His deeds must learn he can be easily
Destroyed by them. So my advice
To you is do not try to flee
This battle-ground when in the midst
Of fire and flame there's greater safety
To be found than in the most secure
Mountain. There is no way that man
Can cheat the cruel blows of fate,
And so, although you think you can
Escape, there's nothing you can do
If destiny dictates that death's
In store for you.

CLARION *dies.*

BASILIO.
                              There's nothing you
Can do if destiny dictates
That death's in store for you.
I am persuaded that this corpse
Provides the evidence of my
Own ignorance, and that its bleeding
Wounds are mouths that eloquently speak
Of how man's efforts to avoid
His fate may often bring about
The opposite; for I who tried so hard
To save my country from its enemies
Have of my own accord condemned
It to that very tyranny.

CLOTALDO.
It's true, your majesty, that fate
Can often mould the lives of men,
And, even though he hides amongst
Impenetrable rocks, destroy
Its chosen victim. But it is wrong,
And surely un-Christian too,

To think that for such things
As these there is no remedy,
When he who's wise and sensible
Can by his ingenuity
Avoid what seems inevitable.
If you are now pursued by fate,
Your safety lies in swift escape.

ASTOLFO.
Clotaldo speaks to you, my lord,
As one experience has made wise,
And I as someone who has fought
As best I could at your side.
We have a horse amongst the trees
Whose speed, it's said, outstrips the wind.
I urge your majesty to get
Away from here at once. My sword,
I promise, will delay your enemies.

BASILIO.
If it is God's decree that I
Should die, to run away from death
Is to confirm my foolishness.
To stay and greet death face to face
Is, on the other hand, a true
Acceptance of my mortal weakness.

Call to arms. SEGISMUNDO *enters with followers.*

SEGISMUNDO.
This is the wood where King Basilio
Hides, convinced its branches offer him
Their safety. Search it well. Examine
Every stone and leaf. Let every
Cranny be the object of your close
Attention.

CLOTALDO.
                    There is no time to waste,
Your majesty. I beg you leave
At once.

BASILIO.
                    There is no point.

ASTOLFO.
                                        My lord,
Make haste. Your enemies approach.

BASILIO.
>Astolfo, stand aside.

CLOTALDO.
>>>>Your majesty,
>What do you have in mind?

BASILIO.
>>>>>I seek,
>Clotaldo, the only remedy
>That now seems possible. No need
>To seek me any further, prince.
>I kneel in front of you and offer you
>The carpet of this silver hair
>Where you may tread and place your feet
>Upon this old and foolish head.
>No need to show respect. Instead,
>I beg you take revenge on me;
>Reject what finer feelings you
>May have; inflict the punishment
>That I have merited, and let
>The world see now how destiny
>Prevails, and heaven fulfils its prophecy.

SEGISMUNDO.
>Illustrious Court, so long a witness
>To these mysteries, I speak to you
>As your prince. Attend me now.
>Such things as are determined by
>The heavens and written by God's hand
>Upon a page of blue whose surface is
>The sky, the letters stars, are by
>Their nature true. They only lie
>To us when man, believing he
>Can know their meaning, foolishly
>Interprets them. My father, seeking
>To control my wild condition,
>Made of me an animal, a beast
>In human form, when I, considering
>My noble line and lineage,
>My royal blood and parentage,
>May well have proved to have a mild
>And truly humble disposition.
>Instead, the kind of cruelty
>Of which I was the victim made

Me what I am, the harshness of
My life the very source of my
Ferocity, and everything
Designed to change the course of fate
Proved quite the contrary. But why
Think there is mystery in this?
For if you say to any man:
'Some fierce animal will be
The death of you', does he provoke
The instincts of the beast that, while
Asleep, is meek and mild, but when
Awake, will quickly prove how wild
It really is? And if it's said:
'This sword you wear will be the cause
Of your death', must we conclude
That to evade that death a man
Should draw that fatal sword and point
It to his breast? Or if again
A man is told: 'Beware the sea,
For one day soon its fierce waves
Will be your tomb', does he then run
Into the sea when it is at
Its stormiest, when waves as high
As mountain-tops are capped by foamy
Crests? All this my father has achieved:
A man who, fearing a beast,
Awakened it; who, threatened by
A sword, exposed the blade; who, warned
Of stormy seas, ignored the waves;
And when my fury could have been
A tame, domesticated animal,
A sword that, blunted, never killed,
A sea that, unprovoked, is ever still,
He chose instead by cruel means
To stir such instincts as would otherwise
Have been suppressed. And so it is
Quite evident that any man
Who seeks to change the course of fortune, does
So only by the exercise
Of common-sense and moderation,
Acknowledging that he cannot
Predict those things that are to come,
And when they do, expect to run

Away from them. Behold this spectacle,
This sight so terrible and yet
So worthy of our admiration,
And learn from it the lesson of
A tyrant-father at my feet,
A once proud monarch in defeat.
The heavens thus wreak their punishment
On one whose arrogance was such,
He thought he could defeat them.
What chance do I have, then, if this
Is so, of overcoming what
The heavens decree, when I am younger still,
And far less wise than he? I beg
Your majesty, arise, give me
Your hand. For since you realize
The way you chose to overcome
The heavens cannot succeed, I choose
To kneel at your feet and offer you
The chance to take revenge upon
A son who, so the stars declared,
Would bring about a king's defeat.

BASILIO.

My son, an action such as this
Confirms that you are born to be
A prince. May all your triumphs now
Be crowned with laurel-leaves, and all
Your actions lead to glorious victory.

ALL.

Hail Segismundo! Long live Segismundo!

SEGISMUNDO.

If I am blessed with valour such
As promises great victories,
The greatest of them all must be
To now become true master of
My destiny. Astolfo, give
Your hand in marriage to Rosaura.
Acknowledge your debt and keep
The promise I have made to her.

ASTOLFO.

It's true I am obliged to her,
My lord, but you must also know
She has no proof of her identity

Or origins. To marry such
A woman is for me . . .

CLOTALDO.
                    Stop! At once!
She is a woman of nobility,
Astolfo, as great as yours,
A lady I am proud to call
My daughter. My sword defends her name.

ASTOLFO.
What does this mean?

CLOTALDO.
                    It means I had
Good reason to conceal her name
Until I saw her honourably
Married. A long and tedious story,
But all the same she is my daughter.

ASTOLFO.
If that is so, I have no reason
Not to marry her.

SEGISMUNDO.
                    Well said,
Astolfo. But now Estrella, lest
She grieve too much in losing such
A good and noble prince as you,
Must seek some compensation in
Another husband, if possible
As equal in his qualities
As in his fortune. Give me your hand.
Estrella.

ESTRELLA.
            I gladly do so and
Am doubly honoured.

SEGISMUNDO.
                    Clotaldo,
You served my father loyally.
You have my love, and any favour
You should ask of me.

SOLDIER.
                    Why favour him,
My lord, if he refused to help?
I was the one who set you free

And helped you win this victory
Against your father. What's my reward?

SEGISMUNDO.

I think the tower. You shall remain
There till you die. When treachery
Is over, it would be foolish to
Reward the traitor.

BASILIO.

My son, this is
A sign of true wisdom!

ASTOLFO.

That he
Who was a beast is now a man!

ROSAURA.

And now at last is capable
Of true discretion!

SEGISMUNDO.

Why be amazed
When I have learned that what is but
A dream may soon be over, and I,
Though now a King, may once again
Become a prisoner? It is enough
To know that our joy today
May by tomorrow be our lasting
Sorrow, and from this lesson learn
To use as best we can the time
Still left to us. Let each man seek
Forgiveness for his sins, and others learn
That they do best to pardon him.

Three Judgements in One

Characters

DON LOPE DE URREA, *the elder*
DON LOPE DE URREA, *his son*
DON MENDO TORRELLAS
DOÑA BLANCA, *a lady*
DOÑA VIOLANTE, *a lady*
DON GUILLÉN DE AZAGRA
THE KING, DON PEDRO OF ARAGÓN
BEATRIZ, *servant*
VICENTE, *servant*
ELVIRA, *servant*
OUTLAWS

Act One

Gunshot off. Enter DON MENDO *and* DOÑA VIOLANTE,
backing away from a group of outlaws amongst whom is VICENTE.

DON MENDO.
>You monstrous creatures! Hold your ground!
>I am afraid of neither sword
>Nor gun. I'd rather die than willingly
>Be overcome by such as you.
>You do not frighten me.

DOÑA VIOLANTE.
>$\qquad\qquad\qquad$ Can no one
>Save us?

OUTLAW.
>$\qquad\quad$ See there. The mountain is
>From peak to plain a theatre
>That warns the traveller the leading
>Player in its company is death.
>Though you attempt to be as brave
>As Mars, you cannot save yourselves.

VICENTE.
>Hey, look, the girl's a real beauty.
>Her brightness far outshines the sun.
>As from today, we'll see if she
>Can't bring a little fun to our captain.

DON MENDO.
>Before you touch a single hair
>Of that fair head, I swear you'll see
>Me dead at your feet. And then
>Posterity can say of me
>That even though I could not save her life,
>I made the greatest sacrifice.

OUTLAW.
>We'll help you on your way.

DOÑA VIOLANTE.
>$\qquad\qquad\qquad$ I beg
>You, spare his life!

DON MENDO.
> Come on! Why this

Delay?

Enter DON LOPE DE URREA, *the younger, dressed as an outlaw.*

DON LOPE.
> Stop this! What's going on?

VICENTE.
> We came across this lady, sir,
> There when the branches spread themselves
> In such confusion, as if the Spring
> Seeks some protection from the sun.
> She'd stepped down from her carriage, but
> Her people, overcome with fear
> At the sight of us, just made a dash
> For it, except this old one here
> Who seems to think that he can save her.

DON LOPE.
> How do you think, old man, you can
> Defend yourself against as many men
> As these?

DON MENDO.
> It would be madness if
> My only end were life; but since I now
> Propose to die, defiance makes
> More sense to me. So now you've come,
> You must pass sentence on my life.
> I shall not ask for pity;
> Rather that you put an end to me.

DON LOPE.
> Arise. I feel compassion such
> As I have never felt before
> For any other human life.
> The lady you protect, is she
> Your wife?

DON MENDO.
> She is my daughter, sir.

DOÑA VIOLANTE.
> And I so much my father's child
> In blood and courage, any thought

That you might have of taking me,
Upon his death, is best rejected now.
These hands, placed tight around my throat,
Would do the work of any sword.
Or else I'd throw myself from this
High peak and dash myself in pieces
On the road below.

DON LOPE.
                    My lady, put
An end to thoughts as dark as these.
Such is your beauty, I could be
Excused more cruel and ignoble deeds.
Instead, it stills my mind and hand.
I feel a pity and respect
No other woman in this land
Has ever made me feel. Where are
You headed for?

DON MENDO.
                    The town of Saragossa.
There I have some influence. One day,
Perhaps, the favour you have shown
To us will find some recompense.

DON LOPE.
Who are you, sir?

DON MENDO.
                    My name, Don Mendo
Torrellas. For many years I've served
The King, Don Pedro of Aragón,
In Naples, France and Rome, and now
Am summoned to the Spanish Court.
I give my word that, if the life
You lead is due to some unhappy
Accident, you may rely on me
To represent your cause and, if
The opportunity presents itself,
To seek redress on your behalf.
The world shall know we owe our lives to you.

DON LOPE.
I'd gladly place my faith in such
A promise, sir, if only all
My crimes did not prevent the prospect

Of such happiness. For them I am
Condemned to death and see no end
To all my suffering. I am,
With every passing day, the plaything
Of despair, and losing further hope,
Am driven to commit more daring
Crimes, that in their turn grant me
A few days more of hopeless life.
My wretchedness is such that each
Offence becomes a refuge from
The last, and one more confirmation
Of my wicked past.

DON MENDO.

                Do not despair.
Have faith, and one day you shall see,
Perhaps, that I will prove to be
The instrument of your freedom.
Good fortune smiles on me and yet
Is less to me than my resolve
To see improvement in your wretched fortunes.
I shall do everything to find
You favour with the King. But first
You have to tell me who you are
And what you've done.

DON LOPE.

                  If that is what
You wish, my friend, though I am quite
Convinced there is no point in it.
Leave us alone.

Exit all.

              My history is this.
I, Don Mendo, am the only son
Of Lope de Urrea, my name
The same as his, of noble birth
And origin. If only everything
That's happened to me since had something
Of the same good fortune!

DON MENDO.

                Why, this
Is in itself most fortunate!
Don Lope and myself were once

The very best of friends. For me
To put an end to your misery
Would be the happiest of fates.

DON LOPE.
I am inclined to think the contrary
Is true; for if you are my father's friend,
And I have so offended him
That he regards my life as but
A source of constant pain, to which
Each day adds further suffering,
I think it much more likely you,
His friend, will prove to be my enemy.
Though if the truth be told, my father is
The real cause of my unhappy life.

DON MENDO.
How can that be?

DON LOPE.
                    It is quite easily
Explained.

DON MENDO.
               Proceed. I cannot wait
To hear the rest of such a history
As this.

DOÑA VIOLANTE (aside).
               At least there seems good cause
To think our safety guaranteed.

DON LOPE.
My father, as I was to hear
So many times in future years,
Was never from an early age
Inclined to marry. Rightly or wrongly,
He resisted it, but in the end,
Persuaded by his family
That he must have a son if such
An old and noble line were not
To die with him, agreed, and so,
Though now advanced in years and still
Instinctively opposed to marriage,
Finally proceeded with the plan
To take a wife. His choice was someone whose
Nobility was equalled only by

Her perfect and unrivalled virtue.
And yet they were unequal in
Their years. The lady, Doña Blanca
Soldevilla, was fifteen; Don Lope
Had already seen the winter of
Advancing years begin to place
That snow upon his head, which seems
In men the withered flowers of
A full and happy youth already dead.

DON MENDO (*aside*).
He tells me what I know! Oh, what
I'd give in order not to know!
Why must these thoughts torment me so?

Aloud.
I beg you, sir. Please continue.

DON LOPE.
The girl resisted marriage too,
As though she knew instinctively
That youth and age are not designed
To mix harmoniously; but since
Most noblewomen are denied
A choice, she too was in the end
Obliged to sacrifice herself,
And, in obedience to her parents,
Accepted what for her was but
An empty marriage of convenience.
How often are two people joined
And forced to live as man and wife,
When both of them are quite convinced
They cannot have a happy life!
For him the marriage merely brought
Unhappiness; for her it lacked
The tenderness and joy she sought.
Imagine, then, how any child
Conceived in constant lovelessness,
Must in itself be living proof
Of all its parents' joylessness.
They thought that I, as other sons
Have done, would fill their lives with peace
And harmony. Instead, I proved
To have on them the contrary effect,
And brought a greater animosity
To both their lives, my mother showing me

A love as great as any mother can,
My father brooding on instinctive hate.
Against all Nature's laws, he showed
No love for me, and saw those childish faults
That many fathers think endearing
As one more cause why he should hate
Me more. Because of him I had
No teacher in my early years
And therefore lacked that discipline
Which such a man, through either fear
Or love, can bring to children's lives,
Just as an animal which seems
Untameable is made by love
Or punishment controllable.
As soon as I had reached that age
When reason dawns and I at last
Could make decisions of my own,
I formed such friendships as could do
Me only harm, but were condoned by both
My mother's love and father's lack
Of interest. With such permission
To indulge my appetites, I made
The most of every opportunity
That came my way, and set my sights
On every crime that now appealed to me.
As I grew older still, my pleasures were
Attractive women and my skill
At cards, and all my days and nights
Were spent in dutiful pursuit
Of their cause. Such was the course
I took, the edifice I built,
That, founded not on solid ground
But sand, would soon, when shaken by
The wind, show every sign of falling down.
With every passing day I found
Myself more lost in these activities,
Such was the hold that such a way
Of life by that time had on me.
At last my father realized
The error of my ways, and much too late
Attempted to eradicate those faults
For which he was himself to blame,
And make the twisted tree grow straight
Once more. I must confess, I wanted

To obey, but in the end ignored
Whatever he would say to me.
In consequence of this our lives
Were spent, if not in openly declared
Hostility, at least in mutual
Dislike, and both of us a source
Of deep and constant worry to
My poor mother. Since then her heart
Has always been a victim of
Divided loyalties, for where
I went it always went with me;
And if some night I went to visit her
– the only way our grief could find
Relief or remedy – I used
The key I had to let myself
Into the house as silently
As possible, and so conceal
My presence from my father.
Who ever would believe such honest love
As binds a mother to her son,
Her son to her, would be obliged,
As though it were some common thief,
To so deceive the world? But if
You wish to know what final blow
Of fate condemned me to my misery,
We'll set aside the cards and love-affairs
That made me enemies and caused
My father constant poverty,
And speak instead of someone else
Who then lived near me. She was
A girl who was as much a miracle
Of beauty as a prodigy
Of prudence, for in her person were
Combined for once in perfect harmony
Those two most precious but opposing
Qualities that long have been the fiercest
Of enemies: the purest perfection of
Good looks matched equally by sweet
Discretion. And so she soon became
The single object of my new devotion,
Of which at first the only indication were
Unspoken signs, which soon were sighs,
Then words, which in their clumsiness

Could not express true passion's force.
I told her in my letters of
The love I felt for her, and she,
Affected by these sentiments,
Responded with the pity that
Devotion such as mine deserved.
Her window soon became our meeting-place,
A nightly witness to such heart-
Felt pleas as were designed to melt
Its iron bars with tenderness.
The lady seemed not so displeased
With my attentions as at ease
With them, for if the truth be told,
No lady who agrees to listen to
A lover's flattery is then aggrieved
By it entirely. Encouraged by
Such favour as she'd shown to me,
My thoughts began to turn towards
Those things that for the ardent lover are
The true reward of love. And yet
This true reward, this perfect bliss
So-called, is but appearance,
And love itself a tyrant so
Complete in its intransigence
That what at first seems happiness
Becomes the very source of our distress.
She soon allowed me entry to
Her house, though first commanding me
That I must offer her my hand
And keep the promise I now made
To her of marriage. How easily
Are such vows made! How quickly do
They fade from our memory!
For I, no sooner had I conquered her
And tasted such delight, began
To see her differently, as if
A blindfold had been taken from
My eyes, and she, reflected in
Another glass, seemed not as virtuous
As I had thought, but far too easy.
Oh, honour, fiery basilisk!
No sooner do you gaze upon
Yourself, you risk your very life!

The love I felt for her was matched
Now equally by my regret;
Her beauty dazzled me, and yet
I could not easily forget
How I had overcome what I
Considered perfect, honest virtue.
And so, in order to enjoy
Her still but at the same time keep
At bay the plans for marriage she
Now spoke of constantly, I thought
It wise to emphasize to her
My duty as an only son
To my own family, and so
Delay, as long as possible,
Our wedding-day. Needless to say,
It was not long before she saw
The cunning of my plan, and making me
Believe that she was still deceived,
Began to scheme against myself
With such smooth treachery as I
Thought quite impossible in any woman of
Such obvious moral qualities.
She had a brother who, it seems,
Had been obliged, for robbery
And murder of a wealthy man,
To flee from Saragossa, seeking
Safety in the mountains. He, at her
Command, came back, and hidden in
Her house, was made to listen to
Her story of offended honour.
So enraged was he by all he heard,
He now resolved to take revenge,
And so engaged two other friends,
Two criminals, to help him in
His task. As for myself, I went
That very night to see her once
Again quite unsuspectingly.
No sooner had I passed the stables than
The three of them leapt out at me
At once, swords drawn, and I, attempting
To defend myself by parrying
Their thrusts, instead of one, deflected three.
I quickly drew my gun to save

Myself – it seems that they, for fear of
The noise such weapons make, had none –
And taking aim . . .

Cries off.

VOICES (*off*).
                Search the valley!

VOICES (*off*).
                        Search

The road! As quickly as you can!

DON MENDO.
    What's this? What's happening?

Enter VICENTE.

VICENTE.
                  The servants, sir . . .

DON LOPE.
    What is it?

DON MENDO.
        Speak!

DOÑA VIOLANTE.
             What can it be?

VICENTE.
The ones who ran away from here,
They've gone and fetched the law, I swear
They have! Believe me, sir. Look there!

DON LOPE.
To the mountains, quickly!

DON MENDO.
             I guarantee
Your safety, friend. I'll speak to them.
As for the rest, have faith in me.
I intend to keep my word.

DON LOPE.
            And I

Accept it.

DON MENDO.
       I only ask of you
Some token that, if anyone
Should wish to speak to you on my

Behalf, shall let him safely pass.

DON LOPE.

There's nothing I can really give . . .
Except, perhaps, this hunting-knife.
Whoever wants to speak to me
And carries it, need have no fear
For his life.

DON MENDO.

Why point the knife at me?

DON LOPE.

Perhaps because it points the best
To my brutality.

DON MENDO.

Then I
Shall do my best to blunt that point.

DON LOPE.

Take the knife. Goodbye.

DON MENDO.

May God go with you!

DON LOPE.

Oh, this is most unfortunate!

DON MENDO.

What have you done?

DON LOPE.

In handing you
The knife, I've cut my hand . . . See how
My blood now runs! Oh, what confusion fills
My mind! The knife in your hand
Tells me that I one day shall find
You seeking vengeance on my life!

DON MENDO.

Come now, this is a fear bred
By fanciful imagination . . .

VOICES (off).

They are approaching fast.

DOÑA VIOLANTE.

Please go
At once. The risk that you might run
On our account is more than my

Poor soul could bear!

DON LOPE.

                For your sake
I shall, even though to stay would be
Much greater fun! (*Aside.*) Such things as I
Have seen today confuse imagination!

DOÑA VIOLANTE (*aside*).

Whoever would have thought that crimes
Could have a pleasant face like this?
The things that I have seen today
Shall be a source of constant solace.

They leave.
Enter DON GUILLÉN *and* DON LOPE DE URREA, *the elder.*

DON GUILLÉN.

As you well know, my lord, I was
Don Lope's childhood friend. If there
Is something I can do to put
An end to such distress, command
Me now.

DON LOPE, the elder.

              I am most grateful, Don
Guillén. Most understanding of you.
When did you get to Aragón?

DON GUILLÉN.

Just yesterday, my lord. From Naples.
I have some business to attend to.

DON LOPE, the elder.

I have an audience with the King today,
Though I much doubt he'll give me what
I want or let me have my way.

DON GUILLÉN.

He approaches now.

Enter the KING *with attendants.*

DON LOPE, the elder.

               Your majesty.
I am Don Lope de Urrea. You may
Remember me . . .

KING.

              Of course, Don Lope.

DON LOPE, the elder.

> I do not come to ask of you
> What I have asked for many times
> Before, your majesty. I come
> Beset by other ills, and would
> Implore you now to listen to
> A heart-felt plea.

KING.

> You may proceed.

DON LOPE, the elder.

> I do so gratefully, and yet
> My grief is such, to speak of it
> Is but a source of shame and deep
> Embarrassment. My son, Don Lope
> De Urrea, promised a certain lady he
> Would marry her, but then, because
> He had not asked for my consent,
> And thinking therefore he would be
> The object of my own resentment –
> It hurts me as a father to admit it –
> Delayed the marriage longer than
> He reasonably should. The girl,
> In turn, mistook such caution for
> A change of heart and so informed
> Her brother who, enlisting two
> Companions, took her part in the affair,
> And lay in wait, resolved to kill
> My poor son. The boy does not
> Lack courage, and even though he was
> Himself outnumbered and attacked
> By three of them, instinctively
> Fought back and, in the struggle that
> Ensued, killed one of them. In such
> A case the law has always viewed
> Such action as completely just,
> And taken as its parallel
> The kingdom of the animals,
> Where to defend oneself is seen
> As both correct and natural.
> The boy then ran into the street
> And was unfortunate enough to meet
> And wound one of your constables.
> I know he has offended you,

Your majesty, and yet the fact
He chose to flee and not take part
In further criminal activities
Is not so much a sign he flouts
The law as greatly fears it.
I do admit, as well, he'd serve
You better as a soldier in the fields
Than thus incur disfavour as
An outlaw in the mountains;
Yet you well know the custom is,
In Aragón, when honour is
Offended, the man who lays a claim
To it must in the end defend it.
As for the girl, she was in this
Affair on two occasions most
Unfortunate – not only did
She lose my son, she was as well
The sister of the murdered man –
And so, in order to improve
Her wretched state, appealed to me.
Her wish, which she repeated many times,
And earnestly entreated me
To help fulfill, was that I help
Her, with a gift of money, seek
Seclusion in a convent. And so,
Although I am a poor man,
And need the little money I still have
To feed my family, I sacrificed
My need for hers, and found enough
To guarantee not just her entry there,
But, if she wished, as many years
Of life as are still left to her.
Such is my poverty I am
Obliged today, your majesty,
To live in dark and humble rooms,
And set aside the best of them
For those who come to stay with me.
How else can I fulfill my proper
Duty to my guests, as I am now
Obliged to do to my old friend,
Don Mendo Torrellas. I beg of you,
Prostrated at your feet in all
Humility, that you, as I

Have done, find pity in your soul
To offer to my erring son
A pardon such as only your
Authority can truly give.
And if you think that neither he
Nor I deserve such mercy, think
Of all those great and noble men,
Those worthy ancestors of mine,
Who plead with you for pity too.
I beg you, turn your eyes to them,
Behold what noble and heroic deeds
Those honourable men achieved
In your name. Feel pity for
This snow-white hair. See how
The mere mention of such cares
Provokes a father's burning tears.
And if my love is not enough
To earn forgiveness for my son,
Then let a mother's grief show how
A royal pardon may be won.
Consider how the noble lady is
Distressed for him. I ask you grant
This favour as our King.

KING.
                              Consult
My Minister of Justice.

DON LOPE, the elder.
                              I must
Conclude that destiny will never smile
On me in this; for when I come
To ask a favour of the King,
He recommends me to the Minister
Of Justice.

KING.
          If it is true the law
Must pass its judgement on all crimes,
Must it not grant all pardons too?

DON LOPE, the elder.
Of course, your majesty. But with
The death of Don Ramón, there is
No minister. The post stands empty.

KING.
>Not so, Don Lope. The post is filled
>As from today.

DON LOPE, the elder.
>   Oh this is joy
>Indeed! Enough to put an end
>To all my fears!

KING.
>   To hear a father plead
>Like this! It almost drives a man to tears!

Exit the KING, *his retinue and* DON GUILLÉN.

DON LOPE, the elder.
>Oh, honour, what demands you make
>Upon a noble, pure heart!
>What things we are obliged to do
>So other people cannot start
>To slander us! All this without
>A father's true and deep-felt love!
>It does not mean I do not love
>The boy, and yet I would have done
>These things with greater joy if I
>Loved him as deeply as I should.
>The truth is I do everything
>For Doña Blanca's sake, such is
>My love for her, and try as best
>I can to make her happy even though
>She doubts my love. I would, if I
>Were called upon, be quite prepared
>To sacrifice my life for her . . .

Noise off.

>Who comes accompanied by all
>These people? If I am not deceived,
>It is my friend of many years
>Ago, Don Mendo Torrellas.
>I must not let him see me so
>Distressed, and yet he is to stay
>With me – oh this is true cause for
>Regret! I'll have to speak to him.
>But no, perhaps there is no need.
>The King, informed Don Mendo has
>Arrived, appears again. He has agreed,

It seems, to offer him an audience.

Enter the KING *from one side of the stage,* DON MENDO *from the other. Servants.*

DON MENDO.
>I kneel before your majesty
>In humble recognition of
>My loyalty.

KING.
>   Arise, Don Mendo,
>Lord Chief Justice of Aragón.

DON MENDO.
>Give me your hand, your majesty.
>Grant me the necessary strength
>To bear the burden you have placed
>Upon these undeserving shoulders.
>God grant you everlasting life.

KING.
>I trust you are quite well, Don Mendo.

DON MENDO.
>The honour you have blessed me with
>Gives me new life.

KING.
>   The journey will
>Have tired you. When you have had
>Sufficient rest, we'll speak again.
>Tomorrow we'll discuss why I
>Have brought you to my Court.
>And offered you such high office.

DON MENDO.
>Your majesty, my life and soul
>Are in your hands; your every wish
>From this day forth is my command.

Exit the KING.

DON LOPE, the elder.
>If it is true a nobleman
>Does not forget what previously
>He valued most, let this be proof,
>Don Mendo, you remember me.

DON MENDO.
>How could I possibly forget
>The warmth and generosity
>Of our friendship?

DON LOPE, the elder.
>   I kiss your hand,
>My lord, in recognition of
>My true humility: firstly because
>As someone recently arrived,
>Both I and Doña Blanca offer you
>Our hospitality; and then because,
>As Lord Chief Justice of Aragón,
>You may be good enough to hear
>My own petition.

DON MENDO.
>   Whatever plea
>You make, Don Lope, shall be judged
>Most sympathetically.

DON LOPE, the elder.
>   The King
>Before you came, commanded me
>To speak to you.

DON MENDO.
>   Regard me as
>Your loyal friend, as someone you
>Can always trust implicitly.

DON LOPE, the elder.
>The case concerns my son . . .

DON MENDO.
>   Of course,
>Don Lope, and one I am familiar with.
>I see how deeply it affects you.
>They say your son has little love
>For you and acts most disrespectfully.

DON LOPE, the elder.
>It seems that many people think,
>My lord, that I have little love
>Or sympathy for him. The truth
>Is I refuse to do for him
>What he does not deserve. Because
>He has committed serious crimes,

> I am now despised by everyone,
> The whole world now makes fun of me,
> And I, because of this ungrateful son,
> Am now obliged to live in poverty.

DON MENDO.

> Do not concern yourself so much,
> My friend. I can at least employ
> The power I now have to try
> To satisfy what people ask
> Of me. The cruel fortune your son
> Has been subjected to has come
> Full circle. He has saved my life,
> And so, obliged to him, I can
> Reward him with his life. But we
> Shall speak of this again as soon
> As we have reached your home. Because
> The King's command came suddenly,
> I rode ahead and left my daughter,
> Violante, quite alone. She is
> My only child, I am concerned
> For her. I wish to know if she
> Has reached your house ahead of me.

DON LOPE, the elder.

> It means so much to us to have
> You share our home, my friend. My good
> Lady, Doña Blanca, offers you
> Our every hospitality,
> You'll find her more than pleased to see
> Your needs are properly attended to.

DON MENDO.

> I cannot wait to greet a lady of
> Such estimable quality.

Aside.

> Oh, heavens! To make me meet again
> The lady I once knew is but
> Another sign of your cruelty!

Exit both.

Enter DOÑA VIOLANTE, *dressed for the road, and* DOÑA BLANCA *from the other side of the stage.*

DOÑA BLANCA.

> To have the opportunity
> Of offering my home to such
> A lovely guest is more than I
> Deserve. If there is something you
> Or your servants need, rely
> On me to serve you to the best
> Of my ability. You are
> Most welcome, Violante.

DOÑA VIOLANTE.

> And I
> Most happy to be here, madam.
> For though I've never been to Aragón
> Before, I cannot think that anyone
> Can feel more happy or at home
> Than I do now. My only worry is
> To have to greet you here in this
> Reception-room. My servants will
> Have put away my things quite soon
> And we can speak more comfortably.

DOÑA BLANCA.

> I have to say the fault lies not
> So much with your servants as
> Yourself, for having come to us
> So unexpectedly.

DOÑA VIOLANTE.

> But not as soon
> As I had hoped. I swear there was
> No single moment on the mountain
> I did not long to be elsewhere.
> I truly feared for my life
> A second time.

DOÑA BLANCA.

> You mean there was
> A first?

DOÑA VIOLANTE.

> There was, the very worst
> Of my entire life. To think
> Of it still makes my heart beat fast.

Aside.

> To tell the truth, it beats more quickly now

Than it did then.

DOÑA BLANCA.
                    So what exactly
Happened?

DOÑA VIOLANTE.
                    To seek protection from
The sun, whose rays beat down as if
They thought the mountains were their own
Worst enemy, I left my carriage for
The greater consolation of a cool
And shady bank, a fortress where
The flowers, well-defended by
The steep sides of a stream, resisted both
The merciless attacks of sun
And wind. Then, unexpectedly,
A group of men appeared, as if
The centre of the mountain gave them birth,
And threatening my honour and
My father's life, confirmed that neither had
For them the slightest worth. And so
It would have proved had not a young
Man then appeared on the scene
And boldly intervened on our
Behalf . . . But what is this? Why do
You weep, my lady?

DOÑA BLANCA.
                    The story of
Good fortune such as this reminds
Me only of my own misfortune.

DOÑA VIOLANTE.
In that case I shall say no more.
The very last thing I would wish
Is that my story be the cause
Of bitter memories for you.

DOÑA BLANCA.
Your father must have seen the man,
The one you just described as young?

DOÑA VIOLANTE.
Oh, yes. But, more than that, he owes
Him both his life and honour.

DOÑA BLANCA (*aside*).
      A curse on him! If only he
      Had seized the opportunity
      To take the vengeance I deserve,
      The world . . . (*Aloud.*) What am I saying? Please
      Forgive me! I feel an anguish in
      My soul so deeply rooted I
      Forget myself, and sometimes say
      The most unreasonable things.
      You must not be upset. You see,
      The young man is my only son,
      And almost everything he's done
      Has been the cause of his unhappiness,
      His father's lack of sympathy
      And my own sadness.

DOÑA VIOLANTE.
                        He told us who
      He was, but I was at that moment so
      Confused, I did not understand
      The true relationship of all
      The names he gave to us, or I
      Would not have mentioned it or been
      So foolish as to draw attention to
      Such things.

Enter DON MENDO *and* DON LOPE, *the elder*.

DON LOPE, the elder.
                  Greetings, Blanca. I think
      This house shall witness from today
      New joy and happiness.

DOÑA BLANCA.
                        Then it
      Shall grow accustomed to the joy
      That it has missed for far too long.

DON LOPE, the elder.
      Young lady, please excuse my lack
      Of courtesy. How foolish of
      Me not to offer you the welcome you
      Deserve. The news I bring, dear wife,
      Concerns the guest we serve most happily
      Today. The King has made Don Mendo
      Lord Chief Justice of Aragón.

If that were not sufficient happiness,
He's recommended that I speak
To him and hopefully obtain
For our son a final pardon.

DOÑA BLANCA *(aside)*.
Who'll give me patience to endure this?

Aloud.

My lord, I swear I would not miss
The opportunity of serving you
That this most happy change now offers me.
As for my son . . . you know where duty lies . . .
Though, as I understand, from what
Your daughter, Violante, tells
Me now, you have already met
The boy and he has saved your life,
Thereby incurring your debt to him.

DON MENDO.
You may rely on me to serve
You both and equally, my dear
Blanca. My debt is such, it is
Not quite so easily forgotten.

Enter ELVIRA.

ELVIRA.
Your room is ready for you now,
My lady.

DOÑA VIOLANTE.
If you'll excuse me, Doña
Blanca, I need to rest awhile.

DOÑA BLANCA.
Then I, if you allow me to, shall serve
You to the best of my ability.

DON LOPE, the elder.
And I, as most befits a man
So old in years, accept the role
Of squire, and so insist that I
Accompany you to your room.

DOÑA VIOLANTE.
If that is your wish, you may,
Of course, my lord, but only as

The master of this household. God
Be with you, Blanca.

DOÑA BLANCA.
And with you too,
Violante.

DOÑA VIOLANTE (*aside*).
The thoughts that now
Assault me give me life yet at
The same time, serpent-like, attempt
To murder me with deadly poison.

DON LOPE, *the elder, takes* DOÑA VIOLANTE *by the hand
in order to accompany her to her room.*

DON MENDO.
I give you leave to go with her,
My lord, so I may now enjoy
The company of Doña Blanca.

Aside.

Before she says a word, I'll see
If I can't draw the sting of her
Complaints.

Exit DON LOPE, *the elder,* DOÑA VIOLANTE *and* ELVIRA.

DOÑA BLANCA (*aside*).
I'll need the patience of
A saint to deal with this! (*Aloud.*) What would
You wish of me, my lord?

DON MENDO.
Simply
To offer you my humble services.
I've waited long for this occasion.

DOÑA BLANCA.
I can't think why, if I have no
Intention of accepting them.

DON MENDO.
I am distressed to see you feel
Such bitterness, though I confess
You would be wholly justified
In telling me that I bear most
Responsibility for this.

DOÑA BLANCA.
>Quite honestly, my lord, you leave
>Me at a total loss for words.
>I can't think what 'my bitterness'
>Can be or any reason why
>You wish to talk to me like this.
>I have no memory of you,
>Nor do I think we've ever met before.

DON MENDO.
>My dear Blanca!

DOÑA BLANCA.
>   My dear Don Mendo!
>I ask you not to talk to me
>Of something I, quite frankly, find
>Embarrassing. You are, I think,
>Confusing me with someone else,
>In which case silence is by far
>The best solution. I really do
>Suggest you now forget what you
>Have said to me. I certainly
>Shall never mention it again.

DON MENDO.
>Who ever would have thought, my dear
>Blanca, that ingenuity
>Could so inspire failing memory?

DOÑA BLANCA.
>I've no idea what you mean.

DON MENDO.
>I think you do. It's perfectly clear.

DOÑA BLANCA.
>Then we shall not discuss it further.

DON MENDO.
>In that case, Blanca, I obey.
>I have no choice. What other way
>Do you suggest I offer you
>My services?

DOÑA BLANCA.
>   By saying nothing.

DON MENDO.
>How can I do that?

DOÑA BLANCA.
                    By suffering
    In silence.
DON MENDO.
                    That's not easy.
DOÑA BLANCA.
                        Learn
    From me.
DON MENDO.
                You'll teach me how?
DOÑA BLANCA.
                            Immediately.

    Calling.

    Beatriz!

    Enter BEATRIZ.

BEATRIZ.
            Madam?
DOÑA BLANCA.
                Please show the gentleman
    His room. (*Aside to him.*) I promised you you should
    Not speak to me!
DON MENDO.
                    You choose instead
    To deepen my anxiety!

    They leave.

    Enter DOÑA VIOLANTE *and* ELVIRA, *carrying a lamp.*

DOÑA VIOLANTE.
    Please lock the door, Elvira. If
    My father asks for me, tell him
    I'm still asleep. I do not wish
    To see or speak to anyone.
    Solitude shall be my sole companion.

ELVIRA.
    I can't think why your mood's as dark
    As this, madam.
DOÑA VIOLANTE.
                I doubt I could

Describe, Elvira, what I feel.
Help me undress. Just place my clothes
Across the chest.

They move to the side of the stage.

ELVIRA.
                              So did you find
The outlaws just as fierce as they say
They are?

DOÑA VIOLANTE.
                    One of them especially;
His form, his face, his eyes, engraved
Upon my memory as if
I see him still; and everywhere
I turn my eyes, his image seems
To fill the void and follow me.

Enter DON LOPE and VICENTE, concealing themselves.

DON LOPE.
How can this be? Why is this room

To VICENTE

So elegantly furnished?

VICENTE.
                              Maybe
It's someone else's house. I thought
You said your father's very poor,
Doesn't have a stick of furniture.

DON LOPE.
Wait.

VICENTE.
        I'm waiting.

DON LOPE.
                        Look.

VICENTE.
                              I'm looking.

DON LOPE.
A woman there . . .

VICENTE.
                        I fancy two
Of them.

DON LOPE.

>   . . . the one now daringly
> Removing all her clothes, as if
> They are the meaningless accessories
> To perfect beauty, thus proclaiming she,
> Much more than Pallas armed for war,
> Is in her nakedness a Venus armed
> For love.

VICENTE.

>   I see her perfectly.
> If she takes off some more, she'll drive
> Me crazy.

DON LOPE.

>   Who can she be?

VICENTE.

>   She can't
> Be your mother, nor mine either, come
> To that!

DON LOPE.

>   I'll see if I can't see
> Her face.

VICENTE.

>   And me.

DON LOPE.

>   And hear what she
> Is saying. Tread more softly!

VICENTE.

> Softly? You shan't hear a sound.
> As if I'm walking on a grave,
> My feet, they barely touch the ground.

ELVIRA.

> It all seems very strange, my lady.

DOÑA VIOLANTE.

> In short, I seem to see him still
> So clearly, that everywhere
> I look I swear he's standing there . . .
> Heavens!

ELVIRA.

>   They cannot have your teeth
> Removed for swearing what is true,

My lady. I swear it too!

VICENTE (*aside*).

And I,
That I had never come with you!

DON LOPE (*aside*).
But it's the girl I saw before.

Aloud.

Oh, lovely prodigy! Oh, miracle
Of beauty! Tell me who you are!

DOÑA VIOLANTE.
Oh form created by my fantasy,
Illusion now reality,
Oh phantom of my fevered thoughts,
Projected image firmly caught,
Illusion, image, phantom, form,
Who have no voice, no soul, no flesh,
And yet have flesh and soul and voice,
How did you enter here?

DON LOPE.

Oh vision clothed
By my imagination, let
Me ask my question first, so you
Dispel my doubt: what are you doing here?

DOÑA VIOLANTE.
This is my home.

DON LOPE.

Mine too, and so . . .

DOÑA VIOLANTE.
No more! Don't lie to me!

DON LOPE (*to* ELVIRA).

Then you,
So she is properly informed,
Must listen to me now.

ELVIRA.

Why me?
You speak to her, you ghostly fellow.
She's the one who seems to fancy you,
Not me.

DON LOPE.

I beg you, do not be

So ruled by fear. I am the son
Of this respected household, come
To tell my mother Blanca everything
That's happened. I know she'll want to ask
Don Mendo for the favour that
He's offered me. I used this key
To enter, never imagining
That someone else would venture here
Before me. So now I've rescued you
From your astonishment, you have
To do the same for me, and by
Your explanation bring about
My disillusionment.

DOÑA VIOLANTE.

                              What you
Are saying now, I knew. The fear
I felt was more to do with what
I thought than what I knew; and yet
Your explanation does not put
An end to fear. No sooner does
It fade, another greater fear fills
My heart, and what seemed empty then
Becomes a dread more deep and genuine,
Which, true or false, becomes more frightening.
I am a guest. My servants came
Ahead of me to find a place
Where I might stay and rest awhile.
Your father has, I'm told, another room,
Which I suggest you find as soon
As possible. I think you'll serve
Me best by leaving me alone.

DON LOPE.

Such is the beauty you possess,
I do confess my worship has
Become idolatry, though it
Is at the same time filled with such
Respect and sympathy, such deep
Concern and true humility,
That any love that I may feel
Is also my desire to obey.
May God be with you now. I'll have
You know no other person in

This world has ever curbed my will
Or shown that he could ever still
My wild impetuosity.

DOÑA VIOLANTE.

May God be with you too. I am
Indebted to your generosity.
No one, I swear, has ever made
Me feel as I do now.

DON LOPE.

I'd offer up
My life in payment of that debt!

DOÑA VIOLANTE.

Then listen how you pay me best.

DON LOPE.

But how?

DOÑA VIOLANTE.

By leaving now, at once.

DON LOPE.

No sooner said than done. Vicente!

VICENTE.

Come on, master! Show some sense!
I want to stay the night and get
Some well-earned rest!

DOÑA VIOLANTE (aside).

Oh, heavens! What love
Is this?

DON LOPE (aside).

What beauty this?

DOÑA VIOLANTE (aside).

. . . That now
Attracts without desire?

DON LOPE (aside).

Appeals without love's burning fire?

DOÑA VIOLANTE.

May God
Go with you, Lope.

DON LOPE.

God be with
You, Violante.

Act Two

Enter DON LOPE *and* VICENTE, *dressed for the road, and, from the opposite side of the stage,* DOÑA BLANCA *and* DON LOPE, *the elder.*

DON LOPE.
    Let this become the happiest
    Of days, my lord. And let me kneel,
    In recognition of my love,
    At your feet.

DON LOPE, the elder.
              Arise, my son.
    We welcome you as parents who
    Have waited long to have you home
    With us.

DON LOPE.
        Unless you let me kiss
    Your hand, my lord, to do as you
    Command would be remiss of me.

DON LOPE, the elder.
    Then kiss my hand, and may you prove
    To be as good a son as I
    Would have you be. Now kiss your mother's hand.

DON LOPE.
    I come before you, madam, filled
    With fear and shame, and knowing too
    That for the tears those eyes have shed
    I bear the greatest blame.

DOÑA BLANCA.
               You bear
    The blame, my son, not just for those
    But these as well, though if the truth
    Be told and tears seem the same,
    They were the outward signs of grief
    And these of joy. You are most welcome home.

VICENTE.
    And will you let another man,

A true companion to the devil,
Living rough amongst the rocks,
And suffering for someone else's knocks,
Now also kiss your hand, madam?

DON LOPE, the elder.
What kind of spectacle are you?
Don't tell me you've come with him too!

VICENTE.
My lord, I am his saddle-bags,
A seat to sit on when he flags,
A back to bear him like some nag's.
It follows, then, as day and night,
He always has me in his sights.

DON LOPE, the elder.
I'm sure company as fine
As this must guarantee my son's
Improvement!

VICENTE.
                    I do agree, my lord.
By Christ, my company is excellent.

DON LOPE, the elder.
Control your language!

VICENTE.
                                    The custom and
The usage, sir, of that disreputable life
I led. I beg you, madam, let
Me kiss your hand, or otherwise
The ground your lovely feet now tread.

DOÑA BLANCA.
You shall not kneel. I wish to thank
You for the steadfast loyalty
You've shown my son, despite what you,
On his account, have borne.

VICENTE.
                                        That is,
Madam, because I am a servant born
Into this world 'ad perpetuam
Rei memoriam'.

Enter BEATRIZ.

BEATRIZ.
> Has my lord come?
> Forgive me, sir, if I, despite
> Your presence here, do welcome him like this.

DON LOPE.
> May God protect you, Beatriz.

DON LOPE, the elder.
> The happiness that fills our hearts
> Fills mine especially; but now
> I think the time has come when we
> Must thank Don Mendo; firstly, Lope, for
> The kindness he has shown to us,
> And then for pleading for your own
> Forgiveness. Beatriz, see if
> Don Mendo's free. Lope, attend
> Me now. We'll speak as man to man.

VICENTE (aside).
> And listen to his boring sermon!

DON LOPE.
> Patience, Vicente. I've told you already.
> The old man preaches constantly.   •

> *Exit* BEATRIZ.

DON LOPE, the elder.
> Consider for yourself, my son,
> The current, wretched state of our fortunes.
> What wealth we had was never great,
> But now the family estate
> Has been reduced to almost nothing.
> The girl, Estefanía, is, of course,
> To blame for much of this, since I
> Have guaranteed her upkeep in
> The convent, and have myself therefore
> On her account become so poor,
> I almost have to beg from door
> To door. But this, I'm glad to say,
> Is in the past and you, my son,
> Through Mendo's generosity,
> Are finally forgiven. So now
> I only ask one thing of you,
> Though tears fill my eyes, though
> All my words are pitiable sighs,

Though I, despite this old, white hair,
Should see myself obliged to ask
It on my knees . . . I only ask,
My son, that from today you live
Your life a good deal differently,
And try to please your father. Let
Us therefore now be friends and seek
To put an end to arguments
And rivalries that in the past
So bitterly divided us.
We'll each of us attempt to live
In greater peace and harmony,
I, for my part, exercising love,
Compassion, tenderness; you, for yours,
Obedience to my wishes. I ask
You this, my son, as your father,
Remembering that who protects
You now may not be able to
If circumstances were to change.
I mean by this that if you take
Advantage of such love as is
Now offered you, this could one day
Become a motive for revenge,
In which your very life might be
The final sacrifice.

VICENTE (*aside*).

               Oh what
A piece of good advice! If only he'd
Included heaven and hell, we'd all
Be converts to religion's spell!

DON LOPE.

My lord, I promise from today
You'll see a transformation so
Complete, you'll think my past mistakes
Deliberately planned to pave
The way for my conversion.

Enter DON MENDO *and* BEATRIZ.

DON MENDO.

               And I
Now guarantee that resolutions made
In such good faith are kept.

DON LOPE, the elder.

My lord!

DON MENDO.

Since both of you now wish to speak
To me, I thought it only fair
That I, as your guest, should seek
You out as quickly as I could.

DON LOPE, the elder.

Not only do you favour us,
My friend. You do so with a grace
And pleasing courtesy that make
The favour even more acceptable.

DON LOPE.

I humbly kiss your hand, my lord.
May God protect you in the service of
The King and always keep you safe
From envy's venomous attacks,
That fierce basilisk that dwells
In courts and palaces. I only ask
That fame may favour you instead
And celebrate your name engraved
Eternally in pure gold.

DON MENDO.

My boy, I offer you my arms.
Such thanks as you now offer me
Are scarcely warranted by anything
I've done; for since I owe you both
My honour and my life and am
Indebted to you twice, this pardon is
But one repayment of the larger sum.

DOÑA BLANCA.

My lord, may Heaven reward . . .

DON MENDO.

There is

No need, my dear Blanca. Not
A word. I think your silence far
More eloquent.

DOÑA BLANCA.

Then I must thank
You sir, for what would otherwise
Have been embarrassment.

Exit BLANCA.

DON MENDO.
> I have to take my leave. The King
> Would speak with me.

DON LOPE, the elder.
>   And I must also see
> To certain matters.

DON LOPE.
>   If it were possible,
> I'd serve you equally, but since
> I am obliged to choose, I shall,
> If I'm allowed, accompany
> Don Mendo.

DON LOPE, the elder.
>   Of course you can, my boy.
> And I applaud and envy such
> A choice. Attend Don Mendo well.
> He merits your loyal service.

Exit DON LOPE, *the elder.*

DON MENDO.
> To have you serve me thus is most
> Agreeable, but more than that
> Extremely sensible. For if
> You come with me, I shall not feel
> The need to stay with you, and thus
> Give satisfaction to my soul
> Whose only pleasure and delight
> Is now to have you always in its sight.

Exit DON MENDO *and* DON LOPE. *Enter* VICENTE *and*
BEATRIZ.

VICENTE.
> Listen, Beatriz.

BEATRIZ.
>   What is it?

VICENTE.
> I thought that since our masters are
> Now gone, and you and me are face
> To face at last, and no one else
> Has really welcomed me, you might . . .

Embrace me.

BEATRIZ.

                        Oh, yes? You know what you
Can do with your fancy!

VICENTE.

                        But Beatriz!
If you knew all the agonies
That I've gone through for you.

BEATRIZ.

                        What I
Know's this. I've waited here what seems
Like half a century. And have
You ever been to look for me
Just once? Oh, no!

VICENTE.

                Now that's not fair.
Was I not here a night or two
Ago, me and my master there
In old Don Mendo's bedroom, just
As if we were at home? And Violante,
Your mistress, half-undressed, and all
That whispering: 'Hang-on, who's that?
Oh, it's a man. No, two of them.
It must be some fantastic vision'.

BEATRIZ.

All right, enough of that. It's not
Some complicated novel's plot.

VICENTE.

In God's name, Beatriz. It is.
It's just as if my master's found
A book he can't put down and so
He reads from dusk to dawn. The way
He carries on, he neither lets
Me eat or sleep, but keeps me wide
Awake with that same boring question:
'Was she better looking when her hair
Was up or down?'

BEATRIZ.

                Do you think you can
Get round me with a tale like that?

VICENTE.
>Oh, come on, Beatriz. No need
>To get so uppity.

BEATRIZ.
>   And you,
>Because your master is in love,
>Don't have to be his secretary.
>I've had my eye on you. I've seen
>How you make up to that Elvira.
>I'm not so sure it's only messages
>You give her!

VICENTE.
>   If you had been as close
>To her as me, I swear, sweet Beatriz,
>She wouldn't give you any cause
>For jealousy.

BEATRIZ.
>   Why wouldn't she?

VICENTE.
>She is the serpent with nine heads
>Personified. Believe me, Beatriz,
>One night I caught her unawares.
>She'd taken off her wig. I saw
>Her smooth and bony skull exposed.

BEATRIZ.
>What do you mean?

VICENTE.
>   No hair she'd call
>Her own.

BEATRIZ.
>   Do you mean bald?

VICENTE.
>   I've never seen
>A hard-boiled egg so smooth. But then
>There's more. I saw quite clearly
>That when she smiled there was inside
>Her mouth a marked deficiency
>Of what you might describe as any mouth's
>True property – in short, no teeth.
>Believe me, Beatriz, the gospel truth!

BEATRIZ.
>I can't believe a girl so beautiful
>Should, when she smiles, display a set
>Of teeth that are so . . . artificial.

VICENTE.
>You ought to see the rest of her,
>Though perhaps it's better if I just
>Keep quiet on the matter. I mean,
>I am a man of infinite discretion.
>I wouldn't want to do no harm
>To any lady's reputation.
>Hey, here's my master. Now old Mendo's gone,
>His thoughts are turning to his daughter.

BEATRIZ.
>I'd better go. Whoever would
>Believe of such a lovely face
>As hers that it could be so ugly?
>I think that what they say may well
>Be right: that when a girl puts on
>Her face, the darkest night is still
>Her best accessory.

Enter DON LOPE. *Exit* BEATRIZ.

DON LOPE.
>Vicente. Have you seen the lady
>Violante waiting at her window?

VICENTE.
>No, my lord. And if I had, I swear
>To you I wouldn't know her.

DON LOPE.
>   How so?

VICENTE.
>It's my new policy. The things
>That don't concern me don't impinge
>Upon my memory. Why fill
>It up, like some great empty room,
>With other people's property?

DON LOPE.
>I cannot think it possible
>You could forget such perfect hair,
>Or how those golden locks were waves

That glittered in the evening air.
In every other case, the sea
Consists of pearls that run across
The golden sand, while here the hair
Upon that snow-white neck was one
Great stream of gold that swept towards
The pearl-like land. Can't you remember?

VICENTE.

Sorry, master, no I can't, nor do
I wish to when I was myself
Completely dazzled by Elvira.
I don't believe that beauty's in
The eye of the beholder. Your
Violante is no match for her.

DON LOPE.

Don't be a fool!

VICENTE.

How can I be
When we are taught by history
That servants are quite often much
Superior?

DON LOPE.

If only I could catch
A glimpse of Violante!

VICENTE.

Have you
Forgotten, sir, you've only just
Been pardoned by your dear father?
To mess about with her's to jump
Out of the frying-pan into the fire.

DON LOPE.

To have my father preach to me
Drives me insane. How can I hold
Myself in check, you fool, if you
Now do the same? Is it the case
I can do anything at all
And not be blamed for it? Who's this?

VICENTE.

It's Don Guillén de Azagra.

DON LOPE.

Say

No more. I'd rather talk to you
Than deal with such a crushing bore.

Enter DON GUILLÉN.

DON LOPE.
   What brings you, Don Guillén,
   To Saragossa?

DON GUILLÉN.
                  I found, my friend,
   I could not stay away a moment more.
   As soon as someone told me you
   Were here, I looked for you: not only so
   That I could say how truly pleased
   I am to see you here, but hopefully
   To hear you say the same of me.

DON LOPE.
   Such warmth and generosity
   As this, Guillén, is but the true
   Expression of the depth of our former
   Friendship. In order to respond
   To it in kind, I bid you too
   The warmest and most generous
   Of welcomes here.

DON GUILLÉN.
                  If only that
   Could be for someone who pursues
   A certain cause devotedly,
   And at the same time knows his hopes
   Are bound to be most cruelly
   Deceived.

DON LOPE.
                  Whatever can you mean,
   My friend?

DON GUILLÉN.
                  It's three years since I went
   To fight in Italy.

DON LOPE.
                  I well
   Remember how you said goodbye
   In Seo square. You were so full
   Of bitter tears and gloomy sighs,

I think in retrospect they must
Have been some kind of prophecy
Of all the future knocks and blows
That fortune had in store for me.

DON GUILLÉN.

I was informed of them and do
Assure you I deeply felt
Such undeserved misfortune. But let
Me speak of mine, which now begin
As yours end. I know that they
Can be resolved with your help,
My friend.

DON LOPE.

Then I shall do whatever you
Demand of me. Your every wish
Is my command.

DON GUILLÉN.

We landed, as
You know, in Naples, where our King
Attempted to avenge the death
Of Conradinus, Caesar's son,
Condemned to public execution by
The King of Naples. But this is by
The way, for what I wish to say
To you concerns a lady I
Saw there. To look upon her was
To see the sun itself contained in one
Small sphere, the Spring embodied in
A flower, the dawn reduced to just
One tear. But even such comparisons
As these are quite unfair once you
Begin to realize the lady I
Saw there was . . .

VICENTE.

Doña Violante, sir.

DON LOPE.

What do you mean? A curse on you!

VICENTE.

I mean I've just this moment seen
Her, master, coming from her room.
She went to come this way, but when

She saw that we were standing here,
She stopped and went away again.

DON LOPE.
I think, Guillén, you ought to wait
Outside. Far better to be patient now
Than cause the lady possible
Embarrassment.

DON GUILLÉN.
                    I do agree.
Besides, I think it best she does
Not see me in your company.

Exit GUILLÉN.

DON LOPE.
By God! I thought he was about
To say the girl that took his eye
Was Violante!

VICENTE.
                    So how was I
To know that you on her account
Were going crazy? You'd better speak
To her before he shows his face
Again.

Enter VIOLANTE *and* ELVIRA.

DON LOPE.
                    My lady! Why is it
You dare to pass this way once more,
When beauty such as yours, contained
In this most perfect sphere, brings both
The dawn and dusk together? For when
You now approach, you are the dawn,
In whose bright sun I quickly burn,
But when you leave you straight away
Become the dusk, informing us
The sun has swiftly gone. No, do
Not go! Proceed. I swear there is
No need for you to be afraid
Of me. Observe that it is day,
Not night, that I do not intend
To frighten you as I did once
Before. I come, instead, to offer you

My thanks, my constant loyalty,
But even more than that, my life.

DOÑA VIOLANTE.
The fear that I felt that night
Stays with me still, and though I see
You now by day more clearly,
I wonder if you are of flesh and blood,
Or some pale ghost resolved to haunt
Me till the day I die. I came
This way to speak to Doña Blanca, when
I suddenly caught sight of some
Mysterious stranger standing here,
Another ghost, perhaps, since he
Preferred the shadows to the light.

DON LOPE.
A friend of mine. He wished to speak
With me, but as he saw you come
Towards us, prudently withdrew
So he would not embarrass you.
The man who most adores you knows
The best defence against disdain
Is timely absence, which, in turn
Provides this opportunity for me
To speak to you . . .

DOÑA VIOLANTE (*to Elvira*).
                          Do you think the man
Was Don Guillén?

ELVIRA.
                          I think it was.

DOÑA VIOLANTE (*aside*).
Then everything that Lope says
He says on Don Guillén's behalf.

DON LOPE.
My dearest wish is that you grant
Me now the opportunity
That here presents itself to prove
My steadfast and undying loyalty.

DOÑA VIOLANTE.
I have to say I find extremes
Of loyalty not so much moving as
Intensely boring.

DON LOPE.
                    You mean you would
    Deny me life?

DOÑA VIOLANTE.
                    You mean your life
    Should be considered equal to
    This opportunity?

DON LOPE.
                    Is it
    Not true that both may equally
    Be lost and not recovered?

DOÑA VIOLANTE.
                    Then I
    Suggest you make the most of it,
    In case you never have the chance
    To speak again. What would you have
    Of me?

DON LOPE.
            I would remind you of
    A debt you owe to someone's memory.

DOÑA VIOLANTE.
    And why must you agree to be
    A mere intermediary
    For someone else?

DON LOPE.
                    Because he is
    Not bold enough to speak to you
    Directly. Where love's concerned, the man
    Who seems so bold is often overcome
    By modesty.

DOÑA VIOLANTE.
                    In that case I
    Refuse to listen any more.
    The truth is that the memory
    To which you say I owe a debt
    Is something that upsets me so,
    I cannot bear to think of it.
    No doubt you thought reminding me
    Of that might waken in my heart
    Sweet thoughts of love; but you are quite
    Mistaken. Tell him that. Goodbye.

DON LOPE.
>   But wait.

DOÑA VIOLANTE.
>   I've nothing more to say.

Exit VIOLANTE.

DON LOPE (*aside*).
>   She knew that I was on the point
>   Of saying what I feel for her,
>   And being just as clever as
>   She's beautiful, resorted to
>   The very stratagem I'd used
>   To tell me what a fool I am
>   In thus pursuing her. Oh, this
>   Is hard to bear! (*To* VICENTE.) If Don Guillén
>   Returns, inform him I'll be back.
>   I'll meet him here.

Exit DON LOPE.

VICENTE.
>   Why, Madam Elvira . . .

ELVIRA.
>   What, you back here
>   Again?

VICENTE.
>   To look upon this face by day
>   Is not to be afraid of me.

ELVIRA.
>   To look upon that face suggests
>   It doesn't matter if it's day or night;
>   It's ugly constantly.

VICENTE.
>   I've come to ask
>   Of you just one great favour.

ELVIRA.
>   Which is?

VICENTE.
>   Be crazy for me. Let me be
>   Your saviour. I never make impossible
>   Demands on any sweet young lady.

ELVIRA.
>I think I might consider it
>If I did not already know
>That for a certain Beatriz
>Vicente had a so-called fancy.

VICENTE.
>Who?

ELVIRA.
>I told you: Beatriz. I do
>Have eyes, you know. You can't deny
>The truth.

VICENTE.
>I don't deny the truth.
>I do deny I fancy Beatriz.
>If you knew her, you'd have the certain proof
>Of it.

ELVIRA.
>Which is?

VICENTE.
>That she was fashioned from
>A mould that, so I'm told, was used
>For making hideous monsters in
>The ancient world. You see how on
>The outside everything about
>Her seems so beautiful. If you
>Get really close to her, you'll get
>Your lungs full of the awful smell
>That tells you that she rots inside.
>And if you think that's bad, there's more
>Besides that I could tell, but since
>I am a man of infinite
>Good taste refuse to dwell on, except
>To say I've seen her put her glass-
>Eye in and fix her wooden-leg on.

ELVIRA.
>I don't believe a word of it.
>The whole thing's just a pack of lies.

VICENTE.
>Well, when you see her next, watch how
>She walks, and have a good look in
>Her eyes.

Enter DON GUILLÉN.

DON GUILLÉN (*aside*).
>   Has Violante gone?
> Did Lope stay behind? If only I
> Could speak to her, perhaps I'd have
> Some peace of mind.

Enter DON LOPE.

DON LOPE (*aside*).
>   Violante's safely in
> My father's company. I'll see
> If Don Guillén still looks for me.

ELVIRA.
> The two of them are coming back

VICENTE.
> I'd better go. I'll speak to you again.

ELVIRA.
> God be with you. (*Aside.*) Whoever would
> Have said of Beatriz, whose looks
> Are praised by everyone throughout the land,
> That, when it comes to close-analysis,
> So many of her parts are second-hand?

Exit ELVIRA.

DON LOPE.
> Forgive me, Don Guillén. I had
> To speak to Violante.

DON GUILLÉN.
>   Do not
> Apologize, my friend. I understand.

DON LOPE.
> Proceed, then, with your story.

DON GUILLÉN.
>   Ah, yes.
> Of course. Where were we?

DON LOPE.
>   As I recall,
> In Naples, and on the point
> Of being fascinated by
> A certain lady.

DON GUILLÉN.
                There's something else
  I should have mentioned to you too.

DON LOPE.
  What's that?

DON GUILLÉN.
                When it was known the war
  Would soon be over, Don Mendo was
  Ambassador in Rome. And since
  He'd served the King for many years
  In France and Italy, and had
  Experience of those things, he was
  At once commanded by King Pedro to
  Proceed to Naples, where he could
  Discuss the treaty to be signed.
  In saying that, I think I have
  Disclosed to you the lady's name.
  For if Don Mendo was the man
  Then sent to Italy; and if
  The girl I saw so fascinated me
  That I have come to Saragossa more
  In hope than certainty, and meeting you
  Again have asked you if you'll help
  Me seek some remedy for love,
  It will be clear to you now
  The one that I adore above
  All else is Violante, deity
  Supreme, upon whose altar I
  Would willingly surrender both
  My life and soul.

VICENTE (aside).
                If you ask me,
  I think we're in a bit of trouble.
  I'll take a bet, before he leaves,
  My master goes and bursts his bubble.

DON LOPE (aside).
  Whoever saw confusion such
  As this? But for the moment let's
  Pretend that nothing is amiss,
  And though the cup is poisoned, drink
  It up, and let him think he has
  Good cause to dream of happiness.

Aloud.

You praise her rightly, Don Guillén.
On any other girl such praise
And flattery as you now pour
On her would certainly be wasted.
But if I am to do what you
Have asked me to, I need to know
If Violante favours you.

DON GUILLÉN.

Two words describe the state of my
Relationship with her.

DON LOPE.

                              They are?

DON GUILLÉN.

The first is love, the second hate;
Which is to say that I love her,
But she does not reciprocate
My love. Instead she hates me.

VICENTE (*aside*).

I do feel sorry for him. Even so,
I'm very keen to hear a little more.

DON GUILLÉN.

As soon as I discovered she
Had come to Saragossa, I resolved
To follow her, and if I could,
With your help, attempt to make
Her favour me. The fact that she
Is now a guest in your house
Means I can visit you and at
The same time hope to see and speak
To her. But even so, I now
Implore you that you intervene
On my behalf, and since there might
Not ever be a better opportunity
Than this, that you explore what ways
You can of handing her a letter I
Propose to write. I have not told
Her I am here, and so prefer
To stay away from her, and not
Allow surprise the chance to make
Her more annoyed with me than she

Already is. I'll write the letter soon.
I'd write it now if only I
Could get into your room. Wait here.
I shan't be long. I'll bring it with me.

Exit DON GUILLÉN.

VICENTE.
I'm off, then, master. See you soon.

DON LOPE.
What do you mean? Off where? Vicente!

VICENTE.
I'll see you in the mountains shortly.
The way that things are going here.
It won't be long before you join me.

DON LOPE.
But there's no need. I have respect
For Violante. The thought that he
Loves her offends me, true, but since
I love her more, I shall behave
Impeccably. It's most unusual
To see that what offends me now
Controls me too. I shall endure it,
And in the meantime try to find
Some cure for this ill that at
The same time leaves him hoping still.

VICENTE.
I'm glad to see such common-sense
At last prevail. Can I suggest
A plan that never fails?

DON LOPE.
                                        What is
It, man?

VICENTE.
                    You just walk out on her.
I mean, you're only at the start of things.
Won't do no harm to clip your wings.

DON LOPE.
Believe me, I would do it if
I could. But now I can't. And if
I did, I know that it would be
In vain.

VICENTE.
>   So if you can't, what will
>   You do?

DON LOPE.
>   The answer is impossible.
>   But wait. Here's Violante.

VICENTE.
>   That
>   Was quick.

DON LOPE.
>   For anyone in love
>   A moment seems a century.

Enter VIOLANTE.

DOÑA VIOLANTE.
>   Don Lope! You here still?

DON LOPE.
>   It is,
>   My lady, nature's principle,
>   That every object always seeks
>   The thing it is attracted to.
>   The river, winding constantly,
>   Will always flow into the sea;
>   The stone, wherever it is thrown,
>   Returns to earth, its proper home;
>   The wind, no matter what its source,
>   Seeks other winds, adds to their force;
>   And fire, though it barely smoulders,
>   Always bursts into a bonfire.
>   And so I too am now that stream
>   That seeks the sea of my anxiety;
>   That stone that, falling to the earth,
>   Cannot deny the force of gravity;
>   That wind that flies with sudden force
>   Towards the world of fantasy;
>   That flame that, bursting into fire,
>   Engulfs me in my misery;
>   And therefore burnt, blown, swept, thrown,
>   Must, like the wind, the stream, the flame, the stone
>   Now seek the earth, the air, the fire, the sea.

DOÑA VIOLANTE.
>   Don Lope, though I cannot claim

To understand philosophy,
I understand the meaning of
Your words, and yet their object is
A mystery.

DON LOPE.

        Then it is easily
Explained, for if I say that where
You are my soul will always be,
My meaning will be plain.

DOÑA VIOLANTE.

                And yet
The sentiment is not, I think,
The same as one that went before.

DON LOPE.

How so?

DOÑA VIOLANTE.

        Because you acted then
As intermediary for someone else,
But now you speak much more directly.

DON LOPE.

The style no longer pleases me.
Besides, it is important now
That what I have to say should not
In any way be clouded by
Obscurity. I must begin
By speaking on behalf of Don
Guillén . . .

Enter DON GUILLÉN. *He listens at the door.*

DON GUILLÉN (*aside*).

        This is my lucky day!
He speaks to her of me.

DON LOPE.

             . . . who's come
From Italy to Aragón.
He is the very sunflower
To your love, his movement governed by
The light you pour on him from up
Above; a kind of human plant
Endowed with reason, who's told me what
To say on his behalf and begs

You listen.

DON GUILLÉN (*aside*).

He is the very best
Of friends, the soul of loyalty!
But someone comes and forces me
To turn away. I cannot hear how she
Replies.

Exit DON GUILLÉN.

DOÑA VIOLANTE.

I cannot think this second style
Is less offensive than the first,
When both of them take liberties.
And yet I think I might perhaps
Forgive the one that seems the more
Agreeable.

DON LOPE.

Then I must know
The one for which you think that sweet
Forgiveness possible. You are
The only one who can resolve
The utter muddle of my thoughts.

DOÑA VIOLANTE.

I want you to reply to Don
Guillén. He seems to think that I
Am interested in him, in which
Case tell him he is quite mistaken.
He knows he's had no luck with me,
And I can only offer misery.

DON LOPE.

And what of me? What must I tell
Myself?

DOÑA VIOLANTE.

I would have thought that in
A case in which the magistrate
Had sentenced someone else, you might
Have guessed . . .

DON LOPE.

Guessed what?

DOÑA VIOLANTE.

He'd sentence you

Quite differently. For had the sentence been
The same, he would have joined
Your name to his, concluding both
Of you were equally to blame.

DON LOPE.
That's true. I could not bring
Myself at first to speak as openly
As I would like.

Enter DON GUILLÉN. *He stops and listens.*

DON GUILLÉN (*aside*).
                         The stranger's gone at last.
Let's see if I am still the subject of
Their conversation.

DOÑA VIOLANTE.
                         And so, for now,
Don Lope, I shall say no more,
Except to say that though I've always been
As hard as diamond, bronze or stone,
Resisting every effort of
The chisel or the file to hone
And smooth the roughness of its surface,
I also know that in the end
The hardest diamond or stone
Will not resist the efforts of
The man who strives sufficiently.

DON GUILLÉN (*aside*).
Thank heavens! Violante speaks of me
In such a way I must conclude
She has developed gentle qualities.

DON LOPE.
I kiss your hands a thousand times
In gratitude for favours such
As these.

DON GUILLÉN (*aside*).
                         This is a friend indeed!
Why, anyone would think that he's
The one in need of love, and she's
His saviour!

DON LOPE.
                         My joy would be complete

    If now, my lady, you could offer me
    A gift as final proof of your favour.

DOÑA VIOLANTE.
    Take this flower. Let it be
    The symbol of my hope, for it
    Proclaims hope's bright and happy colour.

    Exit VIOLANTE.

DON LOPE.
    I swear that this shall live eternally.
    The icy winds that blow from north
    And west shall never blight or stunt
    Its flawless beauty. Happy is
    The man who has this flower!

DON GUILLÉN.
                    Happier still
    The man to whom you now deliver it,
    When Violante is its owner,
    And you her trusted messenger!
    I kneel in gratitude at your feet.

VICENTE (*aside*).
    Whoever saw a pair as sweet
    As this?

DON GUILLÉN.
              And here acknowledge that
    This debt is doubly due, for you,
    Don Lope, have not merely offered me
    Your friendship but the precious gift
    Of this most green and lovely flower.
    I could not take it without first
    Acclaiming that true friendship that is ours.

DON LOPE.
    You'd best get up, Guillén: for if
    This flower is the cause of these
    Extremes, it's also possible
    Its colour may not always be
    What it now seems.

DON GUILLÉN.
              What do you mean?

VICENTE (*aside*).
    The feller can't have heard the song

That says the green of hope becomes
Before too long the green of jealousy.

DON LOPE.
I mean that though the flower in
My hand belongs to Violante,
It doesn't follow it's for you.

DON GUILLÉN.
I heard you speak to her of all
My qualities.

DON LOPE.
Quite true.

DON GUILLÉN.
And then,
Although a stranger interrupted me,
I heard her say this flower should
Be seen as evidence that mountains can
Be moved, the diamond made soft,
The hardest marble in the end made smooth.

DON LOPE.
Then this is one occasion when
The man who listened did not listen to
The story of his own misfortunes.

DON GUILLÉN.
You have to tell me more.

DON LOPE.
It seems,
Before you were distracted, you
Heard everything that flattered you,
But, when you were away, missed other things
That mattered even more, of which
The most important is that Violante finds
Your constant love a constant bore.

DON GUILLÉN.
So who was Violante speaking of
That she regards more tenderly?

DON LOPE.
Why, me, of course!

VICENTE (aside).
He is the soul of honesty!

DON GUILLÉN.
  You?

DON LOPE.
    Yes.

DON GUILLÉN.
    I warn you, Lope, do
  Not make me doubt the constancy
  Of your friendship.

DON LOPE.
        Why doubt the truth
  Of what I say? Why not accept it?

DON GUILLÉN.
  Come now! You've had your bit of fun.
  The joke is over. Give me the flower!

DON LOPE.
  The flower's mine, and being so,
  Is not, I think, designed for you.

DON GUILLÉN.
  Not true! The flower's mine. It's time
  That you surrendered it.

DON LOPE.
        I'd like
  To know exactly how, Guillén.
  You think you'll get it.

DON GUILLÉN.
        Let's go outside.
  We'll see if swords can't now decide
  Whose flower it is, and at the same
  Time punish broken promises.

DON LOPE.
  Just lead the way. Let no one say
  I ever disobey.

    Exit DON GUILLÉN.

    Enter DOÑA BLANCA *and* DONÃ VIOLANTE *from opposite
    sides of the stage.*

DOÑA VIOLANTE.
        Don Lope! What's
  Going on?

DON LOPE.
                    Why, nothing, madam.

VICENTE.
                              Do you think
    That we behave like hooligans?

DOÑA BLANCA.
    I heard two voices arguing.

DOÑA VIOLANTE.
    And I the sound of quarrelling.

DOÑA BLANCA.
    Where are you going?

DON LOPE.
                    Let me pass.
    It's nothing, I assure you.

DOÑA VIOLANTE.
    Don Lope, wait.

DON LOPE.
                    I'll do exactly what
    You want in just a minute.

DOÑA BLANCA.
                              God
    Forbid this is some new dispute!

VICENTE.
    Believe me, madam, not a word
    Of truth in it!

DOÑA VIOLANTE.
                    Then why are you
    So clearly upset?

DON LOPE.
                    I think you let
    Your fears run away with you.
    I'm not upset.

DOÑA BLANCA.
                    Since you arrived,
    There's not a moment yet I've had
    Some peace of mind.

DON LOPE.
                    My lady! (*Aside.*) This
    Is quite impossible! (*Aloud.*) How have I

Offended you?

DOÑA VIOLANTE.

                  I want to know
What you are up to!

DOÑA BLANCA.

                       What it is
You plan to do!

VICENTE.

                    I've told you twice.
It's ages since we had a good to-do!

Enter DON LOPE, *the elder.*

DON LOPE, the elder.

    What noise is this? Why, Lope, are
You so distraught, so angry both
With Blanca and Violante? What's
The cause of it?

DOÑA BLANCA.

               My lord . . . (*Aside.*) Heaven grant
Me ingenuity to hide
From him the truth of this . . . (*Aloud.*) It's just
That Lope and Vicente had
Some angry words, and since we overheard . . .

VICENTE (*aside*).

    My God, I didn't know I was
Involved in it!

DOÑA VIOLANTE.

                We thought that we'd
Resolve it peacefully.

DON LOPE, the elder.

                  Why, Lope, must
You always act so rashly?

DON LOPE.

                       It
Was really nothing, father.

VICENTE.

                    Just
A bit of fuss and bother over what
I owed him.

DON LOPE.
>   All right, Vicente, we'll
>   Forget it.

VICENTE.
>   No, we shan't. I'll have
>   You know I always pay my debts.

>   *Exit* VICENTE.

DON LOPE, the elder.
>   I cannot understand why you,
>   In such a trivial matter, act
>   With total disrespect in front
>   Of Violante and your mother.

DON LOPE.
>   Nor I, my lord. I know no words
>   Can justify my wild behaviour.
>   I therefore have to let my silence be
>   My only answer. (*Aside.*) I have to get
>   Away from here and find Guillén.

>   *Exit* DON LOPE.

DOÑA BLANCA.
>   Please make him stay, my lord.

DON LOPE, the elder.
>   I think
>   It better if he has his way.
>   Forgive him, Blanca! His anger is
>   Most strange. He lacks respect for anyone.

DOÑA VIOLANTE.
>   As far as I'm concerned, he is
>   Forgiven. (*Aside.*) And I'm the only one
>   To blame.

DOÑA BLANCA (*aside*).
>   It was my aim to ensure
>   He stayed, but now I've offered him
>   An open door. What can I do?

DOÑA VIOLANTE (*aside*).
>   I fear some disaster's near.

>   *Sound of swords off.*

DON GUILLÉN (*off*).
>   This is the way I take revenge

On any so-called friend who proves
A traitor.

DON LOPE (*off*).

You mean you haven't heard
All's fair in love and war?

DON LOPE, the elder.

What's that?

Enter ELVIRA *and* BEATRIZ.

ELVIRA.
A sword-fight in the street!

BEATRIZ.

My master's one
Of them. Hurry, sir! It's your son!
What are you waiting for?

DON LOPE, the elder.

I knew
That not a day would pass before
There was some trouble. Oh, let me feel
A father's love! Though if the truth
Be told, I've never in my life
Felt true enthusiasm for anything
Affecting him.

Exit all. Enter DON GUILLÉN *and* DON LOPE, *swords
drawn. People try to intervene. Enter* DON LOPE, *the elder.*

DON LOPE, the elder.

Don Lope, stop!
Don Guillén!

DON GUILLÉN.

A friend who's false . . .

DON LOPE.
The one who's false is . . .

DON LOPE, the elder.

Why, when I
Am here, do you not put aside
Your sword?

DON LOPE.

Because you would deprive
Me of the honour which in fact
You never gave me.

DON LOPE, the elder.

       I swear to God,
You have defiled what honour you
Once had. And since you now show no
Respect for this grey head, I beg
You, Don Guillén, that you instead
Respect me now.

DON GUILLÉN.

       My lord, to show
I have respect, I set aside
My sword and hereby give my word
That what has angered me today
Can be resolved another way.

DON LOPE.

  A nice way to disguise the fact
You are afraid of me!

DON GUILLÉN.

       Just see
If I'm afraid.

They clash again.

DON LOPE, the elder.

      Listen to me! Stop!
You foolish boy! How is it he
Respects me properly and you
Do not? I swear to God you'll learn
To fear me!

DON LOPE.

      I warn you, do
Not threaten me. These hands shall rip
That stick from your grasp.

DON LOPE, the elder.

        A son
So wild and untoward! You need
To ask Guillén to teach you how
You should behave.

DON LOPE.

      He shows respect
For you because he is a coward.
He is afraid of you, and you
Consider that a shining virtue!

DON GUILLÉN.
>The man who says or even thinks
>I am afraid . . .

DON LOPE, the elder.
>   I'll say it for
>You, Don Guillén. He lies.

DON LOPE.
>   Since you
>Insult me in his name, old man,
>I ask of you the satisfaction I
>Would ask of him.

He strikes his father. The old man falls.

VICENTE.
>   What are you doing?

DON LOPE, the elder.
>Heaven punish you for this, as God
>Is now my witness.

ALL.
>   Help him up!
>The son deserves to die who so
>Offends a poor, helpless father!

They exit, struggling with DON LOPE.

VICENTE.
>I don't know what I'm doing here.
>I haven't done a thing to stir
>This up. I'll help you up, good sir.

DON LOPE, the elder.
>Ungrateful son! I call on heaven
>To punish you for this offence.
>The swords that seek revenge shall be
>The bolts that soon shall end your life.
>For when it is our Lord who's wronged,
>A sword becomes his lightning,
>My son the victim of his wrath,
>A father doomed to endless weeping.
>The hand you raised against this snow-
>White head is equally a hand
>With which you've dared to challenge heaven
>Itself. Why, then, does it not tear

Apart this veil? Why, then, does it
Not in its fury rail against
The air you breathe, consume the earth
You tread, and in a single, blinding flash
Of light now strike you dead?

VICENTE.

Good sir,
Your cape and hat. Let's put it on
Your head for you. Oh, yes, and here's
Your stick.

DON LOPE, the elder.

What use is any stick
If it is made of wood, not iron?
No, give it. It shall serve to bring
To heel a wicked son who has
No feeling for his father. For if,
Like me, it now lies helplessly,
It soon, like me, revives, and punishes
A son who practises such tyranny.
Heaven offers me this stick so I
May take revenge . . . but when I try
To take it in my hand and rise,
I find I cannot stand as firmly on
My feet as I would like . . . oh, harsh
And cruel fate! How can I take
Revenge if what I most depend
On to support me now proves not
To be a source of strength, but more
A fateful pointer to my death?

VICENTE.

Don't talk so loud! Do you know
You've got a crowd of people watching you?

DON LOPE, the elder.

Then let them watch! They know I've not
Much more to lose. Yes, let them see
Me here and be acquainted with
My shame: and see my honour by
That son irreparably stained.
You people, look at me! Observe
A father's life now totally
Destroyed by that same boy who owes
To him his birth; who only through

The spilling of his precious blood
Can now regain his honour and
His own true worth. The justice I
Demand of this ungrateful son,
I seek by pleading both that God,
Our supreme Judge, should punish him;
And secondly, his instrument
Of justice on this earth, our great
And glorious Spanish King. I shall
Inform him of these dark and evil things.

Exit all. DON LOPE, *the elder, and* VICENTE *enter again.*

VICENTE.
    I'm not so sure it's a good
    Idea this, bursting straight into
    The palace.

DON LOPE, the elder.
             I'd just as easily
    Burst through the gates of heaven!

    Calls out.

                       Oh, King
    Don Pedro of Aragón, known to
    The wise as just, to all the ignorant
    As cruel . . .

    Enter the KING, DON MENDO *and attendants.*

KING.
            Who speaks my name?

DON LOPE, the elder.
    A man who's most unfortunate,
    And, kneeling at your feet, now seeks
    Your justice.

KING.
           You are Don Lope. You pleaded for
    Your son who was condemned to die,
    And I, most moved by such a plea,
    Showed him compassion. What do you ask?

DON LOPE, the elder.
    If only I were not obliged
    To ask, your majesty! But now,
    As if to prove how constant is

My loyalty, I come to plead
With you not for your pity but
Your royal justice. My son, if he
Can truly be regarded as
My son (forgive me, Blanca, this
Offence against your innocence,
Compared to which the brightness of
The sun itself grows pale!) has now
Most seriously offended God,
His King, and father too. For when
I reprimanded him, he chose
To disobey, ignoring the command
That we must first love God and then
Our parents, raising his hand instead
Against his father. Because in this
Case vengeance is impossible,
I now appeal to you, my King,
And ask that you, on my behalf,
Proceed to punish him. I pleaded with
You once, you offered pity. I ask
For justice now; do not deny me this,
Or I shall ask that heaven itself
Respond to me. The heavens, the world,
All men must know that when a son
Insults his father so, he drives
Him to such cruelty . . .

Exit DON LOPE, *the elder, and* VICENTE.

KING.
                              Don Mendo . . .

DON MENDO.
    Majesty . . .

KING.
              You are my Lord Chief Justice.
    This is a matter you, as my
    Supreme authority in law,
    Must now address. Arrest the boy.
    Until you've done so, do not rest.

DON MENDO.
    I shall do everything I can,
    Your majesty.

KING.

>Please bear in mind
>This matters more to me than you
>Might think.

DON MENDO.

>But why?

KING.

>Because I think
>No king throughout our history
>Has ever been obliged to deal
>With any case as strange as this.

DON MENDO (*aside*).

>What shall I do? I see such pictures in
>My mind . . . But no, I'll find a way . . .

Aloud.

>Your majesty, it shall be done.

KING.

>You have to find me proof that he
>Is really father to the boy,
>And he the father's real son.

Act Three

Enter DON MENDO, *accompanied by armed men.*

SOLDIER.
> This is the place, my lord. It's where
> The mountain streams rush down to join
> The Ebro's foaming flood, and where
> He thinks that he can hide from us.

DON MENDO.
> Then look for him. Examine every rock,
> Each tree and blade of grass.

Exit all except DON MENDO.

>   Whoever found
> Himself in a predicament
> Like this, when I am forced by someone else
> To seek what in the end must be
> The cause of my unhappiness?
> The King — I cannot tell if he
> Is cruel more than merciful —
> Refuses to allow me to return
> Without the boy as prisoner —
> The thought appalls me so, and yet,
> The feelings that I have for him,
> The everlasting debt I owe
> To him, are things I must consider too.
> If I arrest him, I betray
> My love for him; if I do not,
> I risk the anger of the King.
> Oh, heavens, how can I, torn between
> Both love and duty, possibly
> Resolve such different things?

Enter DON LOPE, *his face bloodied, attempting to keep at bay his pursuers.*

ALL.
>   You can't
> Escape. Give up your sword!

DON LOPE.

                                 I know
> I am to die and yet I give
> My word my life will not be spent
> Until this sword is covered in
> Your blood.

DON MENDO.

                        You must not kill him! The King
> Demands I capture him alive.

Aside.

> If I arrest him now, I'll have
> More time to think of how I may
> Arrive at some more cunning scheme
> To save his life. (*Aloud.*) Don Lope!

DON LOPE.

                                My lord,
> I recognized your voice at once
> But could not see your face when I
> Was three-times blinded by confusion, blood,
> And smoking gunpowder. And still
> I do not know if it is your voice
> I hear, or thunder from above
> That pierces my heart and mind,
> And freezes me with sudden fear.
> What do you want, what do you ask
> Of me? You are the only one,
> The only one, Don Mendo, to arouse
> More dread and fear with your voice
> Than all the others with their guns.

DON MENDO.

> The only thing I ask is that
> You give me your sword and then
> Yourself in custody.

DON LOPE.

                    You mean
> You will arrest me?

DON MENDO.

                    Yes.

DON LOPE.

                        I cannot do

So easily.

DON MENDO.

               You have my word . . .

DON LOPE.

    I know, my lord, and yet I cannot.
    Fear shall not rule me.

DON MENDO.

                 Foolish boy!
    What can you hope to do?

DON LOPE.

                  I'd rather die
    By killing you. And yet it is
    Impossible. No sooner do
    I raise my sword, I tremble at
    The sight of you; no sooner do
    You speak a word, I stumble at
    The sound of you. I drown in tears, choke
    In sighs; and when I take my sword,
    Both earth and heaven appear to
    Grow dim before my eyes.

DON MENDO.

                   It is
    The proper way God's justice works
    Upon a guilty man; remorse
    And fear for what he's done.

DON LOPE.

                  Not true.
    For knowing I'm a criminal
    Would still allow me, like some wild
    And cornered animal, to tear
    You all to shreds; but you alone
    Awaken fear and respect in me,
    And force me now to place my head
    At your feet, and offer you
    My sword, this blazing flash of light
    That, blood-stained in my hand, has been
    For all my enemies the source
    Of everlasting night.

DON MENDO.

               Arise,
    Don Lope. The heavens well know that in

A case like this, in which I am
The judge and you the criminal,
I'd gladly take your place if it
Were possible, and thus exchange
The danger that you face for my
Bewilderment and total muddle.
But do not be afraid. That I
Now seem to act towards you angrily
Is less to do with me than with
The fact that I now represent
The King's severity.

DON LOPE.

The King?
How can the King know anything
Of me?

DON MENDO.

Your father went to him
And asked that you be brought to justice.

DON LOPE.
Then I shall need my sword.

DON MENDO.

I have
Your sword. You must accept that this
Is unavoidable. I gave
My word.

DON LOPE.

Oh, cruel heavens!
The sword in your hand is like
Some fatal knife that, raised on high,
Informs me of the end of life.
Why do you make me feel such fear?
Why do you make me tremble more
Than my own father? I know if he
Were on the point of striking me
Again, I would not be afraid
To raise my hand to him.

DON MENDO.

You there!

SOLDIER.
You called, sir?

DON MENDO.

Go and find a cloak
To cover this man's head and then
Escort him to his cell. (*To another*) You there!

SOLDIER.

My lord.

DON MENDO.

Now listen well! There is
To be as little fuss as possible.
I want him taken through the secret door
That leads up to my room. But make
Quite sure that none of this is known
To him. And see to it a doctor tends
His wounds while I inform the King
Of his arrest. (*Aside.*) I feel such pain,
Such anguish, such anxiety,
It seems to dominate my soul entirely.

Exit all. Enter the KING.

KING.

I wait impatiently to see
If Mendo has fulfilled the task
I asked him to. I shall not rest
Until I am informed he's seen
It through. How can a son behave
Towards a father so disgracefully
And not expect to make the King
Extremely angry? My people shall
Today be witnesses of how
I punish him for this display
Of arrogance and pride, so they
Might learn that no one who commits
A crime can then escape and hope
To hide from me. Oh, no! Let no
One think that he can trifle with
King Pedro! But here, I think, Don Mendo comes.

Enter DON MENDO.

DON MENDO.

Your majesty, I kiss your hand.

KING.

I swear, Don Mendo, you deserve

My arms. You serve me well, but more
Than that, as Atlas bears the weight
Of this great world, you share with me
The cares of this unruly state.

DON MENDO.

The best response to such great trust
As you have placed in me, my lord,
Shall be the demonstration of
My constant loyalty.

KING.

                  I take
It that the fact that you are here
Means you now have Don Lope prisoner?

DON MENDO.

I do, your majesty. I have
Him in my house where no one else
May speak to him.

KING.

                  You have performed
The greatest service to your King.
I must preserve the name I have
For being just by taking action in
A crime that must have been amongst
The most unusual the world has ever seen.

DON MENDO.

If I may speak, your majesty,
The judge who's really wise will not
Allow himself to be so easily
Convinced by first impressions. The fact
Is that the truth was less spectacular
Than it appeared in the subsequent
Narration.

KING.

             Even so, the fact
Remains a son commits an act
Of violence against his father, who,
In turn, complains to me that son
Is thus responsible for his
Dishonour.

DON MENDO.

             Admittedly, that was

The case, your majesty, and yet
The evidence suggests the son
Was not, perhaps, as guilty as
He seems.

KING.

                    If only that were true,
Don Mendo, I would welcome it.
To think that anyone would have
The nerve to perpetrate an act
As grave as this and think that they
Can get away with it!

DON MENDO.

                    I quite
Agree, and yet the truth may not
Be quite as simple as at first
It seems. There was an argument,
I gather, between Don Lope and
A certain Don Guillén de Azagra.
We do not know exactly what
The two were fighting over, but
Azagra is my prisoner
As well. The father, it would seem,
Appeared when Azagra was
About to call his son a liar.
He saw how angry he'd become,
And rather than allow him to
Insult his son, spoke up himself.
The boy, however, thought Azagra spoke
The words and, angered further, turned
To strike him at the very moment when
His father tried to intervene.
The old man, thus unfortunately placed
Between them, took the blow, though it
Is clear that his son was not
To know he was about to strike
His father. He, then, considering
That he had been insulted by
His son, was moved by sheer rage
And impetuosity to speak
With your majesty, though I
Am told he now regrets the fact
He acted somewhat hastily.

The fact is he is getting old,
And in complaining of his son's
Behaviour, proves he is afflicted by
An old man's temper. I'd also add
That since antiquity there is
A kind of natural law which states
A son may not be publicly
Indicted by his father or
A father by his son. It is
A reason why I think, your majesty,
We should desist from further action.

KING.
You really think so, Mendo?

DON MENDO.
                                        Yes,
    I do.

KING.
        I am afraid that I
    Do not. For even if we now forget
    The crime, and for the moment set
    Aside the fact that both are in
    Some way to blame, I am determined to
    Discover why it is that any son
    Can act with such hostility
    Towards his father, and any father quite
    So foolishly towards his son.
    I have a plan in mind, which means
    You must detain the father too.
    It's best he's not at home tonight,
    So I can see the matter through.

    Exit the KING.

DON MENDO.
    Your wish is my command, your majesty.
    Heaven help me now and banish this
    Confusion from my heart that is
    At once both icy fear and darkest premonition!

    Exit DON MENDO; *enter* DOÑA VIOLANTE *and* ELVIRA.

ELVIRA.
    But what can be the cause of such
    Deep sorrow?

DOÑA VIOLANTE.
                Fear of what might come tomorrow.

ELVIRA.
    And is there any reason for
    This fear?

DOÑA VIOLANTE.
                The thought of what might happen here.

ELVIRA.
    But what can be the cause of all
    This gloom?

DOÑA VIOLANTE.
                  The feeling I am doomed
    To great unhappiness, and must
    Now face a life of sadness.

ELVIRA.
    What is it spoils your happiness?

DOÑA VIOLANTE.
    My own unhappiness.

ELVIRA.
    And who is it that makes you sad?

DOÑA VIOLANTE.
    The love that ought to make me glad.

ELVIRA.
    And is there nothing to be done?

DOÑA VIOLANTE.
    What else but let misfortune run
    Its course? I find no joy in love,
    And can expect no pity when
    Misfortune, love and misery
    Are all my main adversaries.

ELVIRA.
    Who lies behind this great conspiracy?

DOÑA VIOLANTE.
    My hostile fate.

ELVIRA.
                  Confront it with
    A ray of hope. It's not too late.

DOÑA VIOLANTE.
    My fate extinguishes all hope.

ELVIRA.
>Then you must now eclipse your fate,
>As does the moon the sun.

DOÑA VIOLANTE.
>That cannot be, for my moon wanes,
>And I, deprived of hope, am but
>A victim of a great conspiracy
>Of sun and moon and destiny.

ELVIRA.
>What else prompts such despair?

DOÑA VIOLANTE.
>The thought that now my death is near.

ELVIRA.
>Who is responsible?

DOÑA VIOLANTE.
>My fate declares escape impossible.

ELVIRA.
>My lady, you shall live, you'll see.

DOÑA VIOLANTE.
>It goes against the heavens' decree.
>I cannot hope for anything
>That frees me from my suffering.
>How can I hope for victory
>Against such cruel enemies?
>I beg you, do not ask me more.
>To do so is to bring to mind
>That cruel moment when I saw
>Don Lope taken prisoner.
>The mere thought brings tears to
>My eyes; the answer that you seek
>About the origin of all
>My deep despair and anguished sighs
>Lies there in his imprisonment,
>His wretched state the eloquent
>Embodiment of fear, dread,
>Of constant apprehension; of love,
>Unhappiness, the cruellest misfortune;
>Of sun and moon and stars' decree;
>Of death and fate and destiny.

ELVIRA.
>Your father's room is where they keep

Him prisoner. It seems they took
Him in there by a secret door.

DOÑA VIOLANTE.
If only I could find a way
To end his suffering!

ELVIRA.
                    I'd say
It is enough that such a lady as
Yourself now grieves so much for him.

DOÑA VIOLANTE.
Oh, no, Elvira. It is not enough.
To see him suffering makes me want
To sacrifice this life of mine
If only that would guarantee
New life for him. You have the key
To open up my father's room.

ELVIRA.
Your father has the master-key,
But I have this one.

DOÑA VIOLANTE.
                    I'll try to get
A message through to him. The fears
That once concerned me for my safety are
As nothing now compared with my
Anxiety for him. Stay here,
Elvira. And let me know at once
If anyone should happen to come near.

Exit both. Enter DON LOPE.

DON LOPE.
What reason is there for such great
Unhappiness? Why did they bind
My eyes and bring me to a prison such
As this? Oh, Violante, how
I suffer now for your beauty!
And yet what little of my life
Is left to me grieves for you still.
It matters not my own life's to
Be lost, but that I lose it at
The greater cost of losing you.

DOÑA VIOLANTE *enters by a door.*

DOÑA VIOLANTE (*aside*).
>His face is stained with blood, as if
>Someone has wounded him. (*Aloud.*) Don Lope!

DON LOPE.
>Who's there? Who can it be that calls
>My name? Is there still someone who
>Does not forget or feel complete
>Disdain for me?

DOÑA VIOLANTE.
>   Someone who, moved
>By your plight, feels only pity.

DON LOPE.
>Oh, living shadow of my death,
>Oh, pale reflection of my life,
>Oh, still projection of my thoughts,
>Oh, eager spirit of my fantasy,
>Oh, portrait fashioned in the air
>By my imagination's artistry,
>Oh, voice to which my own dumb words
>Have given shape and living body, I beg
>You do not now torment me with
>This sweet illusion, then deprive
>Me of your lovely vision.

DOÑA VIOLANTE.
>   How can
>I be a vision, Lope, when
>This body, soul and voice suggests
>That I am human?

DON LOPE.
>   The truth is that
>My own confusion makes me think
>That this is just a dream. You tell
>Me it is not, but still I'm not
>Convinced that things aren't what they seem.

DOÑA VIOLANTE.
>Then be convinced that I respond,
>Regardless of the risk involved,
>To that sweet obligation forged
>By love, then strengthened by my deep
>Compassion for your plight, and finally
>Confirmed by my belief that I

Too bear responsibility
For your father's accusation.
Tonight you'll find this door unlocked.
Believe me, safety lies in flight.
Who would have thought that I could now
Give life to anyone when I
Am almost dead from sheer fright?

DON LOPE.
They say there is a wondrous plant,
So rare and exquisite that when
It is applied to any wound,
It cures it, and when there is
No wound, it strangely causes it.
You have, I think, the qualities
Of that same plant, for as you were
My executioner, so now
You are my bléssed saviour: where
There's life you bring me death, and where
There's death, you offer me new life.

DOÑA VIOLANTE.
I also heard of two strange plants
That when they are apart contain
A fatal poison, when they are
Together, a healing medicine.
Consider, then, how in the two
Of us that same effect is true:
You die apart from me, and I
From you; while love itself attempts
To bring the two of us together,
Each one the healing medicine
That saves the other. If it is true
You have provoked the anger of
The King, and there is anything
That I can do . . . (*Noise off.*) What noise is that?

Enter ELVIRA.

ELVIRA.
Your father's coming.

DOÑA VIOLANTE.
                      In that case I had best
Be going.

DON LOPE.
> When shall I see you?

DOÑA VIOLANTE.
> > Soon.
> I'll come tonight . . . to free you.

DON LOPE.
> > I need
> To know, not just because you set
> Me free, but more because I long
> To see you constantly.

Exit DON LOPE.

DOÑA VIOLANTE.
> Elvira, close the door. We have
> To leave before my father finds
> Us here.

ELVIRA.
> > There seems to be no danger,
> Madam. He isn't coming here.
> He's entered Doña Blanca's chamber.

DOÑA VIOLANTE.
> I cannot say that offers me
> More peace of mind. Elvira, go
> At once and see if you can find
> Someone who knows what's happening.
> To know the grave offence committed here
> Is merely to anticipate
> A cold and sudden fear.

Exit DOÑA VIOLANTE *and* ELVIRA.

ELVIRA (*off*).
> The door is closed. I'll see what news
> There is.

Enter VICENTE.

VICENTE.
> > I swear to God, the world
> Has never seen a greater slap
> Than that! Oh, what a whack it was!
> Or better still, to add the sound —
> Effect, a good resounding thwack.
> To call it just a bump's to do

Injustice to it when it was
A solid thump the like of which
No family dust-up's ever seen.
If they had rung the church-bells of
Velilla, the sound of it could not
Have been much clearer . . .

Enter ELVIRA.

ELVIRA.

                        Vicente, what
Are you doing here?

VICENTE.

                    I'm telling you,
Elvira, I have had enough.

ELVIRA.
Enough of what? Of who?

VICENTE.

                       Of everyone;
Of all the things that people do
To one another, and more especially
A certain father and his son.

ELVIRA.
So what has either done to you?

VICENTE.
What bothers me is that I serve
Them both, and having seen the things
Of which they both are capable,
Must now conclude that both of them
Are evidently certifiable.
Whoever saw a son more generous?
Without being asked, he hands it out.
Was there a father more ridiculous?
What he should hide, he shouts about.
I'm furious with my mistress too:
She broods forever on the case,
And 'God protect him' all day long,
And weeps and moans about the place.
As for Don Mendo, your boss,
What he does most is contemplate,
You'd think he'd gone into the Church,
And started his novitiate.
He's not quite sure who has sinned,

Arrests my master and Guillén,
And then, to make a job of it,
The old man too along with them.
Then there's the King. I'm really mad
With him.

ELVIRA.

You must have had too much
To drink. You'll soon be saying things
That you'll regret.

VICENTE.

They beat me up,
You see, but would the King accept
Responsibility? Oh, no!
All he could do was look tight-lipped
And let his eyes breathe basilisks.
Now, as for you . . .

ELVIRA.

Oh, yes? I'd like
To know what I have done to you.

VICENTE.

Not so much what you've done as what
You haven't done. I know you worship me
With all five thousand senses you
Command, and yet you've never sung
To me, nor written me a note,
Nor ever held me by the hand.

ELVIRA.

I've told you it's because you are
Too fond of Beatriz.

VICENTE.

And I've
Told you that all this fuss you make
Of her has got to cease.

ELVIRA.

If that
Were only true, Vicente, I
Would offer you my lips.

VICENTE.

And you
Can have them back again if what
I'm telling you is fibs.

ELVIRA.
>   In that
> Case I agree. There's nothing less
> Will satisfy my modesty.

They embrace. Enter BEATRIZ.

BEATRIZ.
> Praise be to God! You've learned at last
> To love your neighbour.

VICENTE.
>   Beatriz!

ELVIRA.
> Come on, Vicente, just ignore her.

VICENTE (*aside*).
> I dread to think what she will have
> In mind for later.

BEATRIZ.
>   No need to look
> At me like that, my little doves,
> So innocent, when what you really are
> Are dog and bitch both sniffing at
> Each other's scent. But never mind.
> Remember what they always say:
> 'There's always someone needs the shoe
> That someone else has thrown away'.

ELVIRA.
> I'll have you know I've better taste
> Than that. I buy things new, straight off
> The peg. You think I'd want a shoe
> From someone with a wooden leg?

VICENTE (*aside*).
> She's done it now!

BEATRIZ.
>   What do you mean?
> Are you suggesting I'm the daughter of
> Some pirate such as Long John Silver?

ELVIRA.
> Could be him, or someone similar.

VICENTE (*aside*).
> And now the fat's right in the fire!

BEATRIZ.

> You see these hands of mine, my dear?
> They'll scalp the hair right off your head,
> Unless, of course, as I've been told,
> You have to wear a wig instead.

ELVIRA.

> How very droll that you should think
> My hair is false when your eye
> Is made of glass.

BEATRIZ.

> I swear . . .

VICENTE (*aside*).

> I'd better stop
> Them here. (*Aloud.*) Come now! I think that both
> Of you have gone quite far enough.

ELVIRA.

> There's more to say. I'll have her know
> I haven't got duff teeth.

BEATRIZ.

> Oh, yes
> You have. And what a sight they make
> When they pop out and find a second-home
> Inside a glass at night.

ELVIRA.

> You think
> These teeth are false?

BEATRIZ.

> This eye of mine
> Is made of glass?

ELVIRA.

> This hair a wig?

BEATRIZ.

> That I am what they call peg-legged?

VICENTE.

> I beg you, show some modesty.
> We are amongst the aristocracy.

ELVIRA.

> This scoundrel . . .

BEATRIZ.

> Waster . . .

ELVIRA.

                              Rogue . . .

BEATRIZ.

                                        Disaster of

  A man's . . .

ELVIRA.

              To blame for everything.

BEATRIZ.

  So won't mind if we punish him.

  They set about VICENTE.

VICENTE.

  Please, ladies, have a heart.

ELVIRA.

                              I think

  There's someone coming.

BEATRIZ.

                              We'll finish later what

  We've started.

VICENTE.

                    Finish later?

ELVIRA.

                              Now

  That we are friends.

BEATRIZ.

                    And never parted.

ELVIRA.

  'Bye for now then.

BEATRIZ.

                    See you. Cheerio.

  Exit both.

VICENTE.

  The devil take you, silly cows!
  Whoever saw as great an avalanche
  Of blows as they let loose on me?
  What makes it worse, of course, is that
  The bloody King will not accept
  Responsibility.

  Exit VICENTE. *Enter the* KING, *his face concealed, and*
  DOÑA BLANCA.

DOÑA BLANCA.
>   Who can
>   It be that, as the dark of night
>   Descends, dares enter here? Who are
>   You, sir? What do you want of me?
>   You bring me news of some misfortune?
>   Clearly, you do. For in a house
>   Where joy no longer enters, he
>   Who brings bad news must always be
>   The only visitor. (*Aside.*) He hides
>   Both face and voice from me, agrees,
>   But does so silently. (*Aloud.*) Beatriz,
>   A light! (*Aside.*) Oh, heavens! My fears engulf
>   Me like the darkest night.

Enter BEATRIZ *with a light.*

Aloud.

>   Who are
>   You, sir, who dares to enter here,
>   And fill my heart with sudden fear?

KING.
>   As soon as we're alone, you'll know.

DOÑA BLANCA.
>   I'll be quite safe, Beatriz. Please go.

Exit BEATRIZ.

Aside.

>   As soon as one grief disappears,
>   An even greater one appears.

Aloud.

>   Will you not tell me who you are?

KING.
>   First let me see the door's secure.

DOÑA BLANCA (*aside*).
>   Whoever knew confusion such
>   As this? (*Aloud.*) Is no one there?

KING.
>   Do not
>   Call out!

DOÑA BLANCA.
>Then tell me who you are.

KING.

Why, certainly.

The KING uncovers his face.

DOÑA BLANCA.
>Great heavens!

KING.

>I think

You recognize me now.

DOÑA BLANCA.
>Your majesty!
I doubt that anyone could fail
To recognize the sun, however well
Disguised. But why would you now speak
To me, at such an hour, in this
Strange guise? I swear my loyalty,
But at the same time beg you to
Deliver me from what has now
Become a greater doubt and worse
Confusion than before. Must I
Regard this visit as a punishment
Or royal favour?

KING.

>Neither, madam; more
The sign of such an obligation as
The duties of a King impose
On me.

DOÑA BLANCA.
>I cannot think, my lord,
That anything that I have done
Can merit such an obligation.

KING.

I beg you, Doña Blanca, do
Not be quite so emotional.
The things I have to say demand
That you should be both cool
And rational. The facts are these:
Your son offends your husband publicly;
Your husband then approaches me,

Accusing him, which merely gives
The matter more publicity;
And in the end, since you are wife
And mother to them both, reflects,
I do believe, suspiciously on you.
You have good reason to feel so
Concerned; you are quite justified
In feeling so alarmed when such
Events as these have rarely been
Surpassed in human history.
And now I have to know the reason why
A father's anger with his son,
A son's hostility towards
His father can assume such great,
Unnatural proportions as
To make the one so eagerly
Seek vengeance on the other. You,
I am convinced, can best assist
Me in this purpose by agreeing now
To be a willing witness and
Provide a truthful testimony.
You may, though, rest assured that
Whatever information you
Agree to give me now shall not
In any way be used by me
To cast the slightest blemish on
Your name and faultless reputation.
Trust me, Blanca. The two of us
Are quite alone. But if you think
You can conceal from me . . .

DOÑA BLANCA.

                    Your majesty,
I beg of you, please do not pass
So quickly from such gentleness
To cruelty, from mildness to
Such harshness and severity.
It is quite true that I have long
Concealed a secret in my breast,
And vowed for many years I would
Not speak of it to someone else.
But if, as you suggest, I have
Become the object of some foul
Suspicion, it would be as wrong

Of me to keep the secret to
Myself. Respect and honour mean
So much to me, and yet are so
Dependent on the actions of
My family, I cannot stand
Aside and let imagination feed
Itself on vague, unjustified
Suspicion. I therefore ask your majesty,
The world and heaven itself to pay
Attention to the story I
Now tell.

KING.
      Proceed.

DOÑA BLANCA.
            My father was
A poor man and yet had such
Nobility he seemed the sun itself.
He knew he could not hope to match
Such qualities to that material wealth
He lacked, and so decided I
Must marry young, and let my youth
And beauty be my dowry to
Don Lope de Urrea. And so
The two of us were married, he
Already in the snow-white January of
His life and I in early Spring.
I loved him dearly, despite
The difference in our years, and so
Was deeply hurt to find he treated me
Indifferently, as if we were
Two instruments that had been tuned
So they could never play in harmony.
I soon convinced myself a child
Would be the best solution to
His lack of love – how often does
A problem seek its resolution in
Audacious schemes? – and so began
To dream of such a child above
All other things. But God, I think,
Perceived this great desire as
A sin and so resolved to punish my
Excessive longing by denying me
That child. But now, your majesty,

I wish to turn away from this
Account of married life, unhappy as
It was, to speak of someone else:
I had a sister, younger than
Myself, a sweet and tender soul
Who would, if only she would come,
Console me for what joy my marriage to
Don Lope lacked. And so she came
To live with us. But then it was
A certain gentleman became
Obsessed with her – and if I do
Not name him now, your majesty,
It is because it serves no purpose in
My story or might cause offence to you.
But no. This cannot be. Why do
I hesitate when every detail I
Reveal could well exonerate
The honour and good name of all
My family? The man I would
Not name was . . . Don Mendo Torrellas.
Discovering my sister cold
To his advances, he employed
The services of someone in
The house to gain his entrance to
Her room at night by climbing to
Her balcony. There is no doubt
That there – and Heaven will surely bear
Me out in this – he promised he
Would marry her, and having entered as
A thief, emerged the callous victor
Of her honour. It was not long before
This lover married someone else –
As if to prove that all men place
Convenience over and above their sense
Of duty – and then was sent to France
By your father as ambassador.
In short, he knew no more of what
Had passed than I have told you here.
As for my sister, I observed
How often she complained of poor health
And found herself increasingly
In pain. I sought the cause as best
I could, imploring, begging her,

The tears that often burned my cheeks
The outward sign of that concern
And love I felt for her. At last
She told me of the lover I've described
To you and how, in payment for
The error she had made, she had inside
Her now a viper born of her mistake.
It greatly saddened me, and yet,
How could I criticize someone
As close to me as she had now
Become? There seems no point when what
Is done is done, and when the person who
Is guilty of that wrong requires not
So much a sermon as some words
Of sweet and gentle consolation.
How many times I cursed the heavens
For what was done! Who would have thought
That one event could ever be
For both of us the cause of such
Unhappiness or such misfortune,
And what I would have welcomed as
My own true happiness could only be
For her the cause of deep distress?
These were the thoughts that now preoccupied
Me constantly and made me think
How best I could devise some plan
To ease our mutual misery.
At last I realized it might
Be possible, if it was only known
To me, to hide her pregnancy
And thus to publicize my own.
And so the promised day arrived –
The world has never seen its kind! –
She artfully concealed her pain,
And I ingeniously invented mine.
When Laura died in giving birth
It seemed to be her destiny.
The cause was given as disease
For which there is no remedy.
A single servant knew what we
Had done, and from that day to this
The nature of our plan was known
To no one else, and still would not

Be known unless your majesty,
By making me so consious of
My shame, had made me now confess
To what was done. I bear the blame
For everything, your majesty,
And ask that any punishment
That you consider fit should fall
On me entirely. But in
My own defence I also beg
You bear in mind my love for both
My husband and my sister, and nothing that
I did offended love or honour.
I therefore ask your majesty
To show the world, in judging me,
You are not only Pedro, King
Of Aragon, but also that
True paragon of justice you
Are by your subjects thought to be.
I kneel at your feet. I do
Not seek forgiveness; only that
Your sentence now informs the world
That, if I have deceived my husband, I
Have not offended my integrity,
Or damaged my good name, or been
Responsible for anything for which,
As far as honour goes, I am to blame.
I give my word, your majesty,
I may be blamed for indiscretion but
Admit no other accusation.

KING.

You would appear in what you've said
To have dismissed what I had feared most.
If it is true, a son has not
Committed an offence against
A father nor a father sought
To bring a charge against a son.

Aside.

Though now I also think that if
This one great problem is in part
Resolved, there are another two
That must somehow be solved. Despite
What Blanca has revealed and I

Must keep in confidence, the public is
Convinced a son is guilty of
A grave offence against his father.
As for Don Mendo, he is guilty too
Of having, as a younger man,
So callously betrayed his lover.
And thirdly, Blanca, who for all
These years has so deceived a husband who
Implicitly believed in her.
In short, these three offences, each
Quite cunningly concealed, but each
In all its consequences equally
Revealed. It matters not the boy
Is not Don Lope's real son.
I am obliged, because I am
The man I am, to seek a punishment
That will provide for public wrongs
A public satisfaction, and
For private wrongs a private one.

Aloud.

God be with you, Blanca.

DOÑA BLANCA.

                    God protect
Your majesty.

A knock at the door as the KING *is about to open it.*

KING.

                    Open the door.
Whoever's there must not be told
That I am here.

The KING *conceals himself.*

DOÑA BLANCA.

                    Who's there?

DON MENDO (*off*).

                    Don Mendo,
Blanca.

DOÑA BLANCA *opens the door.* DON MENDO *enters.*

DOÑA BLANCA.

Why have you come? (*Aside.*) Whoever saw
Confusion such as this?

DON MENDO.
>   I come
> To tell you not to be afraid.
> I have control of everything.
> No one dares to disobey me now
> In anything.

KING (*appearing*).
>   Except the King.

> DON MENDO *is disturbed*.

DON MENDO.
> Your majesty! I did not think . . .

KING.
> To find me here? You have the key
> To where Don Lope is a prisoner?

DON MENDO.
> This is the key. But first you have
> To know . . .

KING.
>   I need to know no more.
> Blanca, you may go. Don Mendo, stay.

> *Aside*

> Tonight I shall display my justice to
> The world.

> *Exit the* KING.

DON MENDO.
>   What was he doing here?

DOÑA BLANCA.
> I think that heaven sees fit to punish both
> Of us for our errors. Follow him!
> And beg for mercy! Lope is
> My sister's son and yours!

DON MENDO.
> Heaven help me then! To save his life
> I'll gladly sacrifice myself.

> *Exit both. Enter* ELVIRA *and* DOÑA VIOLANTE.

ELVIRA.
> Consider . . .

VIOLANTE. No, it has to be.

ELVIRA.
If you do this . . .

VIOLANTE.
There's no dissuading me.

ELVIRA.
The one . . .

VIOLANTE.
You can't discourage me.

ELVIRA.
Who'll bear the blame for helping him
Escape is your father.

VIOLANTE.
My mind's
Made up. As far as I'm concerned,
It doesn't matter. As for you,
I'll ask you not to interfere.
Open the door, and say no more.

ELVIRA.
I do so, madam, even though
I die of fear. There's someone there.

VIOLANTE.
Then we must take great care to make
Quite sure that nothing's happened which
Will interfere with our plan.
It's possible it's been discovered,
And someone else has entered by
The other door. We'd better listen,
Before we open it.

ELVIRA.
I hear
The sound of voices, but they speak
So quietly, the meaning of
Their words is lost on me.

VIOLANTE.
Then let me listen. No. I cannot hear
The words, nor can I see as clearly
As I would like . . . and yet there seems
To be a crowd of people . . .

Enter DON MENDO.

DON MENDO.

                          Who
Has witnessed anything as terrible
As this?

DOÑA VIOLANTE.

              Why, father! What has happened? Why
Are you distressed?

DON MENDO.

                  I cannot tell
You why. And yet I know that I
Must share with you, my daughter, what
I cannot bear alone, and hope that you
Can offer me some consolation.
Lope is not Blanca's child.
He is your brother, and my son.

DOÑA VIOLANTE.
Sweet heavens! What are you telling me?

DON MENDO.
I am resolved to sacrifice
My life, my name, my honour, if only I
Can set him free.

DOÑA VIOLANTE.

              The cause was then
Unknown to me, but I now understand
Why I was moved to feel such pity.
The sounds I heard inside the room
Have ceased. Let's open it.

DON MENDO.

                    At once,
But carefully.

DON LOPE (*off*).

             Will no one help
Me now?

DON MENDO.

           That voice expresses so
Much suffering, I feel its agony.

DOÑA VIOLANTE.
My hands are trembling so much,
I cannot turn the key.

DON LOPE (*off*).
>   God help
>   Me now!

DON MENDO.
>   Give me the key. Despite
>   Our fears, let's see what's happening.

A knocking is heard at both doors at the back of the stage.

DON MENDO.
>   Who can be knocking at both doors
>   At once?

DOÑA VIOLANTE.
>   God grant me patience to endure this!

DON MENDO.
>   We have no choice. We have to open it.

Then open the doors. DOÑA BLANCA and BEATRIZ enter through the door opened by DOÑA VIOLANTE, DON LOPE, the elder, and VICENTE through that opened by DON MENDO.

DON LOPE, the elder.
>   The King commands me, Mendo, that
>   I ask what justice you have given me.

DOÑA BLANCA.
>   I come to seek, sweet Violante, solace for
>   The sorrows that I see ahead of me.

VICENTE.
>   And I to see what comes of it,
>   Because I'm full of curiosity.

DON MENDO.
>   The King has not instructed me
>   To punish him.

DOÑA VIOLANTE.
>   How can I speak
>   Consoling words when I myself
>   Am most in need of them?

DON MENDO.
>   It could well be the nature of
>   The punishment will be revealed
>   As soon as we have opened this
>   Locked door.

He opens the door, up-stage centre, and DON LOPE *is seen
garrotted, a paper in his hand, candles on either side.*

DON MENDO.
                    What's this I see?

DOÑA BLANCA.
    This awful spectacle?

DOÑA VIOLANTE.
                            This sight
    So terrible?

VICENTE.
                    Too gruesome to be true!

BEATRIZ.
    Oh hideous tragedy!

ELVIRA.
                            Oh cruel destiny!

DON LOPE, the elder.
    The source of my hostility that now
    Becomes the object of my pity!

DON MENDO.
    The paper in his hand contains
    The judgement which the King thought I
    Should pass on him. See what it says,
    Though none of us can now do anything.
    Aside.

    It is the punishment for all my sins,
    But I am forced to keep my secret hidden.

DOÑA BLANCA (*aside*).
    It is the judgement on my own deceit,
    But I must never speak aloud of it.

DON LOPE, the elder (*reads*).
    'The man who strikes and thus offends
    Whom he believes to be his father, dies;
    Observed by one for whom to stain
    Another's honour is the greater prize;
    And grieved by one who thinks it best
    To cover cunning and deceit with lies.'

ALL.
    Our play ends here. For all its faults,
    Excuse its author.